D

The Suez Crisis

Cc   6 and
the   thony
Ec   ce the
of   : crisis
its   s fully
ex   d on a
gl

A   textual
ar   graphs,
ca   s. The
si   ns – is
h

D1423495

ROUTLEDGE SOURCES IN HISTORY
Series Editor
David Welch, University of Kent

OTHER TITLES IN THE SERIES
Resistance and Conformity in the Third Reich
Martyn Housden

FORTHCOMING

The Russian Revolution
Ronald Kowalski

Italian Fascism
John Pollard

The Holocaust
John Fox

The German Experience
Anthony McElligott

The Rise and Fall of the Soviet Union
Richard Sakwa

The Suez Crisis

Anthony Gorst and Lewis Johnman

London and New York

First published 1997
by Routledge
11 New Fetter Lane, London EC4P 4EE

Simultaneously published in the USA and Canada
by Routledge
29 West 35th Street, New York, NY 10001

Typeset in Galliard and Gill by Keystroke, Jacaranda Lodge, Wolverhampton
Printed and bound in Great Britain by Biddles Ltd, Guildford and King's Lynn

British Library Cataloguing in Publication Data
A catalogue record for this book is available from the British Library

Library of Congress Cataloging in Publication Data
Gorst, Anthony.
    The Suez Crisis / Anthony Gorst and Lewis Johnman.
        — (Routledge sources in history)
    Includes bibliographical references
    and index.
    1. Egypt—History—Intervention, 1956. 2. Great Britain—Foreign
relations—1945– I. Johnman, Lewis. II. Title. III. Series.
    DT107.83.G68 1997   96–5892
    962.05′3—dc20   CIP

ISBN 0–415–11449–7
        0–415–11450–0 (pbk)

Contents

Series editor's preface

Sources in History is a new series responding to the continued shift of emphasis in the teaching of history in schools and universities towards the use of primary sources and the testing of historical skills. By using documentary evidence, the series is intended to reflect the skills historians have to master when challenged by problems of evidence, interpretation and presentation.

A distinctive feature of *Sources in History* will be the manner in which the content, style and significance of documents is analysed. The commentary and the source are not discrete, but rather merge to become part of a continuous and integrated narrative. After reading each volume a student should be well versed in the historiographical problems which sources present. In short, the series aims to provide texts which will allow students to achieve facility in 'thinking historically' and place them in a stronger position to test their historical skills. Wherever possible the intention has been to retain the integrity of a document and not simply to present a 'gobbet', which can be misleading. Documentary evidence thus forces the student to confront a series of questions which professional historians also have to grapple with. Such questions can be summarised as follows:

1 *What* type of source is the document?
- Is it a written source or an oral or visual source?
- What, in your estimation, is its importance?
- Did it, for example, have an effect on events or the decision-making process?
2 *Who* wrote the document?
- A person, a group or a government?
- If it was a person, what was their position?
- What basic attitudes might have affected the nature of the information and language used?
3 *When* was the document written?
- The date, and even the time, might be significant.
- You may need to understand when the document was written in order to understand its context.
- Are there any special problems in understanding the document as contemporaries would have understood it?
4 *Why* was the document written?
- For what purpose(s) did the document come into existence, and for *whom* was it intended?

- Was the document 'author-initiated' or was it commissioned for somebody? If the document was ordered by someone, the author could possibly have 'tailored' his piece.
5 *What* was written?
- This is the obvious question, but never be afraid to state the obvious.
- Remember, it may prove more revealing to ask the question: what was *not* written?
- That is, read between the lines. In order to do this you will need to ask what other references (to persons, events, other documents, etc.) need to be explained before the document can be fully understood.

Sources in History is intended to reflect the individual voice of the volume author(s) with the aim of bringing the central themes of specific topics into sharper focus. Each volume will consist of an authoritative introduction to the topic; chapters will discuss the historical significance of the sources, and the final chapter will provide an up-to-date synthesis of the historiographical debate. Authors will also provide an annotated bibliography and suggestions for further reading. These books will become contributions to the historical debate in their own right.

In *The Suez Crisis*, Anthony Gorst and Lewis Johnman plot the history and strategic importance of Suez and the events that led to Britain's withdrawal from the Persian Gulf. Their skilful analysis of the sources they have selected reveals how Britain slowly came to recognise that it would have to scale down its global commitments and accept a more regional role focused on Europe. It is the contention of the authors that while the Suez crisis may not have caused the major changes in Britain's status in the world, it did act as a powerful catalyst of change. As this volume clearly indicates, Suez cruelly exposed the assumptions shared by most British politicians of the 1950s that the country remained a great power. After Suez the 'illusion' of Britain as an independent world power could no longer be sustained.

David Welch
Canterbury 1996

Acknowledgements

In a work of this type it is inevitable that the authors have incurred debts to many individuals. Our thanks are due to Professor Peter Hennessy of Queen Mary and Westfield College, University of London, to Dr W. Scott Lucas of the School of History at the University of Birmingham and to Dr John Kent of the International History Department of the London School of Economics. Gail Smith kindly drew the maps. Crown copyright is reproduced with the permission of the Controller of HMSO. For permission to quote from the *Foreign Relations of the United States* series, the State Department is duly acknowledged. Cartoons are reproduced by permission of *Punch*. For permission to quote from *Suez 1956* and the Selwyn Lloyd papers at Churchill College, Cambridge, thanks are due to the literary executors of Lord Selwyn Lloyd. Material from J. Eayrs *The Commonwealth and Suez* (1964) is reproduced by permission of Oxford University Press. The appendix from Keith Kyle's *Suez* is reproduced by permission from Weidenfeld & Nicolson. For permission to cite *The Observer* editorial on the crisis thanks are due to *The Observer*. The extract from Harold Macmillan's 'Winds of Change' speech of 4 February 1960 is © Times Newspapers Ltd 1960. For permission to quote from N. Frankland (ed) *Documents on International Affairs 1956* thanks are due to Oxford University Press and the Royal Institute of International Affairs. While the publishers have made every effort to contact copyright holders of material used in this volume, they would be grateful to hear from any they were unable to contact.

At Routledge we would like to thank Heather McCallum, Catherine Turnbull and Sarah Conibear and the Series editor, Professor David Welch. All errors remain the responsibility of the authors.

Introduction

The Suez Crisis of 1956 occupies a fundamental position in the historiography of twentieth-century Britain. Contemporary commentators, politicians and historians have tended to view the crisis as a discontinuity in British history. Prior to 1956, it is argued, Britain was confident of her continuing great power status: after 1956 Britain became a second-class power, a fact symbolised by the rapid disintegration of its remaining imperial position. Only recently has this view of Suez been challenged by the assertion that the major developments that affected Britain's position in the world were already in train before the Suez Crisis took place. On this view, for example, British decolonisation in Africa was not a product of the Suez Crisis but a working out of trends that had been long established **(Darwin, 1991, pp. 70–74)**. It is the contention of this book that while Suez may not have caused the major changes in Britain's status in the world, it both highlighted and accentuated developing trends. Suez on this reading is a catalyst rather than a harbinger of change.

For the authors, the interest of Suez lies in the conjunction of economic weakness and Britain's pronounced post-war 'decline' from great power status. Suez highlights the atavistic assumptions shared by most British politicians of the 1950s that the country remained a great power and could act as such – Suez would cruelly reveal this not to be the case as Britain was brought sharply to heel by economic pressure from her American allies. Suez highlights the central fact of post-war British history that it no longer possessed an economy that was capable of sustaining a great power role: the humiliating cease-fire and withdrawal in November 1956 clearly illustrated the vulnerability of Britain to economic pressure. In this sense, the bulk of the present work focuses on the events of 1956 with an emphasis on the interplay of the diplomatic and economic forces that shaped British policy in the Suez Crisis. The work is therefore not concerned, for example, with the minutiae of military planning; nor is it concerned with American, Egyptian, Israeli or French policy except in so far as this affected British actions.

The central chapters are framed by two shorter chapters which briefly analyse the background to the crisis and the aftermath of the crisis respectively. The first chapter examines the presumed importance of the Suez Canal to Britain and why it was that the Middle East in general was such a strong and continuing area of British interest. The second of these chapters analyses the aftermath of the crisis, until 1968 paying particular attention to the interplay of British overseas interests and the ability of the economy to sustain such commitments. The final section of the book highlights the main areas of debate which have developed in the historiography of the Suez Crisis; this is complemented by an annotated bibliography.

The documentary record pertaining to the Suez Crisis is vast and spans several languages. Given the focus of the book we have chosen to concentrate on British and American sources. Even here, however, the task of selection has been a complicated and at times a difficult one. While seeking to preserve the narrative flow of the British decision-making process, which inevitably means a concentration on British government documents, we have tried to provide a range of documents illustrating the diversity of material available to the student of British policy during the Suez Crisis.

Notes on Sources

PRO refers to material held at the Public Record Office, Kew; SELO refers to the Selwyn Lloyd Papers held at Churchill College, Cambridge.

The origins of the crisis
Britain, Egypt and the Middle East 1881–1955

1.1 The Crossroads of Empire 1881–1945

The Universale Company of the Suez Maritime Canal was formed in December 1858 by Ferdinand de Lesseps who had in 1854 gained from Mohamed Said the Viceroy of Egypt – Egypt then being part of the Ottoman Empire and nominally ruled by the Turkish Sultan – a ninety-nine-year concession to dig and operate a sea-level canal through the isthmus of Suez to link the Mediterranean and Red Seas. De Lesseps made determined efforts to sell shares in this ambitious enterprise but met with little success. In Britain, for example, the House of Commons voted by 290 votes to 62 against participation in the scheme and were resolutely opposed to a venture which they saw as essentially speculative and organised by a representative of a power with whom Britain had a long history of poor relations (in fact the British government organised a boycott of support of the Canal enterprise). Accordingly, the company was formed of French shareholders, French capital and French management with Egypt supplying unpaid forced labour, substantial land grants and customs exemptions. It would be a consistent Egyptian claim that their contribution to the Canal in terms of money, labour and lives was far greater than that of any other country. Indeed, Said was obliged to take up far more shares on Egypt's behalf (some 44 per cent of the total) than originally envisaged as a consequence of the international boycott.

Document 1.1.1 Construction of the Suez Canal *c*. 1860s

In 1866 the Turkish Sultan demanded alterations to the concessions but the new Viceroy or *Khedive*, Ismail, had to pay financial compensation to the Company. In 1875 the *Khedive*, facing bankruptcy, sought a purchaser for his shares. The British Prime Minister, Benjamin Disraeli, ignored the opposition of both his Chancellor of the Exchequer and Foreign Secretary and purchased these shares for £4 million. The purchase of the shares provoked an outburst of nationalism in Britain which was to set the tone towards the Canal for many years to come: descriptions of the Mediterranean as 'an English lake' and the Suez Canal as 'another name for the Thames' in 1875 differed little from Anthony Eden's description of the Canal in 1929 as 'the swing door of Empire' and Lord Hankey's view in 1953 that the Canal remained the 'jugular vein of world and Empire shipping' **(Kyle, 1991, pp. 14,**

Source: Hulton-Deutsch Collection

17 and 42). This image was used by the British government in the inter-war campaign to encourage people to buy goods produced in the Empire. The Canal was portrayed as the link that tied together the Empire and also symbolised the maritime tradition of Britain.

Document 1.1.2 Charles Pear, 'Suez Canal', 1927

Such emotive expressions and terms were to be echoed in the Suez Crisis of 1956. These metaphors were, however, misplaced as an expression of reality. The Canal Company did not own the Canal itself – it ran through the sovereign territory of first the Ottoman Empire and later Egypt – but was a private joint-stock company only possessing a concession to operate the Canal until 1968 on which date the Canal and all its facilities would revert to Egyptian control. Moreover, the Company itself remained essentially French, the French government itself being the largest shareholder, and its headquarters were in Paris.

By the beginning of the 1880s Egypt's international debt position had worsened to such an extent that Ismail had been deposed by the British and French who had imposed financial controls over the Egyptian government. The response to this act was an upsurge of Egyptian nationalism which in its turn provoked a joint ultimatum from Britain and France who claimed that their property and the lives

Source: Constantine, 1986, plate 6

of their nationals were in danger. Following anti-European rioting in Alexandria in June 1882, the Royal Navy bombarded Alexandria and a British military expedition under Sir Garnet Wolseley used the Canal to invade Egypt, landing at Ismailia and achieving a resounding victory at Tel al-Kebir. Egypt was now under British occupation. The British quickly moved to dismantle the vestiges of joint Anglo-French control in Egypt and although Turkey remained *de jure* the sovereign power the de facto situation was that the *Khedive* was under British control and Egypt was part of the British Empire albeit as a 'protectorate'.

In 1888 the Convention of Constantinople was signed between Turkey and the European powers regarding the operation of the Canal.

Document 1.1.3 The Suez Canal Convention of April 1888

ARTICLE I

The Suez Maritime Canal shall always be free and open, in time of war as in time of peace, to every vessel of commerce or of war, without distinction of flag.

Consequently, the High Contracting Parties agree not in any way to interfere with the free use of the Canal, in time of war as in time of peace.

The Canal shall never be subjected to the exercise of the right of blockade. . . .

ARTICLE II

The High Contracting Parties likewise undertake to respect the plant, establishments, buildings and works of the Maritime Canal and of the Fresh Water Canal.

ARTICLE IV

The Maritime Canal remaining open in time of war as a free passage, even to ships of war of belligerents, according to the terms of Article I of the present Treaty, the High Contracting Parties agree that no right of war, no act of hostility, nor any act having for its project to obstruct the free navigation of the Canal, shall be committed in the Canal and its ports of access, as well as within a radius of three marine miles from those ports, even though the Ottoman Empire should be one of the Belligerent Powers.

Vessels of war of belligerents shall not revictual or take in stores in the Canal and its ports of access except in so far as may be strictly necessary. The transit of the aforesaid vessels through the Canal shall be effected with the least possible delay, in accordance with the regulations in force, and without any other intermission than that resulting from the necessities of the service.

Their stay at Port Said and in the roadstead of Suez shall not exceed twenty-four hours, except in case of distress. In such case they shall be bound to leave as soon as possible. An interval of twenty-four hours shall always elapse between the sailing of a belligerent ship from one of the ports of access and the departure of a ship belonging to the hostile Power. . . .

ARTICLE VII

The Powers shall not keep any vessel of war in the waters of the Canal (including Lake Timsah and the Bitter Lakes).

Nevertheless they may station vessels of war in the ports of access of Port Said and Suez, the number of which shall not exceed two for each Power.

This right shall not be exercised by belligerents. . . .

ARTICLE VIII

The Agents in Egypt of the Signatory Powers of the present Treaty shall be charged to watch over its execution. In case of any event threatening the security or the free passage of the Canal, they shall meet on the summons of three of their number under the presidency of their Doyen, in order to proceed to the necessary verifications. They shall inform the Khedival Government of the danger which they may have perceived, in order that that Government may take proper steps to insure the protection and the free use of the Canal. Under any circumstances they shall meet once a year to take note of the due execution of the Treaty.

The last-mentioned meetings shall take place under the presidency of a Special Commissioner nominated for that purpose by the Imperial Ottoman

Government. A Commissioner of the Khedive may also take part in the meeting, and may preside over it in case of the absence of the Ottoman Commissioner.

They shall especially demand the suppression of any work or the dispersion of any assemblage on either bank of the Canal, the object or effect of which might be to interfere with the liberty and the entire security of the navigation. . . .

ARTICLE X

Similarly, the provisions of Articles IV, V, VII and VIII, shall not interfere with the measures which His Majesty the Sultan and His Highness the Khedive, in the name of His Imperial Majesty, and within the limits of the Firmans granted, might find it necessary to take for securing by their own forces the defence of Egypt and the maintenance of public order.

In case His Imperial Majesty the Sultan, or His Highness the Khedive, should find it necessary to avail themselves of the exceptions for which this Article provides, the Signatory Powers of the Declaration of London shall be notified thereof by the Imperial Ottoman Government.

It is likewise understood that the provisions of the four Articles aforesaid shall in no case occasion any obstacle to the measures which the Imperial Ottoman Government may think it necessary to take in order to insure by its own forces the defence of its other possessions situated on the Eastern Coast of the Red Sea.

ARTICLE XI

The measures which shall be taken in the cases provided for by Articles IX and X of the Present Treaty shall not interfere with the free use of the Canal. In the same cases, the erection of permanent fortifications contrary to the provisions of Article VIII is prohibited.

ARTICLE XII

The High Contracting Parties, by application of the principle of equality as regards the free use of the Canal, a principle which forms one of the bases of the present Treaty, agree that none of them shall endeavour to obtain to respect to the Canal territorial or commercial advantages or privileges in any international arrangements which may be concluded. Moreover, the rights of Turkey as the territorial Power are reserved.

ARTICLE XIII

With the exception of the obligations expressly provided by the clauses of the present Treaty, the sovereign rights of His Imperial Majesty the Sultan and the rights and immunities of His Highness the Khedive, resulting from the Firmans, are in no way affected.

ARTICLE XIV

The High Contracting Parties agree that the engagements resulting from the present Treaty shall not be limited by the duration of the Acts of Concession of the Universal Suez Canal Company.

Source: Parliamentary Papers, C5623, 1889

This formal diplomatic agreement between the main European powers and Turkey is written in very legalistic language. While the document may seem somewhat dry, it represents the basis on which Anglo-Egyptian relations were first framed and contains within it issues that were to become the nub of the 1956 crisis. Under Articles I and IV the Canal was to be free and open whether in war or peace to the vessels of all countries whether mercantile or naval. In theory, under Article X the Convention could not interfere with the *Khedive*'s need to take any measures which he saw fit to secure the defence of Egypt. In reality this meant any measures which the British saw fit to take to secure the defence of Egypt; this article would be invoked consistently by the British during the two world wars. Article XIV deemed the Convention to be paramount and not bound by the limits of the concession. Much, however, rested on the interpretation of this. To the British, European management meant effective internationalisation, while to the Egyptians the principles of free and open navigation being established in international law implied no connection between the Convention and the concession. In nationalising the Suez Canal Company in 1956 Nasser did not breach the Convention; this was to cause the Eden government great difficulty in the search for a pretext for intervention. In a very real sense the British undercut their own position. The French insisted that Article VIII machinery should be established for international supervision in the event of a crisis, but due to British opposition this machinery was never established.

While the Company itself remained substantially French, the *Entente Cordiale* of 1904 removed any future French official interest in the governance of Egypt. Moreover, Turkey's sovereignty was effectively ended by the First World War: the *Khedive* was deposed and Egypt became a formal protectorate within the British imperial system with the Suez Canal being treated as a territorial possession. The result was, as Douglas Farnie has observed, that 'Britain infringed almost every article of the convention' **(Farnie, 1969, p. 549)**. The end of the war witnessed the creation of the League of Nations and with it the oft-trumpeted principle of national self-determination. In Egypt, the nationalist movement in the form of the Wafd party demanded an end to British occupation; in February 1922, after three years of uneasy relations, the British proclaimed Egypt independent with Sultan Faud as king. It was, however, a strange form of independence as the British government reserved four areas to its own discretion: the protection and security of imperial communications (meaning the Suez Canal), the defence of Egypt (Britain could reoccupy the whole of Egypt in the event of war), the protection of foreign interests and minorities (British), and the issue of the government of the

Sudan which Egypt claimed as part of its integral territory. All of these matters of discretion would allow for renewed British intervention as they saw fit: it was therefore a highly circumscribed form of independence.

These discretionary exceptions to full sovereignty were to some extent codified when in 1936 the Anglo-Egyptian Treaty was signed by the then Foreign Secretary, Anthony Eden.

Document 1.1.4 The Anglo-Egyptian Treaty of 26 August 1936

ARTICLE I

The military occupation of Egypt by the forces of His Majesty The King and Emperor is terminated. . . .

ARTICLE IV

An alliance is established between the High Contracting Parties with a view to consolidating their friendship, their cordial understanding and their good relations.

ARTICLE V

Each of the High Contracting Parties undertakes not to adopt in relation to foreign countries an attitude which is inconsistent with the alliance, nor to conclude political treaties inconsistent with the provisions of the present treaty.

ARTICLE VI

Should any dispute with a third State produce a situation which involves a risk of a rupture with that State, the High Contracting Parties will consult each other with a view to the settlement of the said dispute by peaceful means, in accordance with the provisions of the Covenant of the League of Nations and of any other international obligations which may be applicable to the case.

ARTICLE VII

Should, notwithstanding the provisions of Article 6 above, either of the High Contracting Parties become engaged in war, the other High Contracting Party will, subject always to the provisions of Article 10 below, immediately come to his aid in the capacity of an ally.

The aid of His Majesty the King of Egypt in the event of war, imminent menace of war or apprehended international emergency will consist in furnishing to His Majesty The King and Emperor on Egyptian territory, in accordance with the Egyptian system of administration and legislation, all the facilities and assistance in his power, including the use of his ports, aerodromes and means of communication. It will accordingly be for the Egyptian Government to take all the administrative and legislative measures including the establishment of martial law and an effective censorship, necessary to render these facilities and assistance effective.

ARTICLE VIII

In view of the fact that the Suez Canal, whilst being an integral part of Egypt, is a universal means of communication as also an essential means of communication between the different parts of the British Empire His Majesty the King of Egypt, until such time as the High Contracting Parties agree that the Egyptian Army is in a position to ensure by its own resources the liberty and entire security of navigation of the Canal, authorises His Majesty The King and Emperor to station forces in Egyptian territory in the vicinity of the Canal, in the zone specified in the Annex to this Article with a view to ensuring in co-operation with the Egyptian forces the defence of the Canal. The detailed arrangements for the carrying into effect of this Article are contained in the Annex hereto. The presence of these forces shall not constitute in any manner an occupation and will in no way prejudice the sovereign rights of Egypt.

It is understood that at the end of the period of twenty years specified in Article 16 the question whether the presence of British forces is no longer necessary owing to the fact that the Egyptian Army is in a position to ensure by its own resources the liberty and entire security of navigation of the Canal may, if the High Contracting Parties do not agree thereon, be submitted to the Council of the League of Nations for decision in accordance with the provisions of the Covenant in force at the time of signature of the present treaty or to such other person or body of persons for decision in accordance with such other procedure as the High Contracting Parties may agree. . . .

ARTICLE XV

The High Contracting parties agree that any difference on the subject of the application or interpretation of the provisions of the present treaty which they are unable to settle by direct negotiation shall be dealt with in accordance with the provisions of the Covenant of the League of Nations.

ARTICLE XVI

At anytime after the expiration of a period of twenty years from the coming into force of the Treaty, the High Contracting Parties will, at the request of either of them enter into negotiations with a view to such revision of its terms by agreement between them as may be appropriate in the circumstances as they then exist. In case of the High Contracting Parties being unable to agree upon the terms of the revised treaty the difference will be submitted to the Council of the League of Nations for decision in accordance with the provisions of the Covenant in force at the time of signature of the present treaty or to such other person or body of persons for decision in accordance with such procedure as the High Contracting Parties may agree. It is agreed that any revision of this treaty will provide for the continuation of the Alliance between the High Contracting parties in accordance with the principles contained in Articles 4, 5, 6 and 7. Nevertheless, with the consent of both High Contracting Parties negotiations may be entered into at any time after the expiration of a period of ten years after the coming into force of the treaty, with a view to such revision as aforesaid.

Source: Parliamentary Papers, Cmd 5360, 1937

This formal treaty signed between the sovereign governments of the United Kingdom and Egypt formed the basis of Anglo-Egyptian relations until 1954. Although notionally an agreement between equals, the document shows the fundamental imbalance in the relationship between Egypt and Britain. Article 7 gave British forces sweeping powers in war-time and Article 8 created the Suez Canal Zone under British occupation. In the Second World War the British invoked these articles: Egypt became the base for Allied forces in the Middle East following Italian entry into the war in 1940 and was once again treated as a British possession. Moreover, this military reoccupation had a political dimension when the Egyptian government of the nationalist politician Ali Maher Pasha, considered to be pro-Fascist by the British, was removed from office in 1940. In 1942, on the orders of the British Ambassador Sir Miles Lampson, British tanks surrounded the Royal Palace and forced King Farouk, who had succeeded Faud in 1936, to choose between abdication and appointing a government headed by Nahas Pasha. This high-profile exercise of imperial might bit deep into the consciousness of the Egyptian populace, especially that of the younger sections of the military. Although the treaty was for twenty years, under Article 16 renegotiation could take place with the consent of both parties after ten years with the mediation of the League of Nations if necessary. In fact, after the Second World War, although it was to prove difficult to renegotiate terms acceptable to both sides, the successor to the League of Nations, the United Nations, was not called in to mediate.

1.2 The Three Pillars 1945–1951

At the end of the Second World War the new Labour government of Clement Atlee had to redefine Britain's role in the world in response to the seismic changes in its position as a Great Power. Preliminary discussions had already taken place, even while the war was continuing, within the higher echelons of the Foreign Office and the Chiefs of Staff that were concerned with British external policy and in March 1945 a paper on the Middle East was produced to define Britain's post-war security needs. It formed part of a series covering different areas of British interests and was predicated on the assumption of a potential threat from a hostile Soviet

Union occurring in the mid-1950s after it had recovered from the ravages of the Second World War.

Document 1.2.1 British Military views on 'Security in the Eastern Mediterranean and Middle East', 27 March 1945

54(a) On the maintenance of our position in the Middle East depends the security of: –

 (i) Our oil resources, which will be vital to the development of the full war effort of both the British Commonwealth and the USA.

 (ii) Our sea and air communications through the Mediterranean to India, the Far East and Australasia.

 (iii) A main administrative base, and the most suitable location for an Imperial Strategic Reserve.

 (iv) British territories and states for the defence of which we accept commitments.

(b) A hostile USSR would constitute a very grave potential threat to our interests, in particular to our oil supplies. We therefore have a vital interest in retaining her friendship.

(c) In order to avoid provoking Soviet hostility, it may be necessary for us to forego certain of the measures which we would otherwise wish to take, to ensure against the possibility of aggression by the USSR. We should, however, aim; –

 (i) To increase the depth of our defensive system as far as possible to the north of the areas of greatest strategic interest to ourselves.

 (ii) To obtain early assistance in strength from Allies, particularly from the USA, who should be encouraged to assume definite responsibilities in this area.

 (iii) To maintain mobile forces in the Middle East which could delay the enemy and gain time for the deployment of reserves.

 (iv) To provide depth in rear to our defences by a system of alternative bases in safer areas.

(d) In view of the vulnerability of the Iraq and Persian Gulf oilfields, it would probably prove impossible to defend them successfully against a full-scale Soviet assault. We must, therefore, take steps in peace to reduce to a minimum our dependence on these sources of oil in time of war.

(e) It is essential that we should obtain general recognition of our predominant interest in the Middle East and of our right to play the leading role in this area. This implies ultimate responsibility for the maintenance of internal security which entails a formidable military commitment. It is, therefore, essential that our policy should aim at eliminating every cause for dispute and should ensure the integrity and peaceful development of the Arab states.

(f) A successful World Organisation would be greatly to our advantage inasmuch as it would: –

(i) Foster Anglo-Soviet relations

(ii) Increase the likelihood of the USA participating in defence measures in the Middle East.

55 Our further conclusions are:–

(a) We should endeavour, in agreement with the USSR, to establish Persia as an independent state, in fact as well as in name.

(b) In the Middle East France should be encouraged to co-operate in measures for the security of our common interests, but not in a manner which might seriously antagonise the Arab world. The use of French facilities in North-West Africa will be of especial value in providing depth for our defences and in maintaining our sea and air routes to the Middle East.

(c) We should maintain our traditional friendship with Greece, renew our friendship with Italy and should endeavour to ensure that the USSR does not obtain a greater influence than ourselves over Turkey.

(d) Our present treaties with Egypt and Iraq will not, if strictly interpreted, cover our future requirements in peace.

(e) Trans-African air routes should be maintained and developed, even if such a policy cannot be justified on commercial grounds.

Source: PRO FO 371/50774, 27 March 1945

Compare with the importance attached to the Middle East in 1947 in document 1.2.5, pp. 20–21.

Despite being produced by an interdepartmental planning team of diplomats and military figures, this series of papers ran into substantial opposition from both the Foreign Office and the military, with the result that it was shelved at the end of the war and never formed the basis of policy. None the less, the document is of substantial interest to the historian as it clearly demonstrates the centrality of the Middle East to Britain's strategic position. Moreover, it acknowledged that Britain alone could not defend the Middle East against Soviet penetration and advocated the creation of an alliance system to defend the region. Although it envisaged such an alliance encompassing the regional powers such as Greece, Turkey and France, and indeed Italy, the cornerstone was to be the United States. This was to prove somewhat difficult in the post-war period. In 1947, Britain was forced on financial grounds to abdicate responsibility for the support of Greece and Turkey, thus forcing the United States to adopt a more interventionist role in these countries through the promulgation of the Truman Doctrine in the same year. However, the United States was reluctant to become too identified with any wider Middle East defence system which had the air of colonialism about it.

The Foreign Office commentary on this paper acknowledged that

this war and the last have shown very clearly that the Egypt–Suez–Palestine area is strategically essential to the security of the British Empire . . . the other two Great Powers (America and Russia) are rapidly consolidating their hold on the areas which they consider vital to them. . . . We should keep pace and dig ourselves in, politically and strategically, in the areas shown to be essential to us.

(PRO FO 371/50774)

Foreign Office thinking on the difficulties likely to confront Britain in the post-war world was further amplified in a discussion paper by Orme Sargent, a senior figure within the Diplomatic Service who was later to become the Permanent Under-Secretary at the Foreign Office.

Document 1.2.2 'Stocktaking After VE Day', 11 July 1945

3 . . . It suits us that the principle of co-operation between the three Great Powers should be specifically accepted as the basis on which problems arising out of the war should be handled and decided. Such a co-operative system will it is hoped, give us a position in the world which we might otherwise find increasingly difficult to assert and maintain were the other two Great Powers to act independently. It is not that either the United States or the Soviet Union do not wish to collaborate with Great Britain. The United States certainly find it very convenient to do so in order to fortify their own position in Europe and elsewhere: and the Soviet Union recognise in Great Britain a European Power with whom they will certainly have to reckon. But the fact remains that in the minds of our big partners, especially in that of the United States, there is a feeling that Great Britain is now a secondary Power and can be treated as such, and that in the long run all will be well if they – the United States and the Soviet Union – as the two supreme World Powers of the future, understand one another. It is this misconception which it must be our policy to combat. . . .

10 It must be an essential feature of our European policy to maintain close and friendly relations with Italy, Greece and Turkey, so as to secure our strategic position in the Eastern Mediterranean, especially now that Russia, stretching down from the North, is once again exerting pressure on this all-important link between Great Britain on the one hand, and India, Malaya, Australia, New Zealand and our Persian and Iraq oil supplies on the other. It ought to be possible for us to maintain our position in these three countries by building them up as bastions of 'liberalism' even though this may involve us in responsibilities and commitments of which we otherwise would be only too glad to be rid. It will be all the more important to do so if Russia remains in political control of Bulgaria and acquires physical control of the Straits. . . .

13 It should not prove impossible for us to perform the double task of holding the Soviet Government in check in Europe and at the same time, amicably and fruitfully co-operating with the Soviet and United States Governments in the resettlement of Europe if once the United States Administration realise both the political and economic implications of the European situation. But the process of inducing the United States to support a British resistance to Russian penetration in Europe will be a tricky one, and we must contrive to demonstrate to the American public that our challenge is based on upholding the liberal idea in Europe and not upon selfish apprehensions as to our own position as a Great Power . . . we shall therefore be well advised consciously and consistently to enlist American support upon some principle and perhaps even to exercise some restraint in not pursuing cases where a principle cannot easily be shown. In particular, the diplomatic interventions in the internal affairs of other countries, which may be necessary in certain contingencies must not seem to be motivated by personal hostility to, or support of, individuals in the State in question unless these are pretty obviously the opponents or champions of the 'liberal' idea. Such common material interests as oil development in Persia would not be an issue in which we could count on American support very far. This is not to say that United States policy is always based on principle, far from it, but it is a fact that a British policy is suspect if it is based on anything else, and particularly so at the moment in regard to Russia. . . .

15 In considering how best to co-operate with the United States in world affairs we must also take into account the whole series of economic and financial questions which remain to be settled between us and the United States Government, such as the financial accommodation we require after the end of the Japanese war, our financial and commercial policy in the context of Article 7 of the Mutual Aid Agreement, and the problem, of the consideration to be given to the United States in respect of the Lease–Lend deliveries and services we have received. The spirit in which these questions are handled is bound to be reflected in the realm of Anglo-American co-operation throughout the world. Moreover, with the end of the war with Germany they have become urgent and their settlement cannot be further delayed without great danger to Anglo-American relations generally. . . .

19 To sum up:–

(a) We must base our foreign policy on the principle of co-operation between the three World Powers. In order to strengthen our position in this combination we ought to enrol France and the lesser European Powers and also the Dominions as collaborators with us in this tri-partite system.

(b) We must not be afraid of having a policy independent of our two great partners and not submit to a line of action dictated to us by either Russia or the United States, just because of their superior power or because it is the line of least resistance, or because we despair of being able to maintain ourselves without United States support in Europe.

(c) Our policy, in order not to be at the mercy of internal politics or popular fashion, must be in keeping with British fundamental traditions and must be based on principles which will appeal to the United States, to the Dominions, and to the smaller countries of Europe, especially in the West. It must be definitely anti-totalitarian, and for this purpose must be opposed to totalitarianism of the Right (Fascism &c), as much as to the totalitarianism of the Left (Communism &c). In pursuance of this policy of 'liberalism', we shall have to take risks, and even live beyond our political means at times. We must not, for instance, hesitate to intervene diplomatic-ally in the internal affairs of other countries if they are in danger of losing their liberal institutions or their political independence. In the immediate future we must take the offensive in challenging Communist penetration in as many of the Eastern countries of Europe as possible, and we must be ready to counteract every attempt by the Soviet Government to communise or obtain political control over Germany, Italy, Greece, or Turkey.

(d) We must exert every effort to grapple with the economic crisis in Europe – not only in our own interests (a prosperous Europe is Great Britain's best export market) but in order to use the material resources at our and America's disposal as a makeweight throughout Europe against Communist propaganda, which the Soviet Government will use for their own ends wherever possible.

(e) In the Far East, while collaborating with the United States and the Soviet Union, we ought to try to organise under our leadership the lesser colonial Powers who have a stake in that part of the world, i.e., France, the Netherlands and Australia.

Source: PRO FO 371/50912, memorandum by O.G. Sargent, 11 July 1945

See documents 1.2.6 and 1.2.7 (pp. 22–23, 24–25) for the views of the Foreign Secretary on this in 1948 and 1949.

This briefing paper represented the thoughts of one senior Foreign Office official on Britain's position in the post-war world. Written in the summer of 1945 after the end of the war in Europe and with hostilities with Japan still continuing, the paper reflects the uncertainties in Britain's relationship with its two senior and more powerful partners in the Grand Alliance. Following the optimism of the Yalta Conference, at which agreement had seemingly been reached on the vexed question of East–West relations over the future of Eastern Europe, it is clear that the Foreign Office was beginning to have doubts about the intentions of the Soviet Union. While not ruling out a continuation of the Grand Alliance, which would considerably ease Britain's strategic dilemmas, Sargent was not at all sanguine about the possibility of co-operation in the post-war world. The paper somewhat optimistically envisages an independent role for Britain, but paradoxically recog-nises the need for American support. The document acknowledges the differences between British and American interests, particularly in the economic sphere (paragraphs 13 and 15), but hoped by using the cover of support for 'liberalism' to ensure an American commitment to future co-operation. These themes were to recur in the early post-war years as the new Labour government sought to construct a policy that reconciled independence and alliance.

All of this 'grand strategy', however, was rendered somewhat fanciful by the growing realisation of Britain's economic weakness. The Treasury had become increasingly concerned throughout 1944–1945 about the dichotomy between British post-war plans at both domestic and international levels and the country's ability to finance them. The grave weakness of the balance of payments position came to dominate Treasury discussions in 1945, culminating in an apocalyptic warning by Lord Keynes to the Cabinet in August 1945.

Document 1.2.3 'Our Overseas Financial Prospects', 13 August 1945

1 Three sources of financial assistance have made it possible for us to mobilise our domestic manpower for war with an intensity not approached elsewhere and to spend cash abroad, mainly in India and the Middle East, on a scale not even equalled by the Americans, without having to export in order to pay for the food and raw materials which we were using at home or to provide the cash which we were spending abroad.

2 The fact that the distribution of effort between ourselves and our Allies has been of this character leaves us far worse off when the assistance dries up than if the roles had been reversed. If we had been developing our exports so as to pay for our current needs and in addition to provide a large surplus which we could furnish free of current charge to our Allies as Lend–Lease or Mutual Aid or on credit, we should, of course, find ourselves in a grand position when the period of providing the stuff free of current charge was brought suddenly to an end.

3 As it is the more or less sudden drying up of these sources of assistance shortly after the end of the Japanese war will put us in an almost desperate plight, unless some other source of temporary assistance can be found to carry us over while we recover our breath – a plight far worse than most people, even in Government Departments, have yet realised.

4 The three sources of financial assistance have been:–
    (a) Lend–Lease from the United States.
    (b) Mutual Aid from Canada.
    (c) Credits supplemented by sales of our pre-war capital assets from the Sterling Area including Credits under Payments Agreements with certain countries especially in South America which are outside the Area but have made special arrangements with it.

5 In the present year, 1945, these sources are enabling us to overspend our own income at the rate of about £2100 millions a year. . . .

6 This vast, but temporary, assistance allows us for the time being to over-play our own financial hand by just that amount. It means conversely that others are under-playing their hands correspondingly. How vividly do departments and Ministers realise that the gay and successful fashion in which we undertake liabilities all over the world and slop money out to the importunate represents an over-playing of our hand, the possibility of which will come to an end quite suddenly and in the near future unless we obtain a new source of assistance? It may be that we are doing some things which are useless if we have to abandon them shortly after V.J. and that our external policies are very far from being adjusted to impending realities. . . .

24 To an innocent observer in the Treasury very early and very drastic economies in this huge cash expenditure overseas seems an absolute condition of maintaining our solvency. There is no possibility of our obtaining from others for more than a brief period the means of maintaining any significant part of these establishments, in addition to what we shall require to meet our running excess of imports over exports and to sustain the financial system of the Sterling Area. These are burdens which there is no reasonable expectation of our being able to carry. . . .

25 Even assuming a fair measure of success in rapidly expanding exports and curtailing Government expenditure overseas, it still remains that aid of the order of $5 billions is required from the United States. We have reason to believe that those members of the American Administration who are in touch with our financial position are already aware that we shall be in Queer Street without aid of somewhere between $3 and $5 billions and contemplate aid on this scale as not outside practical politics. But this does not mean that difficult and awkward problems of terms and conditions do not remain to be solved. The chief points likely to arise are the following:–

(a) They will wish the assistance to be described as a *credit*. If this means payment of interest and stipulated terms of repayment, it is something that we cannot undertake in addition to our existing obligations. It would be a repetition of what happened after the last war and a cause of further humiliation and Anglo-American friction, which we should firmly resist. If however the term credit is no more than a camouflage for what would be in effect a grant-aid, that is another matter.

(b) The Americans will almost certainly insist upon our acceptance of a monetary and commercial financial policy along the general lines on which they have set their hearts. But it is possible that they will exercise moderation and will not overlook the impropriety of using financial pressure on us to make us submit to what we believe is to our grave disadvantage. In fact the most persuasive argument we can use for obtaining the desired aid is that only by this means will it lie within our power to enter into international co-operation in the economic field on the general principle of non-discrimination.

(c) Bases, islands and air facilities and the like may conceivably come into the picture.

26 Nor must we build too much on the sympathy and knowledge of the members of the American administration with whom we are in touch. It will be a tough proposition, perhaps an impossible one, to sell a sufficiently satisfactory plan to Congress, and the American people who are un-acquainted with, and are never likely to understand, the true force of our case, not only in our interests but in the interests of the United States and the whole world. For the time being Ministers would do well to assume that no arrangement which we can properly accept is yet in sight, and that until such arrangement is in sight, we are, with the imminent cessation of Lend–Lease, virtually bankrupt, and the economic base for the hopes of the public non-existent.

27 It seems, then, that there are three essential conditions without which we have not a hope of escaping what might be described, without exaggeration and without implying that we should not eventually recover from it, a financial Dunkirk. These conditions are (a) an intense concentra-tion on the expansion of exports, (b) drastic and immediate economies in our overseas expenditure, and (c) substantial aid from the United States on terms which we can accept. They can only be fulfilled by a combination of the greatest enterprise, ruthlessness and tact.

28 What does one mean in this context by a 'financial Dunkirk'? What could happen in the event of insufficient success? That is not easily foreseen. Abroad it would require a sudden and humiliating withdrawal from our onerous responsibilities with great loss of prestige and acceptance for the time being of the position of a second-class Power, rather like the present position of France. From the Dominions and elsewhere we should seek what charity we could obtain. At home a greater degree of austerity than we have experienced at any time during the war. And there would have to be an indefinite postponement of the realisation of the best hopes of the new Government. It is probable that after five years the difficulties would have been largely overcome.

29 But in practice one will be surprised if it ever comes to this. In practice, of course, we shall in the end accept the best terms we can get. And that may be the beginning of later trouble and bitter feelings. That is why it is so important to grasp the reality of our position and to mitigate its potentialities by energy, ingenuity and foresight.

Source: PRO CAB 129/1, memorandum by Lord Keynes, 13 August 1945

This document, although ambiguously entitled *Our Overseas Financial Prospects*, was circulated by Hugh Dalton, the new Chancellor of the Exchequer, with a warning that his Cabinet colleagues should be 'informed, without delay, of this most grim problem'. Lord Keynes, who had been economic adviser to the Treasury during the Second World War, highlighted the central fact that Britain had only survived the war in economic terms by heavy borrowing from the United States and by the liquidation of assets. These were temporary expedients which would not continue into the post-war era. The full magnitude of the country's economic plight was revealed by the balance of payments position which was massively in deficit. Accordingly Keynes's prescription was that the country first had to substantially reduce its expenditure and second had to obtain assistance from the United States on the best terms which could be negotiated. The first expedient could only be found in external affairs (paragraph 27), given the Labour government's commitment to the establishment of the new welfare state, while the second was liable to be fraught with difficulty (paragraphs 25 and 26). The use of the emotive image of 'a financial Dunkirk' illustrates Keynes's perception of the gravity of the situation.

Following Cabinet consideration of this memorandum, Keynes was sent to Washington to negotiate American economic assistance to ease the immediate financial difficulties confronting Britain. After several months of difficult negotiations this resulted in the Anglo-American Dollar Loan Agreement of 1946. Britain was to receive $3.75 billion and $650 million in final settlement of Lend–Lease, interest was to be 2 per cent and repayment, beginning in five years, was to last fifty years. This seemed to provide the necessary resources to give Britain the breathing space identified by Keynes **(Cairncross, 1985, p. 105; Pressnell, 1985, pp. 262–329)**. However, as a condition of the loan Britain had to make sterling convertible in 1947. This was viewed by the United States as essential in achieving the full operation of the Bretton Woods system of fixed exchange rates. The attempt to make the currency convertible would result in the early expiry of the Anglo-American loan and create a major economic crisis in the United Kingdom in August 1947 which was not resolved until the devaluation of the pound in 1949. Economic factors, therefore, were to be a major constraint on policy for the lifetime of the Labour government; nowhere was this to be more apparent than in the area of external policy.

The Labour government was faced with the need to redefine British policy in the Middle East. Consideration of, *inter alia*, the future of the ex-Italian colonies, the British position in Egypt and Palestine, together with a review of future defence policy was to reveal profound differences of opinion between Attlee and Bevin, the new Foreign Secretary. The immediate difficulty facing the new administration in the autumn of 1945 was the future of the ex-Italian colonies which were under temporary British control.

Document 1.2.4 'Future of the Italian Colonies', 1 September 1945

2 Quite apart from the advent of the atomic bomb which should affect all considerations of strategic area, the British Commonwealth and Empire is not a unit that can be defended by itself. It was the creation of sea power.

With the advent of air warfare the conditions which made it possible to defend a string of possessions scattered over five continents by means of a Fleet based on island fortresses have gone. In the 19th century the passage of the Mediterranean could be secured by sea power with Gibraltar, Malta and Egypt as its bases. In the air age the neutrality, if not the support of all countries contiguous to the route are needed. This is only one example.

3 The British Empire can only be defended by its membership of the United Nations Organisation. If we do not accept this, we had better say so. If we do accept this we should seek to make it effective and not at the same time act on out-worn conceptions. If the new organisation is a reality, it does not matter who holds Cyrenaica or Somalia or controls the Suez Canal. If it is not a reality we had better be thinking of the defence of England, for unless we can protect the home country no strategic positions elsewhere will avail.

4 Apart from strategic considerations I can see no possible advantage to us in assuming responsibility for these areas. They involve us in immediate loss. There is no prospect of their paying for themselves. The more we do for them the quicker shall we be faced with premature claims for self-government. We have quite enough of these awkward problems already.

5 After the last war, under the system of mandates, we acquired large territories. The world outside not unnaturally regarded this as a mere expansion of the British Empire. Trusteeship will appear to most people as only old mandates writ large.

6 Cyrenaica will saddle us with an expense that we can ill-afford. Why should we have to bear it? Why should it be assumed that only a few great Powers can be entrusted with backward people? Why should one or other of the Scandinavian countries not have a try? They are quite as fitted to bear rule as ourselves. Why not the United States?

7 British Somaliland has always been a dead loss and a nuisance to us. We only occupied it as part of the scramble for Africa. If we now add Ogaden and Italian Somaliland we shall have a troublesome ward with an unpleasant neighbour in Ethiopia. The French are on the spot in French Somaliland. Why not let them have it if they like? It will be a sop to their pride, and may help them to put up with the loss of their position in the Levant. There would, of course, be the sentimental objection to giving up a piece of the Empire, but otherwise it would be to our advantage to get rid of this incubus.

Source: PRO CAB 129/1, memorandum by Mr Attlee, 1 September 1945

In this document, produced for discussion in Cabinet, the new Prime Minister showed an unsuspected radical turn of mind as he challenged the core assumptions of both the Foreign Office and the Chiefs of Staff that the British position in the Middle East could and should be reconstructed on the basis of continued

British dominance. For Attlee, if not the British military, the lesson of the war was that the British position in the Middle East was indefensible except through membership of the United Nations. Echoing Keynes's memorandum, the Prime Minister was also worried about the expense of acquiring and administering new territories.

In response to this dramatic intervention, which implied a wholesale change in Britain's stance, Bevin, with the support of the Chiefs of Staff, maintained his assumption that His Majesty's Government would continue to assert their political predominance in the Middle East and the overriding responsibility for its defence. A prolonged and heated debate involving the Prime Minister, the Foreign Secretary and the Chiefs of Staff raged for some eighteen months, but faced with a united front from his main political ally, the Foreign Secretary, and his chief military advisers, Attlee was forced to acquiesce. In the summer of 1947 the Defence Committee of the Cabinet approved a new strategy put forward by the Chiefs of Staff based on the 'three pillars' that underpinned Britain's position.

Document 1.2.5 'Future Defence Policy', 22 May 1947

(a) The defence of the United Kingdom and its development as an offensive base.
(b) The control of essential sea communications.
(c) A firm hold in the Middle East and its development as an offensive base.

These three pillars of our strategy must stand together. The collapse of any one of them will bring down the whole structure of Commonwealth strategy. . . .

15 The area in which Russian expansion would be easiest and at the same time would hurt us most would be the Middle East. We may be sure that if we abandon our position there in peace Russia will fill the vacuum.
16 Our experience in other areas such as Eastern Europe has shown that when Russia gains control our economic interests are forfeited and our communications are cut. The first impact of Russian expansion into the Middle East would therefore be upon our oil supplies and upon Common- wealth sea and air communications. The importance to us of present and potential oil supplies in the area is as great, if not greater, than ever, particularly in peace. The importance of the Middle East as a centre of Commonwealth communications remains, and will remain, beyond question.

If the use of the Middle East communications was denied to us it would be necessary to divert our supplies round the Cape or across Central Africa, which would increase immeasurably on our resources. Moreover our strategic signal communications would be disrupted.
17 The powerful position which Russia would acquire by linking the Middle East countries to her influence and economy would prepare the way

for further infiltration into both Asia and Africa. If Russia were to establish herself in the Middle East in peace or war, her power and influence would dominate the Moslem world and would be likely to spread eastwards through India, Burma and Malaya; southwards through the Sudan; and westwards in North Africa.

18 In all these areas cells of communism exist, but so far in isolation. Once Russia is established in the Middle East she will create from these isolated cells a comprehensive and unified organisation. This would seriously undermine our strategy and economic interests in all these areas. Her eastward expansion would threaten the security of India, our control of sea communications in the Indian Ocean and our resources of oil, tin and rubber. Her westward expansion would create a new threat to our Atlantic sea communications already likely to be gravely endangered.

19 Moreover, by ejecting the influence of the Western Powers from the Middle East, Russia would be securing her most vulnerable flank. It is from the Middle East area that her own vital oil industry and new industrial centres can most effectively be threatened. At the same time we should be placed in the position of having to be prepared to meet direct attacks on our own territories and interests in Africa, Aden, the Mediterranean and India and on our communications in the Indian Ocean.

20 *To sum up:* if Russia secured control of this area not only would we lose very important resources and facilities but she would acquire a position of such dominating strategic and economic power that it would be fatal to our security. It is therefore vital that we must retain a firm hold on the Middle East. This can only be achieved by our physical presence there in peace and by tangible evidence of our intention to remain.

An important contribution to the security of our position will be the continued independence of Greece and Turkey.

21 The need to retain our strategic and economic position in the Middle East is of equal importance if we should be engaged in war with a power other than Russia. This is demonstrated by the fact that in two world wars we have had to defeat Germany in the Middle East.

Source: PRO CAB 21/1800, report by the Chiefs of Staff, 22 May 1947 (emphasis in the original)

This document, which reflected the victory of the British military, harks back to the position papers of 1944–1945 in its emphasis on the centrality of the Middle East to British security. It was to form the basis of British policy until the 'Radical Reviews' of the early 1950s. It is clear that the Chiefs of Staff felt that a firm foothold in the Middle East was necessary in peacetime in order to forestall Soviet penetration through the Middle East into Africa and Asia. In war, the Middle East had to be held in order to protect Britain's oil supplies in the Persian Gulf and its communications through the Mediterranean as well as providing the air bases for an atomic armed strategic bombing offensive against the Soviet Union.

The key to the British position in the Middle East, following the referral of the Palestine question to the United Nations in 1947, was Egypt which alone possessed the bases and facilities to sustain a British military presence in the area. Anglo-Egyptian relations still rested on the 1936 Treaty, which was to remain in operation for twenty years from its signature, but the Egyptian government had from December 1945 been demanding its renegotiation on the basis that British troops should be withdrawn from Egypt in time of peace. Bevin, supported by the Chiefs of Staff, argued that a renegotiated treaty should be drafted in such a way as to bring Egypt into a regional defence system for the Middle East as a whole so that facilities for the British armed forces could be maintained under this cover. These negotiations were to break down over the issue of Egyptian claims to the Sudan and remained in abeyance for some time thereafter.

By early 1948, Bevin had become fully convinced of both the hostility of the Soviet Union and the threat that communism posed to British worldwide interests. In order to meet this perceived threat the Cabinet concluded in January 1948 that 'there was general support for the proposal that positive steps should be taken to consolidate the forces of the Western European countries and their Colonial possessions'. They therefore approved the following paper by the Foreign Secretary.

Document 1.2.6 'The First Aim of British Foreign Policy', 4 January 1948

It must be recognised that the Soviet Government has formed a solid political and economic block behind a line running from the Baltic, along the Oder, through Trieste to the Black Sea. There is no prospect in the immediate future that we shall be able to re-establish and maintain normal relations with European countries behind that line . . . these countries are dominated by the Communists although they are only a minority in each country. Indeed we shall be hard put to it to stem the further encroachment of the Soviet tide. It is not enough to reinforce the physical barriers which still guard our Western civilisation. We must also organise and consolidate the ethical and spiritual force inherent in this Western civilisation of which we are the chief protagonists. This in my view can only be done by creating some form of union in Western Europe, whether of a formal or informal character, backed by the Americas and the Dominions.

THE SITUATION

. . . It is clear that from secure entrenchments behind their line the Russians are exerting a constantly increasing pressure which threatens the whole fabric of the West. In some Western countries the danger is still latent but in Germany, France, Trieste, Italy and Greece the conflicting forces are already at grips with one another. In each country the issue is still in doubt and we must act resolutely if we are to prevail. The Soviet Government has based its policy on the expectation that Western Europe will sink into economic chaos and they may be relied upon to place every possible obstacle in the path of American aid and of Western European recovery.

THE WESTERN UNION

I believe therefore that we should seek to form with the backing of the Americas and the Dominions a Western democratic system comprising, if possible, Scandinavia, the Low Countries, France, Portugal, Italy and Greece. As soon as circumstances permit we should of course wish also to include Spain and Germany, without whom no Western system can be complete. This may seem a somewhat fanciful conception, but events are moving fast and the sense of a common danger drives countries to welcome tomorrow solutions which appear unpractical and unacceptable to-day. . . .

The policy I have outlined will require strong British leadership in order to secure its acceptance in Europe on one hand and in the Dominions and the Americas on the other. Material aid will have to come principally from the United States, but the countries of Western Europe which despise the spiritual values of America will look to us for political and moral guidance and for assistance in building up a counter attraction to the baleful tenets of communism within their borders and in recreating a healthy society wherever it has been shaken or shattered by the war. I believe that we have the resources with which to perform this task.

Provided we can organise a Western European system such as I have outlined above, backed by the power and resources of the Commonwealth and of the Americas, it should be possible to develop our own power and influence to equal that of the United States of America and the USSR. We have the material resources in the Colonial Empire if we develop them and by giving a spiritual lead now we should be able to carry out our task in a way which will show clearly that we are not subservient to the United States of America or to the Soviet Union.

Source: PRO CAB 129/23, memorandum by the Secretary of State for Foreign Affairs, 4 January 1948

Compare with Churchill's influential speech at Fulton, Missouri, of 5 March 1946 which observed that 'from Stettin in the Baltic to Trieste in the Adriatic, an iron curtain has descended across the Continent'.

The increasingly pugnacious Bevin here defined a distinctive role for Britain within the accelerating Cold War. This was the 'Third Force' idea which was to underpin British policy for the next eighteen months. The central thesis of this was that Britain was not doomed to a subordinate role to the United States, but that, in conjunction with the Commonwealth and Empire and like-minded European powers and their empires, Britain could form a counterweight to the Soviet Union that was independent of American power. Part of the rationale for this was Bevin's belief that the democracies of Western Europe were antipathetic to the raw materialism espoused by the 'capitalist' United States and could only be mobilised behind a more 'social democratic' ethos personified by the Labour government. It is, however, noteworthy that even Bevin recognised the necessity for American material assistance in order to establish a Western Union. Moreover, the whole concept was ultimately dependent upon Britain's ability to lead this group and the willingness of others to be led.

In the context of the Czech coup of March 1948 and the Berlin Blockade of 1948–1949 Bevin's fears of Soviet intentions may well have been accurate. However, in the light of the withdrawal from India, Palestine, Greece and Turkey in 1947–1948 and the continuing economic strains upon Britain, the Foreign Secretary's ambitions were somewhat grandiose if not wholly unrealistic. As part of the Anglo-American Dollar Loan Agreement, sterling was made convertible in August of 1947. This led to an immediate drain on Britain's reserves as holders of sterling rushed to convert into dollars. The Treasury was forced to take emergency action and the country was subjected to an austerity programme for the following eighteen months. This crisis of Britain's external economy was symptomatic of the general stresses and strains on the British economy wherein the search for savings in government expenditure came to be the paramount objective of policy. Nowhere was this more evident than in the field of defence expenditure where short-term estimates of £662 million for 1948 were estimated to rise to £1,500 million in the mid-1950s but had to be held down to £600 million per annum in 1948–1949 **(Gorst, 1991, pp. 190–209)**. The implications for an independent British role in the Cold War were obvious, given the economic constraints.

Thus, by October 1949, Bevin was forced to concede that Britain's future role had come to depend on 'the closest association with the United States'. In a paper to the Cabinet he reached the following conclusions.

Document 1.2.7 'European Policy', 18 October 1949

(1) The Commonwealth alone cannot form a Third World Power equivalent to the United States or the Soviet Union.

(2) Commonwealth solidarity is more likely to be promoted by the consolidation of the West than by the formation of a Third World Power independent of America.

(3) A weak, neutral Western Europe is undesirable and a strong independent Western Europe is impracticable at present and could only come about, if at all, at the cost of the remilitarisation of Germany.

(4) The best hope of security for Western Europe lies in a consolidation of the West on the lines indicated by the Atlantic Pact.

(5) During the next 10–20 years, Western Europe provided it continues on its policy of co-operation, should emerge from economic and even from military dependence on the United States but the two areas will remain interdependent.

(6) The United Kingdom will have an increasingly important part to play in the consolidated West, and must also seek to maintain its special relations with the United States of America.

Source: PRO CAB 129/37 Pt I, memorandum by the Secretary of State for Foreign Affairs, 18 October 1949

This policy paper, approved by the Cabinet, marks the clear recognition that, at least in the short term, the idea of a Western Union under British leadership and independent of the United States was totally impractical. Therefore Britain had to seek to sustain its world role through an increasingly close relationship with the United States.

Despite the formation of NATO in 1949, the difficulties in basing British policy on a 'special relationship' with the United States were to become rapidly apparent. The Korean War, which broke out in the summer of 1950, demonstrated the political and diplomatic problems that arose from Britain's increasingly subordinate position. Moreover, the associated rearmament programme, to which Britain committed itself in the belief of American economic support which was not forth-coming, strained the British economy to the limit of its capacity and slowed an export-led economic recovery. In many ways the Far East could be seen as an American sphere of influence, but, more worryingly for the British government, the same trend of American assertiveness was to raise its head in the Middle East, which was accepted as an area of British responsibility, during the Abadan crisis of 1951. This crisis, sparked off by the nationalisation of the holdings of the Anglo-Iranian Oil Company by the Iranian Prime Minister Dr Mossadeq, both demonstrates the 'reality' of the 'special relationship' and presents interesting parallels with the Suez Crisis.

Document 1.2.8 'Abadan Memorandum' 1962

1 The decision in 1951 to relinquish control at Abadan of the greatest single British investment overseas was one of the heaviest decisions taken by any British Government since the Second World War. Nor has its political importance diminished in subsequent perspective. . . .

6 British economic and military weakness after the Second World War spelt British weakening in the Middle East, though not its abandonment as suggested by the Prime Minister. The relative British decline and American ascendancy in the Middle East generally (e.g., Saudi Arabia, Palestine, Greece, Turkey) extended to Persia and underlay the Abadan crisis. Its importance in this wider context of the British presence in the Middle East was appreciated, and was at the time, though not always, emphasised in the Foreign Office. . . .

7 The potential repercussions of the Abadan crisis upon the British presence in Egypt and her aspirations towards nationalising the Suez Canal were appreciated at the time in the Foreign Office and elsewhere . . . in October

[1951] the British relinquishment of Abadan was promptly followed by Egyptian unilateral denunciation of the Anglo-Egyptian Treaty of 1936 and by a grave crisis in the Canal Zone. . . .

8 It may be that in 1950/51 the background of British power and prestige (e.g., Second World War, Indian Empire) was too close to permit a full adjustment to changed circumstances wherein Great Britain might need to reinforce her position of strength in relation to lesser powers such as Persia by exploiting the techniques of bargaining from weakness with greater powers such as the United States. . . .

25 At the beginning of 1951 the Foreign Office was rightly concerned by the Persian threat of oil nationalisation, but early British reactions were somewhat slow and understandably embarrassed. The Persian demand for nationalisation placed the British Labour government in a logical dilemma which hampered its handling of the crisis. His Majesty's Government was, however, much less inclined towards accepting such nationalisation than was the United States Government which in 1951 steadily pressed His Majesty's Government towards appeasement of Persia. . . .

36 Behind the Abadan crisis lay Britain's financial dilemma in 1951: serious deterioration of her balance of payments made it increasingly important to retain Persian oil, but at the same time increasingly difficult for His Majesty's Government to resist pressure from the American Government on whose financial aid it might become dependent. It was also estimated in June 1951 that, at any rate initially, British oil companies would be dependent on the Americans for three-quarters of the oil needed to replace Persian supplies. . . .

41 . . . His Majesty's Government was however conscious, perhaps almost to a fault, that any decisive support must come from the reluctant Government of the United States, . . .

44 . . . By the end of the month [May 1951] British policy had to reckon that the United States Government would, for most practical purposes, disapprove of such British measures as economic sanctions, military intervention, or political approach to the Shah. After the earlier negativism of the Anglo-Iranian Oil Company, room for British manoeuvre was now restricted between the negative obduracies of Dr Musaddiq and of the State Department. . . .

50 . . . The main British objective, from having been the economic one of keeping the oil flowing, became a political one, at once narrower and broader; to cling to some foothold in Abadan in order to ride out the crisis and maintain the menaced prestige and power of Great Britain throughout the Middle East. . . .

64 During the Abadan Crisis His Majesty's Government constantly found itself pressed into adopting an immediately weaker course towards Persia in hope that, in the likely event of its failure, solid American support would thereby have been secured for stronger measures thereafter. This hope was repeatedly proved false. . . .

68 The two great British reverses over nationalisation at Abadan in 1951 and at Suez in 1956, contrasting yet largely complementary, indicated that within the context of the Cold War led by the United States against the Soviet Union for the adherence of the uncommitted and under-developed peoples in the aftermath of the Second World War, Great Britain had not as yet discovered fully satisfactory means of reconciling the decline of her Imperial heritage with the resurgence of aggressive nationalism in the Middle East and in the continents beyond.

Source: PRO FO 370/2694, memorandum by Dr Butler, September 1962

This memorandum was written in 1962 by the historian Dr Rohan Butler who was working for the Foreign Office producing briefs on particular crises in order that the Foreign Office could absorb any lessons. This document is obviously written with the benefit of hindsight with full access to contemporary papers. Therefore while it should be treated with some care it is also an invaluable source for the student. This analysis clearly brackets Abadan and the Suez Crisis together as major turning-points in Britain's post-war external relations. By highlighting the economic dependency of Britain on the United States, Rohan Butler also indicates the military and diplomatic dependency of Britain within the context of an international order riven by the Cold War.

By 1951 British policy had retreated from a range of high ambitions exemplified by the position papers of 1945 and the Third Force idea to a recognition that within the new realities of the Cold War Britain had to rely upon the somewhat undefined 'special relationship with the United States'. That this relationship was fraught with difficulties was well illustrated by the Abadan Crisis. Giving more cause for concern, due to the importance of the Middle East to Britain, were the unresolved difficulties with Egypt.

1.3 The Road to Suez 1951–1955

This four-year period saw the return to office of the Conservative Party with Churchill forming a government, that included the experienced Eden as Foreign Secretary, in October 1951. The government inherited a complex situation in the Middle East; there had been no substantive progress on a renegotiation of the 1936 Treaty with Egypt and the creation of the state of Israel in 1948 had further complicated the situation by removing an alternative base area while introducing a wholly new and dangerous antagonism into the volatile area. For much of this period, the British were striving to achieve a new relationship with Egypt that would safeguard their interests in the Middle East, a difficult task that was compounded by the coup in July 1952 in Egypt which replaced King Farouk with a more nationalist military regime under General Neguib.

Given continuing economic problems there was an urgent need to rationalise Britain's overseas commitments while continuing to preserve Britain's interests and prestige as a great power. Serious consideration of these issues took place in 1952 with a review of Britain's overseas obligations. The strategy envisaged was a British withdrawal from the Canal Zone in return for Egyptian participation in a Middle East Defence Organisation. Even this, however, proved impossible to achieve as in the course of negotiations from 1952–1954 it became apparent that the Egyptians were unwilling to join an organisation which they saw as a continuing imperial presence in the Middle East. Ultimately, the 1954 Suez Base Agreement would concede that the costs of retaining a large British military presence in the Canal Zone outweighed any perceived benefits. At the same time the British proceeded to organise a defence organisation, the Bagdad Pact, that did not include Egypt (compare with document 1.3.3 pp. 32–33).

The return of Eden as Foreign Secretary led, at least on the surface, to the development of some radical perspectives on Britain's world role. Eden submitted a pivotal paper to the Cabinet which began with a basic definition of British foreign policy.

Document 1.3.1 'British Overseas Obligations', 18 June 1952

4 The essence of a sound foreign policy is to ensure that a country's strength is equal to its obligations. If this is not the case, then either the obligations must be reduced to the level at which resources are available to maintain them, or a greater share of the country's resources must be devoted to their support. It is becoming clear that rigorous maintenance of the presently-accepted policies of Her Majesty's Government at home and abroad is placing a burden on the country's economy which it is beyond the resources of the country to meet. A position has already been reached where there is no reserve and therefore no margin for unforeseen additional obligations.

5 The first task must be to determine how far the external obligations of the country can be reduced or shared with others, or transferred to other shoulders, without impairing too seriously the world position of the United Kingdom and sacrificing the vital advantages which flow from it. But if, after careful review, it is shown that the total effort required is still beyond the capacity of existing national resources, a choice of the utmost difficulty lies before the British people, for they must either give up, for a time, some of the advantages which a high standard of living confers upon them or, by relaxing their grip in the outside world, see their country sink to the level of a second-class Power, with injury to their essential interests and way of life of which they can have little conception. Faced with this choice, the British people might be rallied to a greater productive effort which would enable a greater volume of external commitments to be borne. . . .

28 . . . there are few ways to effect any reductions in our overseas commitments which would provide immediate relief to our economic difficulties. . . .

29 If, on a longer view, it must be assumed that the maintenance of the present scale of overseas commitments will permanently overstrain our economy, clearly we ought to recognise that the United Kingdom is over-committed, and reduce the commitment. The only practical way of removing this permanent strain would be for the United Kingdom to shed or share the load of one or two major obligations, e.g., the defence of the Middle East, for which we at present bear the responsibility alone . . . our present policy is in fact directed towards the construction of international defence organisations for the Middle East and South East Asia, in which the United States and other Commonwealth countries would participate. Our aim should be to persuade the United States to assume the real burdens in such organisations while retaining for ourselves as much political control – and hence prestige and world influence – as we can. . . .

30 The success of this policy will depend on a number of factors, some favourable, some unfavourable. The United States is the only single country in the free world capable of assuming new and world-wide obligations; being heavily committed to the East–West struggle they would not readily leave a power-vacuum in any part of the globe but would be disposed, however reluctantly, to fill it themselves if it was clear that the United Kingdom could no longer hold the position (as they did, for example, in Greece). On the other hand, the history of the Middle East Command negotiations and the unwillingness of the United States Chiefs of Staff to commit forces to it illustrates the American reluctance to enter into new commitments in peacetime. In South East Asia only the sketchiest form of co-operation exists. Moreover, distrust of the British and fear of becoming an instrument to prop up a declining British Empire are still strong. (This is truer among Republicans than Democrats, but we must clearly prepare ourselves to deal with either Government.) As regards the United Kingdom part, a policy of this kind will only be successful with the United States in so far as we are able to demonstrate that we are making the maximum possible effort ourselves, and the more gradually and inconspicuously we can transfer the real burdens from our own to American shoulders, the less damage we shall do to our own position and influence in the world. . . .

[It is] clearly beyond the resources of the United Kingdom to continue to assume the responsibility alone, for the security of the Middle East. Our aim should be to make the whole of this area and in particular the Canal Zone an international responsibility. Hence every step should be taken to speed up the establishment of an Allied Middle East Defence Organisation. It should, however, be recognised that the setting up of such a defence organisation will not result in any immediate alleviation of the burden for the United Kingdom. The United States have refused to enter into any precise commitments in the Middle East or to allocate forces and it should be the constant object of Her Majesty's Government to persuade them to do so. In addition, every possibility should be explored of committing the

United States militarily, e.g., to the building of bases, the provision of material, the sharing and reconstruction of airfields. During the present crisis, any reduction in the British forces in Egypt is a military problem in which the need for safeguarding British lives and property in case of an emergency must be the first consideration. The dilemma is that until we can come to an agreement with Egypt no effective international defence organisation for the Middle East can be established; and so long as there is no settlement with Egypt and no international defence organisation we are obliged to hold the fort alone.

Source: PRO CAB 129/53, memorandum by the Secretary of State for Foreign Affairs, 18 June 1952

This paper should be compared with those of Ernest Bevin in 1948–1949, Documents 1.2.6 and 1.2.7 (pp. 22–23, 24–25).

In Document 1.3.1, Eden placed before the Cabinet his thoughts on the key issues that had bedevilled British foreign policy since the Second World War, if not earlier, and which the Labour government of Clement Attlee had been unable to solve. In the introduction Eden took an apparently hard look at the balance between Britain's commitments and the means of paying for them and recognised that Britain's economy could not support her pretensions. The stark realism of this introduction was, however, obscured as Eden foresaw two options: maintaining the obligations with others paying the cost (the United States) and/or substantially improving the performance of the British domestic economy to enable the costs to be borne. Neither was likely to be an easy option. With regard to the Middle East, this policy, which was in essence a gigantic con-trick, was likely to prove very difficult to carry out because of the reluctance of the United States to assume responsibilities in an extremely volatile region. Furthermore, Egypt's reluctance to participate in any defence organisation for the region was unlikely to be overcome by any notional transfer of responsibility. This was exactly the problem: Britain could not continue to hold the line indefinitely but finding willing substitutes was fraught with difficulties. Egypt would sanction neither a continued British presence nor the joining of any defence organisation and the United States was to show a marked reluctance to take over British responsibilities. Eden's 'grand design' therefore, while recognising these difficulties, could only rest on the Micawberish hope that 'something would turn up' to rescue the situation.

In the meantime, Eden pressed ahead with a new treaty with Egypt and the establishment of a defence organisation. By 1953 Eden had concluded that holding the fort alone was no longer a reasonable option.

Document 1.3.2 'Egypt: The Alternatives', 16 February 1953

We cannot afford to keep 80,000 men indefinitely in the Canal Zone. Already our overseas current expenditure – mainly military – has risen from £160 millions in 1950 to £222 millions (provisional estimate) in 1952.

With our limited resources, it is essential that we should concentrate on the points where our vital strategic needs or the necessities of our economic life are at stake and that we should utilise our strength in the most economical way. It is not possible for our present forces in the Canal Zone to support our peace-time interests elsewhere in the Middle East. If we leave them there in defiance of the Egyptians they will be wholly absorbed in coping with the situation which their very presence creates.

Source: PRO CAB 129/59, memorandum by the Secretary of State for Foreign Affairs, 16 February 1953

In this statement to the Cabinet Eden once again acknowledged that Britain's economic circumstances were increasingly impressing themselves upon Britain's strategic position and that some rationalisation of her position was urgently required. Eden was therefore committed to a new treaty that would redefine the relationship between Britain and Egypt. This was, however, to be a painful process that was to tax the skills and patience of the Foreign Secretary to the limit both in the negotiations with Egypt and in attempting to circumvent opposition from two sources within the Conservative Party. A group of Conservative backbenchers headed by Charles Waterhouse, and including Julian Amery (the son-in-law of Harold Macmillan), Fitzroy Maclean and Enoch Powell, and supported from the Lords by the former Cabinet Secretary Lord Hankey and the former Ambassador to Egypt Lord Killearn (Miles Lampson), had formed the 'Suez Group' in 1952 with the aim of preventing a policy of 'scuttle' from the Suez Canal Zone **(Troën and Shemesh, 1990, pp. 110–126)**. They received private support from the Prime Minister himself who, although he had intimated to Eisenhower as early as February 1953 that the Canal Base did not justify the expenditure in manpower or money **(Boyle, 1990, p. 29)**, had begun to have doubts about the direction of his Foreign Secretary's policy, complaining to his private secretaries of Eden's 'appeasement', and stating that if Eden were to offer his resignation he would accept it. **(Schuckburgh, 1986, pp. 75–76)**. In the event the Foreign Secretary mounted a strong defence of his policy at a meeting of the 1922 Committee, arguing with the support of Churchill that an agreement on the Sudan would enable a satisfactory outcome to the negotiations with Egypt **(Rhodes James, 1987, p. 383)**.

Although a previous obstacle to a settlement, the Egyptian claim to the Sudan was swiftly conceded by the Egyptian government; they were, however, even less inclined than their predecessors to make concessions on the continued presence of British troops in the Canal Zone or to contemplate Egyptian membership of a western-dominated regional military organisation. Ultimately, Eden admitted that Egypt could not be forced against its will to accept either of these conditions, and, accordingly, in 1954, an agreement solely on the Suez Canal Base was reached with the new Egyptian Prime Minister, Colonel Gamal Abdul Nasser, which brought to an end the British presence in Egypt.

Document 1.3.3 'The Suez Canal Base Agreement', 19 October 1954

The Government of the United Kingdom of Great Britain and Northern Ireland and the Government of the Republic of Egypt,

Desiring to establish Anglo-Egyptian relations on a new basis and firm friendship,

Have agreed as follows:–

ARTICLE I

Her Majesty's forces shall be completely withdrawn from Egyptian territory in accordance with the Schedule set forth in Part A of Annex 1 within a period of twenty months from the date of signature of the present agreement.

ARTICLE II

The Government of the United Kingdom declare that the Treaty of Alliance signed in London on 26 August 1936 with the Agreed Minute, Exchanged Notes, Convention concerning the immunities and privileges enjoyed by the British Forces in Egypt and all other subsidiary agreements is terminated.

ARTICLE III

Parts of the Suez Canal Base . . . shall be kept in efficient working order and capable of immediate use in accordance with the provisions of Article 4 of the present agreement. . . .

ARTICLE IV

In the event of an armed attack by an outside Power on any country which at the date of signature of the present Agreement is a party to the Treaty of Joint Defence between Arab League States signed in Cairo on the 13th of April 1950, or on Turkey, Egypt shall afford to the United Kingdom such facilities as may be necessary in order to place the Base on a war footing and to operate it effectively. . . .

ARTICLE V

In the event of the return of British Forces to the Suez Canal Base area in accordance with the provisions of Article 4 these forces shall withdraw immediately upon the cessation of the hostilities referred to in that article. . . .

ARTICLE VIII

The two Contracting Governments recognise that the Suez Maritime Canal, which is an integral part of Egypt, is a waterway economically, commercially and strategically of international importance, and express their determination to uphold the convention guaranteeing the freedom of navigation of the Canal signed at Constantinople on the 29th of October 1888. . . .

ARTICLE X

The present Agreement does not affect and shall not be interpreted as affecting in any way the rights and obligations of the Parties under the Charter of the United Nations.

Source: Parliamentary Papers, Cmd. 9586, 1954

See Document 1.1.3 (pp. 3–6).

This formal treaty between two sovereign nations attempted to place the relationship between Britain and Egypt on a new footing by removing the long-standing irritation of the British presence in the Canal Zone. Provision was retained, however, in Articles 4 and 5 for the re-entry of British forces. With respect to the Suez Canal, Article 9 of the treaty simply confirmed the 1888 Convention while recognising the contradiction in the status of a waterway that was 'international' but an integral part of a sovereign state; the later nationalisation of the Canal in 1956 did not therefore breach this article.

Eden hoped that this agreement, which removed the major irritant from their relations, would usher in a new era of Anglo-Egyptian co-operation centring around Egyptian participation in a regional defence organisation for the Middle East. **(Kent, 1993, pp. 45–63)**.

In the face of continuing Egyptian opposition to such a scheme Eden was forced to consider an alternative plan emanating from Iraq. The pro-British Prime Minister of Iraq, Nuri es-Said, had proposed in September 1954 that the Anglo-Iraqi Treaty of 1930 should be redefined to provide military facilities for British forces. The British were initially lukewarm about this proposal and adopted a watching brief. However, the forming of a Turco-Iraqi pact in February 1955, that looked to create shared defence arrangements, together with a friendly but unsatisfactory meeting between Eden and Nasser in Cairo also in February, transformed the British attitude to what became known as the Baghdad Pact. Henceforward, it would be British policy to build up the so-called 'Northern Tier' as the western bulwark against the spread of communism in the Middle East, an idea first aired by the

American Secretary of State John Foster Dulles in 1953: to this end Britain acceded to the Turco-Iraqi Pact in April 1955. The British hoped that other Arab states, including Egypt, would join this 'NATO for the Middle East' but were to be disappointed, not least because the United States administration declined to throw its weight behind the organisation citing the opposition of pro-Israeli pressure groups in Congress. Eden, who succeeded Churchill as Prime Minister on his resignation in early April 1955, was disappointed at this lack of American support for a venture which they had inspired but hoped for a change of heart from President Eisenhower which would allow American participation and would encourage a wider Arab membership of the Baghdad Pact.

In under a century the British had moved from a position of outright opposition to the construction of the Canal to a position where her prestige and power were intimately tied up with the maintenance of a position in the Middle East. The occupation of Egypt, following the 1882 invasion led to 'informal' imperial control of the country for over sixty years. The need to control Egypt, and to protect the Canal and the route to India, led to the creation of a vast British base in the Suez Canal Zone. This symbol of imperial power was to become increasingly vulnerable, and arguably irrelevant, in the post Second World War period. Successive British governments strove to achieve an accommodation with increasingly nationalist Egyptian governments which would enable them to retain a position in the Middle East, to defend and secure the oil supplies of the Persian Gulf, while spreading the burden of the defence of the region. By early 1955 this policy had failed in that Britain had been forced to agree to leave the Suez Canal Base by the summer of 1956 and no clear arrangements had been made for the defence of the area against the threat of communism in both peace and in war.

Chronology 1854–1955

1854 Ferdinand de Lesseps gains concession from Viceroy of Egypt to dig and operate the Suez Canal

1858 Universale Company of the Suez Maritime Canal formed

1869 Suez Canal opens

1875 British Prime Minister Benjamin Disraeli purchases major shareholding in Canal Company

1882 British invasion of Egypt

1888 Convention of Constantinople signed

1922 Egypt declared independent by Britain

1936 Anglo-Egyptian Treaty signed

1942 British force removal of Egyptian government

1947 British forces withdraw from Egyptian cities but remain in the Suez Canal Zone

1952 King Farouk overthrown by 'Young Officers' coup led by General Neguib

1954 Anglo-Egyptian Base Agreement signed, British troops to be withdrawn from the Canal Zone by June 1956

1955 January Turco–Iraqi Pact signed

April   Britain accedes to Turco–Iraqi Pact.

From ALPHA to nationalisation

1955–July 1956

In December 1954, Dulles and Eden agreed to attempt a solution to the long-running Arab–Israeli confrontation that they considered to be at the root of the instability in the Middle East, instability that raised the spectre of Soviet penetration of an area still held to be vital to western interests. What emerged was the product of a joint Anglo-American team of senior officials who attempted to formulate proposals that were acceptable to both Israel and, the key to Arab opinion, Egypt. These complex and delicate negotiations, known as Plan ALPHA, were summarised by Macmillan in a paper for the Cabinet written in June 1955.

Document 2.1 'Palestine Settlement', 11 June 1955

3 . . . The idea was that Israel should cede two small triangles, one to Egypt with its base on the Egypt–Israel frontier and one to Jordan with its base on the Jordan–Israel frontier, in the extreme South of the Negeb, a few miles North of Elath. The points of the two triangles would meet on the Israeli Road from Beersheba to Elath; and at this junction, which might need mixed or international supervision, a road from Egypt to Jordan under complete Arab control could pass over (or under) the road to Elath, which would remain under complete Israeli control.

4 This combination of diplomacy and engineering would be a novel but perhaps decisive, feature of the settlement proposed. . . .

5 It was agreed that the Israelis would never surrender the whole Negeb or the greater part of it as the Egyptians desired. They are deeply attached to this territory which has for them a religious significance, insures their access to the Red Sea and allows them to taste the freedom of an area in which they can be out of sight of an hostile frontier. On the other hand, there is little doubt that the Egyptians will not accept a settlement which leaves the whole of the Negeb in Israeli hands. There can be no solution except by the principle underlying the proposal described in paragraph 3 above – that the principle of a point at the junction of two triangles where the sovereignty appertains to both or neither. Solomon could do no better. . . .

9 . . . There are of course several financial uncertainties which could only be cleared up finally in the course of negotiations with Israel and the Arab States;

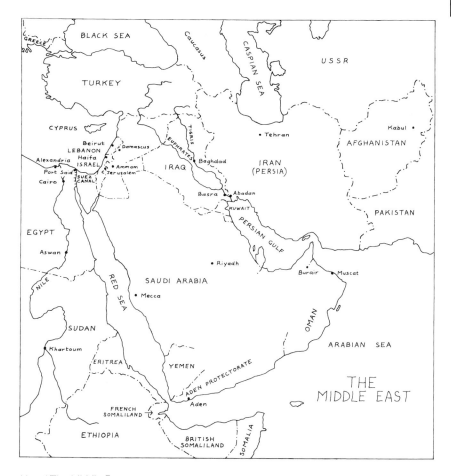

Map 1 The Middle East

for example, it is likely that the parties to the dispute will seek to make the United States Government and ourselves pay for their co-operation in terms of increased financial assistance. . . . Our financial liabilities in connection with the proposed settlement could be limited to the following contributions to the £100 millions compensation which Israel will have to pay to the Arab refugees:–

(a) A loan to Israel, probably on unattractive terms, but spread over ten years, of the order of £15 millions;

(b) Permission for the Israelis to raise about £15 millions over ten years by the sale of Israel Government bonds in the United Kingdom.

10 I ask the authority of my colleagues:–

(a) to co-operate with the United States Government in an attempt, through discussions with Colonel Nasser and subsequently with the other parties to the dispute to bring about a settlement of the Palestine affair. . . .

Source: PRO CAB 129/75, memorandum by the Secretary of State for Foreign Affairs, 11 June 1955

The difficulties in any peace settlement between Israel and Egypt are well illustrated by the novel expedient embodied in paragraph 3 that was the core of ALPHA. These fine calculations were, however, upset by a conjunction of factors. First, Dulles, worried about the effect of such a deal on the forthcoming American election in 1956, decided to make an early statement on ALPHA; this threatened the secrecy on which the success of the ALPHA negotiations was assumed to hinge. Second, and more seriously, rising tension on the Egyptian–Israeli border culminated in a major Israeli attack on *fedayeen* (guerrilla) camps in the Gaza strip in late August 1955. The severity of this action by the new Israeli government headed by David Ben-Gurion led Nasser to the conclusion that the parlous state of the Egyptian armed forces, embargoed by the West, had to be remedied as soon as possible. In the absence of substantial shipments of American and British weapons, Nasser turned to the Soviet Union, who had previously offered arms to Egypt, and on 21 September 1955 announced a deal by which the Soviet Union through Czechoslovakia would supply to Egypt 200 tanks and, more worryingly, 100 high-performance jet aircraft including advanced Ilyushin Il-28 medium-range bombers.

The initial reaction in the West to the arms deal was one of barely concealed fury as the insertion of modern weapons profoundly altered the balance of power in the Middle East and therefore threatened ALPHA. In London, the initial reaction was hostile but also confused; on the one hand, there was a desire to punish Nasser, but on the other it was realised that any punitive action against him was only likely to push Egypt further into the Soviet orbit. Evelyn Shuckburgh, the official in charge of the British side of ALPHA, counselled caution and took the view that the arms deal could be used to advance the cause of ALPHA by pointing out to the participants the danger of a Middle Eastern arms race. This view was soon accepted by the Cabinet.

Document 2.2 Cabinet Discussions of the Czech Arms Deal, 4 October 1955

8 *The Foreign Secretary* said it was now known that the Egyptian Government had entered into a contract for the purchase of arms from the Soviet bloc. There were also indications that the Russians were making overtures for the supply of arms to Saudi Arabia, Syria and possibly other Arab countries. The implications of these developments were serious. It seemed likely that with the situation in the Far East stabilised and a situation of stalemate in Europe, the Russians were turning their attention to the Middle East. . . . As between Egypt and Israel, we and the United States had been

pursuing a policy (through the Middle East Arms Co-ordinating Committee but with increasing difficulty because of the defections of the French) aimed at ensuring that the supplies obtained by each country would be both strictly limited and fairly shared. It would now be necessary to examine how this new Soviet move could effectively be countered. . . .

The Prime Minister said that these developments might seriously affect our interests in the Middle East as a whole. Indeed, the importance of the developments in Egypt lay in their potential effect on the other Arab States. Our interests were greater than those of the United States because of our dependence on Middle East oil, and our experience in the area was greater than theirs. We should not therefore allow ourselves to be restricted over much by reluctance to act without full American concurrence and support. We should frame our own policy in the light of our interests in the area and get the Americans to support it to the extent we could induce them to do so. . . .

In further discussion the following points were also made:–

(a) It would be inadvisable to attempt to subject the Nasser regime to overwhelming pressure. It was doubtful whether such pressure could be made effective and a rebuff would be bad for our prestige in the Middle East.

(b) Our policy should be aimed as far as possible at isolating Egypt among the Arab States. But it was essential that the supply of Western arms to the Arab States allied to us should be expedited for, if this were not done, not all of them could be expected to remain stable in face of offers of Russian arms.

(c) Public opinion at home would expect the Government to have made some representations regarding these Russian moves in the Middle East. It could be made known that a communication had been sent to the Soviet Government. The text of the message need not, however, be published at this stage.

Source: PRO CAB 128/29, CM 34(55), 4 October 1955

The MEACC was an attempt by the Western Allies to prevent the exacerbation of the Arab–Israeli conflict by restricting the flow of arms supplies.

The interest of this Cabinet discussion lies in the statement by Eden that Britain could and should take a line in the Middle East independent of the United States. That this was to be a difficult, if not impossible, prospect was to be illustrated by events in the summer of 1956. There was also a recognition that the situation in the Middle East was delicately poised and that Britain, while supporting its traditional allies with arms supplies, should not marginalise Egypt completely. It should be noted that Eden was beginning to show signs of impatience at the continued policy of moderation being pursued by the Foreign Office, in co-operation with the US

State Department, although for the moment he was seemingly persuaded by Macmillan and Shuckburgh.

This dual-track policy, a continued attempt to promote reconciliation between the West and Egypt and a policy of strengthening the Baghdad Pact through the supply of weapons to encourage a wider membership, was successful in that Iran announced its intention to join the Baghdad Pact on 11 October 1955. But, like Project ALPHA, the Baghdad Pact also suffered from differing expectations. To the British it was a means of bolstering their crumbling position in the Middle East. To the Americans it was an anti-Soviet measure. And to Nasser it simply served as an irritant to his vision of a Pan-Arabist alliance against Israel which was under no obligation to either side in the Cold War.

A Cabinet meeting on 20 October amplified this policy and introduced the High Aswan Dam as the main lever to be used on Egypt.

Document 2.3 Cabinet Discussion of the Aswan Dam Project, 20 October 1955

The Foreign Secretary said that in the Middle East the Russians had clearly embarked on a deliberate policy of opening up another front in the cold war. It would be wrong, however, to be too despondent about the position. The Suez Treaties had created a vacuum in the Middle East and it was a common reaction for a nation which had been controlled by another for a period to turn against it on first obtaining freedom. This initial reaction might be expected to give place eventually to a balanced view. In the meantime we should adopt a policy of moderation in our dealings with Egypt and we should endeavour to persuade the Americans to do the same. We should concentrate on helping other Arab states who behaved loyally, while at the same time demonstrating that there were limits to the extent to which we could be provoked.

The Prime Minister said that the main objective of our policy should be to protect our vital oil interests in the Middle East. From this point of view the strengthening of the Northern Tier defence arrangements was more important than the attitude of Egypt. . . . The allocation of the Egyptian High Aswan Dam project to the European consortium if it could be secured would be of immense value in restoring the prestige of the West and particularly of the older European powers in the Arab World generally, in our dealings with Egypt it could be a trump card.

In discussion the following points were made:

(1) A policy of attempting to reduce tension in the Middle East by limiting the supply of arms could only succeed if the Middle East states could not obtain supplies from countries who were not signatories of the Tripartite declaration of 1950.

(2) It was the normal practice of the International Bank to require

international tenders for any project which they supported; and the risk that this procedure might result in the High Dam contract being let to a Russian or satellite firm could not be excluded. *The Chancellor of the Exchequer* said that he recognised the political advantages of this project being undertaken by the European consortium. He was concerned, however, about the size of the United Kingdom's commitment. In view of the interest of the International Bank in the matter it would be advisable, before any further steps were taken, to consult with the United States Government with a view to securing their support for a policy with regard to international tender which would be acceptable to the bank. In its present context such an approach might also result in getting further direct American support for the Egyptian economy. . . .

Summing up, *the Prime Minister* said that at the forthcoming Meeting of Foreign Ministers in Geneva the Foreign Secretary should take the opportunity of impressing on M. Molotov the dangers of the recent Russian moves in the Middle East which would upset the delicate balance in military strength which the Western powers had been endeavouring to maintain in this area of tension. There was a real danger that war might break out between Israel and Egypt in which the Americans would be likely to support Israel. Once such a war had started it might well spread into a world-wide conflict.

Source: PRO CAB 128/29, CM (36) 55, 20 October 1955

This full Cabinet discussion clearly laid the blame for the deterioration of the situation in the Middle East on the Soviet Union, and also clearly identified the struggle in the Middle East as being part of the Cold War. With respect to Egypt, the policy remained one of conciliation, but with the new element of using the issue of finance for the Aswan Dam as a means of pressurising the Egyptian government into a more pro-western stance. This naturally, as the Chancellor was quick to point out, raised the delicate question of Britain's financial commitment to this project and once again the necessity of American participation was recognised.

Eden was, however, showing signs of frustration at the attempts to persuade Egypt into the western camp, as Ivone Kirkpatrick noted in a letter to Macmillan.

Document 2.4 Letter from Kirkpatrick to Macmillan on Eden and Policy Towards Egypt, 28 October 1995

TOP SECRET

You should know that the Prime Minister is much exercised about the Middle East and is in two minds, oscillating between fear of driving Nasser irrevocably into the Soviet Camp and a desire to wring the necks of Egypt and Syria.

2 He had a meeting on Wednesday with the Minister of Defence and myself to discuss the matter. He decided that the Ministry of Defence should do all they could to accelerate the supply of arms to Iraq and that only a proportion of the arms earmarked for Egypt should at present be delivered. But he was perplexed as to the next step, particularly because he felt that the Jewish lobby would bring increasing pressure to make us cut all arms delivery and economic assistance to Egypt whilst at the same time increasing deliveries to Israel.

3 After some discussion he asked whether it would be any use instructing Sir Humphrey Trevelyan to confront Nasser with a demand for a declaration of his policy and demonstrable evidence of his intention to improve relations with Britain. At the Prime Minister's request I knocked-up a cock-shy draft for him to look at. But I pointed out at the same time that it was no use calling on Nasser to improve his ways unless we have some expectation that he will respond to our appeal. And if he does respond we must be prepared to treat Egypt better than in the past, both in the matter of arms and in the matter of economic aid. If we are not prepared to do this, on account of Israeli susceptibilities, we shall only aggravate relations with Egypt by making an appeal to Nasser. Indeed, the more successful our appeal the worse the damage will be unless we are prepared to respond.

4 I should add that the Prime Minister does not propose to take any action without consulting you. He is at the moment trying in the first place to clear his own mind.

Source: PRO FO 371/113608, letter by Ivone Kirkpatrick, 28 October 1955

It is clear from the heading of TOP SECRET and the restricted circulation of this private letter, to Macmillan and Shuckburgh alone, that the Permanent Under-Secretary at the Foreign Office was becoming increasingly perturbed at the Prime Minister's vacillations which implied a different approach to that which had been agreed by the Cabinet.

This was particularly embarrassing given that Macmillan was meeting Dulles in Geneva on the same day to persuade the Americans to support the Aswan Dam project in an attempt to bring Nasser into the fold. Although Dulles clearly had some reservations, telling Macmillan 'we should not enter upon the construction of the Dam on a blind gamble', by 9 November he appeared persuaded by Macmillan saying that 'he thought that even during the period immediately ahead talks with Nasser on the Aswan Dam should continue' **(FRUS (A), 1988, docs 363 and 391)**. By December it had been agreed that an offer of finance for the Dam should be made to Nasser: Britain and the United States would match the $200 million to be provided by the World Bank with the United States contributing 80 per cent of the funds. This offer was duly accepted by the Egyptian government on 17 December 1955 **(FRUS (A), 1988, doc. 432)**.

On the surface, therefore, at the end of 1955 the situation in the Middle East seemed promising. In reality, however, any progress was highly conditional and ominous cracks were beginning to appear in the two strands of British policy. First, the proposed expansion of the Baghdad Pact to include Jordan received a set-back with the failure of the Templar mission in early December 1955. Worse still, the hostility to General Templar appeared to be orchestrated by the Egyptians and Jordan seemed to be in danger of disintegration **(Lucas, 1991, pp. 76–77; Kyle, 1991, pp. 89–91)**.

Second, the assumptions that underpinned Project ALPHA proved to be highly optimistic and the visit by Robert Anderson, a close friend and adviser of President Eisenhower, to the Middle East in January 1956 proved a failure. As President Eisenhower noted in his diary in mid-March 1956

> he [Anderson] made no progress whatsoever in our basic purpose of arranging some kind of meeting between Egyptian officials and the Israelites. Nasser proved to be a complete stumbling block. ... On the other side, the Israel [*sic*] officials are anxious to talk with Egypt, but they are completely adamant in their attitude of making no concessions whatsoever in order to obtain a peace. Their general slogan is 'not one inch of ground', and their incessant demand is for arms. ... Public Opinion on both sides is inflamed and the chances for peaceful settlement seem remote.

The President concluded mournfully 'It is a very sorry situation' **(FRUS (B), 1988, doc. 187)**.

It was in this air of imminent crisis that Eden left for Washington for summit meetings with Eisenhower and Dulles at which the Middle East would be discussed. He took with him a new Foreign Secretary, Selwyn Lloyd, following a Cabinet reshuffle on 21 December 1955 that moved Harold Macmillan from the Foreign Office to the Treasury. It was at these meetings, at the end of January 1956, that a possible hardening of policy towards Egypt was first discussed. As Eden observed, 'He did not know how long we could go along with Nasser', to which Dulles replied 'We might soon know whether our whole attitude towards Nasser would have to be changed' **(FRUS (B), 1988, doc. 54)**. In effect, Nasser and Egypt were placed on probation subject to good behaviour.

On 1 March 1956, the Jordanian situation took a turn for the worse when King Hussein dismissed General Glubb from his post as commander of the Jordanian Arab Legion and several other senior British officers serving with Jordanian forces. This seemingly precipitate action followed a period of tension in the prickly relationship between the young king and the long-serving Glubb. This came as something of a surprise to the British government – indeed that evening Lloyd, unaware of developments in Amman, had secured an agreement for the cessation of Egyptian propaganda against the Baghdad Pact, the quid pro quo being a British undertaking not to widen membership of the Baghdad Pact **(PRO FO 371/121243)**. The British were quick to discern the hand of Nasser behind Hussein's action and Lloyd was somewhat annoyed with Nasser's protestations of innocence the next day. Lloyd's annoyance was compounded when that afternoon in Bahrein, continuing his Middle Eastern tour, his motorcade to the High Commission was stoned by a crowd.

In London these developments had a dramatic impact on the Prime Minister who saw recent events in the Middle East as part of a pattern with Nasser operating as a Soviet stooge to destabilise the western position in the Middle East, of which the centre piece was the Bagdad Pact. After a meeting of senior ministers, Eden sent a message to Eisenhower which outlined the following arguments.

Document 2.5 Eden to Eisenhower on Events in the Middle East, 5 March 1956

There is no doubt that the Russians are resolved to liquidate the Bagdad Pact. In this undertaking Nasser is supporting them and I suspect that his relations with the Soviet Union are a good deal closer than he admits to us. Recent events in Jordan are part of this pattern.

Our policy should surely be to encourage our friends who will now come under heavy pressure. This means urgent and effective measures to shore up the Bagdad Pact and Iraq in particular ... I feel myself that we can no longer safely wait on Nasser. Indeed if the United States now joined the Bagdad Pact this would impress him more than all our attempts to cajole him have yet done.

Certainly we should accept, I think, that a policy of appeasement will bring us nothing in Egypt. Our best chance is to show that it pays to be our friends.

Source: PRO FO 371/121271, 5 March 1956

This telegram, with its yoking together of Cold War logic and the emotive symbol of 'appeasement', is typical of an increasing trend in the communications between Eden and Eisenhower. The British sought to persuade the Americans of the necessity for a harder line against Nasser by emphasising the threat posed by a Soviet–Nasser axis and the futility of continuing to conciliate the Egyptian leader.

This was reiterated in a telegram from Nutting, Minister of State at the Foreign Office, to Lloyd in Karachi for a meeting of Baghdad Pact ministers the same day.

Document 2.6 Anthony Nutting on Soviet–Egyptian Links, 5 March 1956

implicit in ... [our] ... policy is abandonment of appeasement of Nasser. This may be unwelcome to Americans but fact remains that appeasement has not paid and I suggest you should leave Dulles in no doubt about our suspicions of growing contacts between Egypt and Soviet Russia. Latest information on Aswan Dam negotiations suggests that Egyptians may well be playing double game. Sinister co-incidence of Egyptian and Russian interest in sinking Bagdad Pact may well result in further moves against

Nuri. It is essential therefore that we and Americans do all in our power to support him as our one reliable asset in this gloomy situation.

Source: PRO FO 371/121271, 5 March 1956

Again, as with the previous document, this telegram associates Nasser with Soviet ambitions in the Middle East but also illustrates the threat posed to the linchpin of the western position in the Middle East, Iraq under Nuri es-Said. Although this suggests Nutting's agreement with the Prime Minister's line, in his account written in 1967 Nutting is at pains to point out that his divergence with the Prime Minister's policy towards Egypt that was to culminate in his resignation in November 1956 began at this moment.

Document 2.7 Nutting's Views of Eden, 1967

From now on Eden completely lost his touch. Gone was his old uncanny sense of timing, his deft feel for negotiation. Driven by the impulses of pride and prestige and nagged by mounting sickness, he began to behave like an enraged elephant charging senselessly at invisible and imaginary enemies in the international jungle. . . . a feeling came over me that I was talking to a total stranger. No longer did we see things in the same way; a wide gulf was now between us; and I knew then that nothing about our old relationship would ever be the same again.

Source: Nutting, 1967, pp. 32–33

These extracts (documents 2.7 and 2.8) from the memoirs of a participant written some ten years after the event are significant for a number of reasons. First, Nutting was widely regarded as a coming man in the Conservative Party and had been on close personal terms with the Prime Minister. Second, as Minister of State in the Foreign Office, Nutting was intimately involved with the formulation of British Middle Eastern policy. Third, his volume of memoirs was extremely critical of Eden's and government policy in the Middle East in general; this was all the more damning for being one of the first memoirs written by a participant in the crisis. Within Conservative Party circles it was widely viewed as something of a betrayal and although the book has been subjected to harsh criticism, and indeed was almost proscribed, it remains a valuable source in that the central tenets of its thesis have proved difficult to shake.

In an extraordinary incident Nutting, who was dining at the Savoy Hotel, was called to the telephone where, on an open and insecure line, he was upbraided by the Prime Minister.

Document 2.8 Nutting's Conversation with Eden on the Removal of Nasser, March 1956

'What's all this poppycock you've sent me?' he shouted. 'I don't agree with a single word of it.' I replied it was an attempt to look ahead and to rationalise our position in the Middle East, so as to avoid in the future the kind of blow to our prestige that we had just suffered over Glubb.

'But what's all this nonsense about isolating Nasser or "neutralising" him, as you call it? I want him destroyed, can't you understand? I want him removed, and if you and the Foreign Office don't agree, then you'd better come to the Cabinet and explain why.'

I tried to calm him by saying that, before deciding to destroy Nasser, it might be wise to look for some alternative who would not be still more hostile to us. At the moment there did not appear to be any alternative, hostile or friendly. And the only result of removing Nasser would be anarchy in Egypt.

'But I don't want an alternative', Eden shouted at me. 'And I don't give a damn if there's anarchy and chaos in Egypt.' With this he hung up, leaving me to return to my dinner. I felt as if I had had a nightmare, only the nightmare was real.

Source: Nutting, 1967, pp. 34–35

In some later accounts, Nutting uses the word 'murdered' in place of 'destroyed'. **(Carlton, 1988, p. 29; Kyle, 1991, p. 99)**. Although Rhodes James casts some doubt on Nutting's account, he cites the diary of Eden's wife, Clarissa, as evidence of the mounting strain on the Prime Minister: 'The events in Jordan have shattered A. He is fighting very bad fatigue which is sapping his powers of thought' **(Rhodes James, 1987, p. 432)**.

None the less, in the first Cabinet meeting after Lloyd's return it is clear that sufficient common ground existed between the volatile Prime Minister and the Foreign Office for the Foreign Secretary to put forward a view that was to become the basis of British policy in the Middle East for the next four months.

Document 2.9 Cabinet Discussion on Middle East Policy, 21 March 1956

The Foreign Secretary recalled that, before leaving on his recent tour of the Middle East, he had discussed with the Cabinet the line which he should take in his conversations with the Prime Minister of Egypt. As a result of those conversations he was satisfied that Colonel Nasser was unwilling to work with the Western powers or to co-operate in the task of securing peace in the Middle East. It was evident that he was aiming at leadership of the Arab World; that, in order to secure it he was willing to accept the help of the Russians; and that he was not prepared to work for a settlement of the

Arab dispute with Israel. Despite the conversations in Cairo, there had been no slackening in the Egyptian propaganda against the British position in the Middle East. It was now clear that we could not establish a basis for friendly relations with Egypt. That being so, we ought re-align our policy in the Middle East; instead of seeking to conciliate or support Colonel Nasser we should do our utmost to counter Egyptian policy and to uphold our true friends in the Middle East. Thus, we should seek increased support for the Bagdad Pact and its members. We should make a further effort to persuade the United States to join the Pact. We should seek to draw Iraq and Jordan more closely together. We should try to detach Saudi Arabia from Egypt, by making plain to King Saud the nature of Nasser's ambitions. We should secure further support from Libya, in order to prevent the extension of Egyptian or Communist influence there. We should seek to establish in Syria a Government more friendly to the West. We should counter Egyptian subversion in the Sudan and in the Persian Gulf. There were also possibilities of action aimed more directly at Egypt – e.g., the withholding of military supplies, the withdrawal of financial support for the Aswan Dam, the reduction of United States economic aid and the blocking of sterling balances. In all this we should need the support of the United States Government. The first task would be to seek Anglo-American agreement on a general realignment of policy towards Egypt.

The Prime Minister said that the Foreign Secretary had already discussed with him and some of his senior colleagues the proposals which he had now outlined to the Cabinet. He was in full agreement with this approach to the problem. It might not be easy to secure United States support for a new policy on these lines. We must, however, do our utmost to persuade them of the importance and urgency of checking Colonel Nasser in his bid for leadership of the Arab World. He had therefore authorised the Foreign Secretary to put these proposals to the United States Secretary of State, through H.M. Ambassador at Washington, and he had reinforced this approach by a personal message to the President.

In discussion there was general agreement that every effort should now be made to persuade the United States Government to go forward with us in a new policy towards Egypt on the lines indicated by the Foreign Secretary.

Source: PRO CAB 128/30, CM 24 (56), 21 March 1956

This crucial Cabinet discussion is further evidence of the conclusion drawn about the links between Nasser and the Soviet bloc. What followed from this, according to Lloyd, was the need to strengthen the Baghdad Pact by increasing its membership and by creating better relations with states such as Saudi Arabia. The heavy emphasis on the necessity for Anglo-American co-operation expressed in Lloyd's discourse to the Cabinet was an acknowledgement of the need for a co-ordinated strategy with the United States, a recognition shared by Eden.

Even before the Cabinet met, the Foreign Secretary had sent a telegram to the United States outlining possible measures against Nasser including the delaying of funding for the High Dam. These proposals fell on fertile ground as the State Department was already moving in the same direction. The State Department's suggestions that were put to President Eisenhower by Dulles on 28 March 1956 included the delaying of negotiations by the USA and the UK over the High Aswan Dam, the denial of export licences covering arms shipments to Egypt by both the USA and the UK and a general delaying of other forms of aid **(FRUS (B), 1988, docs 192, 208 and 223–226)**.

At a series of meetings in early April between Eisenhower, Dulles, the British Ambassador in Washington Sir Roger Makins and the British Chairman of the Chiefs of Staff, Air Chief Marshal Sir William Dickson, these measures became a joint Anglo-American policy **(FRUS (B), 1988, docs 232, 234, 240 and 242)**. Lloyd, through Makins, confirmed Britain's agreement with the new policy, noting that he was 'glad to think we are not far apart on the common issues'. With regard to Egypt he made the following statement.

Document 2.10 Anglo-American Discussions on Policy Towards Egypt, April 1956

We agree with the view which you expressed on April 1st to the effect that so far, Nasser had had it all his own way and that it had gone to his head and his leadership of the Arab World even extended to Central Africa. We think it is essential, without coming into the open in any way that we should prove that it is unlucky to play with the Russians. If we could split off the Saudis and build up the Iraqis' position, this would in any case be all to the good and it might lead Nasser to have second thoughts. . . .

We should not publicise this action, it will gradually reveal itself . . . it will be generally a matter of keeping Nasser guessing about our intentions. We should do all we can to strengthen our policy and that of our friends in the area to counter his activities. But, at the same time, it would only arouse his suspicions if we took smilingly his recent propaganda campaign against us. Mr. Lloyd agrees with the view that negotiations with Nasser about the Aswan Dam should be allowed to languish and he welcomes the steps which you and the United States propose to take. . . .

I expect to receive some more detailed proposals in the near future for discussions with you.

Source: FRUS (B), 1988, Makins to Dulles, 5 April 1956, document 243, pp. 467–470

This marks the transition to a more active joint Anglo-American policy framed around economic counter-measures, in particular the withdrawal of support for the Aswan Dam project.

These measures were taken a stage further in April 1956 when the British

Secret Service, MI6, and their Central Intelligence Agency counterparts agreed a programme, codenamed OMEGA, of covert measures to isolate Nasser involving the destabilisation of Nasser's perceived allies in the region including a coup against Syria, Operation STRAGGLE, which was timetabled for the end of October 1956 **(Gorst and Lucas, 1989, pp. 576–595; Kyle, 1991, pp. 101–103)**.

However, tensions in the Anglo-American policy towards the Middle East continued. At a meeting of NATO Foreign Ministers in Paris in early May 1956 wide-ranging discussions took place between Dulles and Lloyd on the Middle East which revealed differences in policy between the two. The United States finally joined the Baghdad Pact, but only its economic and anti-subversion committees; Britain's long-held aim of full American membership remained elusive because the United States wished to maintain some public distance from Britain's imperial image. Discussions on Saudi Arabia revealed substantial differences of opinion surrounding the long-running Buiraimi dispute. However, in the case of Egypt there was common ground.

Document 2.11 Anglo-American Discussions on the Aswan Dam, 3 May 1956

THE SECRETARY OF STATE asked what was the U.S. Government's intention in regard to the High Aswan Dam.

MR DULLES said he thought the policy was to drag our feet but not to let the project drop. The Egyptians had put up some proposals nearly two months ago, and we had not yet answered them. Yet Nasser had not apparently been pressing. He, too, seemed to be in no hurry and was negotiating with the Sudanese about water. Mr Dulles thought that perhaps even the Egyptian Government was beginning to feel that the project was too grandiose and involved too heavy a commitment for their economy over the next twenty years. If so, it was all to the good; but if we gave any indication that we were backing out of our offers of support, he would be almost obliged on prestige grounds, to go to the Russians.

THE SECRETARY OF STATE agreed that we should let the project languish but without giving Nasser any excuse for saying that it was our fault.

Source: PRO FO 371/121273, discussions with Mr Dulles at luncheon, British Embassy, Paris, 3 May 1956

The agreement on the arrangements for the Aswan High Dam marked the coalescence of British and American policy towards Nasser and Egypt, using the stick rather than the carrot. It was, however, also the decision that was to mark the real beginning of what would become the Suez Crisis. Although this decision was not publicised, the Egyptian government became aware very quickly that negotiations on the loan were being dragged out because as the British Ambassador in Cairo Sir Humphrey Trevelyan noted,

If we are to adopt what you call a 'cover policy' and at the same time increasingly take action aimed at deflating Nasser and spoiling his plans, the cover plan is likely progressively to work less and less effectively and Nasser's hostility to us will probably be progressively increased.

(PRO FO 371/118862, 8 May 1956)

Notwithstanding these concerns by the senior British diplomat on the spot the British government continued with its new policy.

Document 2.12 Instructions to British Diplomats in the Middle East, 28 May 1956

As you know, it has become fairly clear that Nasser's activities are, and are likely to continue to be, hostile to our interests. Not only do these conflict with his ambition of eliminating from the Arab world all traces of 'imperialism' (including all British influence and the state of Israel) and then uniting it under his leadership; but since the Western world will not furnish him with the means for realising these aims, he has turned to the Russians. They seem willing to supply him with arms and a certain political support; because in this way he becomes dependent on them for the means of realising policies to which he has publicly committed himself, and also because this opens the way for political and economic penetration of Egypt and through Egypt of many other Arab countries.

We have therefore decided on a number of steps to reduce Nasser's influence in the rest of the Arab World. Some of these measures such as improving the audibility and content of our broadcasting in the area, will be obvious to all. Others will be taken discreetly, or even secretly. Many of these measures will be taken in conjunction with the United States.

Both we and the Americans feel that it is most important not to show Nasser our hand too early. Although he is bound to realise to some extent what we are doing we are anxious to keep him in doubt and to avoid a break with him for as long as possible. For this purpose we are continuing the negotiations about the Aswan Dam, for instance, and avoiding official statements etc, directed against him. Nasser is in a position to do us and our friends great harm at present, both by the influence of his propaganda machine (in countries like Jordan) and economically. Many of the steps which we are putting in hand are designed to minimise the damage which he can do.

It follows from this that you should be careful in conversations with representatives with the local government or with colleagues which might be repeated back to the Egyptians, to avoid giving the impression that we have resigned ourselves to a quarrel with Nasser or are seeking to do him down. You should rather stress our belief that friendly relations between Britain and Egypt are in the interests of both countries and of all the Middle

East and explain our disappointment that, in spite of the generous settlement of the sterling balances, the evacuation from the Canal, and the offer of help for the Aswan Dam, Nasser and his Government have shown themselves so hostile to us and the West, and so willing to involve them-selves with the Communists. The impression you should try to give is that we hope that the course of events will eventually give the Egyptian Government to see realities more clearly; in which case we shall be glad to welcome the chance of collaborating with them again.

Source: PRO FO 371/118862, C.A.E. Shuckburgh to HM Representatives, 28 May 1956

This policy, while containing 'offensive' elements, including a counter-propaganda radio campaign aimed at minimising Nasser's influence in the Middle East, also acknowledged the necessity of not provoking Nasser into precipitate action against western interests in the region. The Foreign Office was clearly anxious to keep the Anglo-American change in policy as low-key as possible. Indeed, as British policy moved towards a harder line with Nasser, the earlier policy of 'appeasement' reached its *denouement* with the final withdrawal of British troops from the Canal Zone base under the 1954 Base agreement in mid-June 1956.

Even though in early May the British and Americans had agreed to 'drag out' negotiations over the dam, opinion, particularly in America, moved rapidly towards a withdrawal of the funding offered in December 1955. This change in attitude was precipitated by signs that Nasser, reacting to western sluggishness, was moving ever-closer to the eastern bloc. On 16 May 1956, Egypt recognised the govern-ment of the People's Republic of China to secure further arms supplies, a move guaranteed to infuriate the United States, still smarting from the 'loss' of China to communism in 1949. Dulles felt that this would make it very difficult to get any funding package through Congress and that it was likely that the Soviet government would move in on the dam project with an offer of aid, a suspicion heightened by the scheduled visit of the Soviet Foreign Minister, Shepilov, in mid-June.

From the middle of April the American Ambassador in Cairo, Henry 'Hank' Byroade, who had been specifically sent to establish good relations with Nasser, made a number of heart-felt pleas for Washington to reconsider its negative policy towards Egypt and Nasser but Dulles and the State Department remained firm **(FRUS (B), 1988, docs 294, 370–371 and 406)**. Indeed, by the end of June Dulles had begun to consider whether it might be to the advantage of the West that the Soviet Union take on the burden of financing the Aswan High Dam as this would both strain the Soviet budget and place the Soviet Union in the role of oppressor of the Egyptian people as, no doubt, the Egyptian economy struggled to repay any loan.

Document 2.13 American Views on Funding the Aswan Dam, 28 June 1956

Mr Allan Dulles said that ... when the new Soviet Foreign Minister Shepilov visited Cairo he had offered to assist the Egyptians to build the High Aswan Dam. Allegedly the offer consisted of a loan of 400 million for sixty years, with no interest. The report states that Shepilov also offered to cancel in toto the Egyptian debt for all bloc arms acquired by Egypt up to this time. Lastly, he had offered to take all of Egypt's cotton crop and to build a steel mill at very low interest rates.

Secretary Humphrey said he was glad to hear of the Soviet offer to build the High Aswan Dam, and he hoped the Egyptians would accept it since that was the best possible thing that could happen for the United States.

With respect to the Russians taking over the High Aswan Dam project, Secretary Dulles commented that the immediate results would be bad for the United States, but that the long-term results might be very good. Whatever nation undertakes to carry through this project was bound to end up by being very unpopular with the Egyptians. The building of the dam was bound to place a heavy burden on the Egyptian economy and standard of living, and the Egyptians would blame the austerities they suffered on the nation which was undertaking this great project. Moreover, the Egyptians would continuously ask for further financial assistance from this nation. In short, the project of building the dam would prove a terrific headache to any nation that undertook it.

Secretary Humphrey again commented that he hoped that the United States would not be saddled with this undertaking. Governor Stassen inquired as to whether the immediate reaction would be bad if the United States actually withdrew its current offer to assist Egypt in building the High Aswan Dam. Secretary Humphrey replied that he did not care how we did it, but if there were any way for the United States to back out of the offer, he desperately hoped that we would seize upon it.

Source: FRUS (B), 1988, memorandum of discussion at the 289th meeting of the National Security Council Washington, 28 June 1956, document 412, p. 755

This wide-ranging discussion, in the main co-ordinating body for American foreign policy, clearly indicates that American policy regarding Egypt and the Aswan Dam was hardening in the direction of a refusal to fund the project. In fact, Nasser turned down a Soviet proposal to finance the dam *in toto* and indicated that the original western offer of December 1955 was now acceptable to him. It was too late; by the middle of July 1956 Dulles had come round to the position of withdrawing the offer as he indicated to the British Embassy in Washington on 18 July **(FRUS (B), 1988, doc. 474)**.

On 19 July 1956, Dulles duly informed the Egyptian Ambassador, Ahmed Hussein, that the December offer had been withdrawn. This came as a considerable shock to the pro-western Hussein although not to Nasser. Nor, despite claims to the contrary in their memoirs was it a shock to Eden and Lloyd; as Kyle has made clear the British government had 17 hours' notice in which to demur if they so chose. They did not, instructing Makins that Dulles's action 'would suit us very well' **(Eden, 1960, p. 422; Lloyd, 1978, pp. 70–72; Kyle, 1991, pp. 128–129)**. At a Cabinet meeting the next day it was agreed that the British offer of funding for the Aswan project would also be withdrawn. Remarkably, this move, which spelt the end of the World Bank's involvement as well, did not result in a Cabinet discussion of any likely reactions by the Egyptians, or possible resulting counter-measures by the British, despite the vulnerability of the Canal Company and its installations. Possibly, as Lloyd suggests, the British were lulled into a false sense of security by the fact that a deal had been made covering the future operations of the Canal company the previous month.

The Egyptian riposte was not long delayed. After a savage attack on American policy in a speech on 24 July 1956, Nasser used the occasion of his annual speech on 26 July, the anniversary of King Farouk's abdication, to respond to the western withdrawal of funding for the Aswan High Dam. Stating that Britain and America were 'punishing Egypt because it refused to side with military blocs' Nasser compared the Director of the World Bank, Eugene Black, with Ferdinand de Lesseps.

Document 2.14 Nasser's Speech Presaging Nationalisation of the Canal, 26 July 1956

I went back in my memory to what I used to read about the year 1854. In this year Ferdinand de Lesseps arrived in Egypt and went to Mohammed Sa'id Pasha, the Khedive, sat next to him and told him: we want to dig the Suez Canal. The Suez Canal will bring you untold benefit. The Suez Canal is a gigantic project which will give Egypt so much.

Whenever Black spoke, I could sense the obstacles behind his phrasing and simultaneously I went back in my mind to Ferdinand de Lesseps. I then told him: look here, we don't like such things. We don't want a Cromer back in Egypt again ruling us. In the past there were loans and interest on the loans and the outcome was that our country was occupied. Therefore I ask you to take this into consideration in your conversation with me. We have a complex as a result of de Lesseps, Cromer and political occupation by way of economic occupation.

Source: Frankland (ed.), 1959, pp. 108–109

This short extract, from a long speech by Nasser, with its repeated use of the name 'de Lesseps', was the signal for Egyptian personnel to take over the offices of the

Suez Canal Company and its installations in the Canal Zone. The seizure of the facilities of the Suez Canal Company was sanctioned by a law nationalising the Canal Company, by which 'all money, rights and obligations are transferred to the State'.

Document 2.15 Suez Canal Nationalisation Law, 26 July 1956

Shareholders and holders of constituent shares shall be compensated in accordance to the value of the shares on the Paris Stock Market on the day preceding the enforcement of this law. Payment of compensation shall take place immediately the State receives all the assets and property of the nationalised company.

Source: Frankland (ed.), 1959, p. 114

Given that full compensation was to be paid to the Canal Company's shareholders, the act represented nothing more than the forced buying out of shareholders in the same manner as the Labour government's nationalisation of coal in 1948. This presented the British government with a thorny dilemma.

Thus the optimism that had underpinned ALPHA had come to nothing and the hopes for peace in the Middle East had resulted in a confrontation with the Egyptian President. Western policy had gradually shifted from accommodation to hostility to meet the perceived intransigence of Nasser. From the British perspective, it was hoped that an Anglo-American strategy would evolve to meet the new situation created by the nationalisation of the Canal, but these hopes were to be dashed.

Chronology June 1955–July 1956

1955

June　　　　Project ALPHA accepted by British Cabinet

September　Egyptian–Czech arms deal signed

1956

January　　Failure of Project ALPHA

1 March　　King Hussein of Jordan dismisses General Glubb, British commander of the Arab Legion

April–May　Anglo-American discussions on Egypt and the Middle East reach agreement that Aswan Dam funding should be allowed to languish

16 May　　Egypt recognises the People's Republic of China

19 July   United States announces withdrawal of funding for the Aswan
High Dam

26 July   Nasser nationalises the Suez Canal Company.

3 The decision to intervene
26 July–30 October 1956

This section covers the events from President Nasser's nationalisation of the Canal on 26 July 1956 until the rejection by Egypt of the Anglo-French ultimatums on 30 October 1956. This three-month period was characterised on the surface by prolonged attempts to secure a peaceful resolution to the dispute. However, simultaneously Britain and France were making strenuous efforts to prepare the ground for a military intervention in Egypt that would both secure the Canal and bring about the downfall of the Egyptian President and his government. The contradictory nature of these policies raised several questions. First, if a peaceful solution were achieved, what would be the effect on Britain's standing in the world; second, how were military requirements to be meshed with the diplomatic process; third, what was the pretext for any military action against Egypt? The tensions in this 'dual-track' policy led the Eden government into a quagmire from which it only extricated itself via a highly dubious policy that was to have damaging repercussions.

News of Nasser's speech of 26 July 1956 was received in London at 10.15 p.m. while Eden and senior ministers were at a dinner for the King and Prime Minister of Iraq. An immediate meeting, including the British Chiefs of Staff, the French Ambassador and the American *chargé* was convened, and, although no official minutes were taken, William Clark, the Prime Minister's press secretary, recorded Eden's determination that Nasser 'must not be allowed to get away with it' **(Clark, 1986, p. 186)**. Accordingly, the British Chiefs of Staff were authorised to begin preparation of contingency plans for the retaking of the Canal. At a Cabinet meeting the following morning a full discussion took place which spelt out the key concerns of the British government.

Document 3.1 Cabinet Discussion of Initial Reactions to the Nationalisation of the Suez Canal, 27 July 1956

The Cabinet considered the situation created by the decision of the Egyptian Government to nationalise the Suez Canal Company.

The Prime Minister said that, with some of his senior colleagues, he had seen the French Ambassador and the United States Chargé d'Affaires on the previous evening and had informed them of the facts as we knew them. He had told them that Her Majesty's Government would take a most serious view of this situation and that any failure on the part of the Western Powers to take the necessary steps to regain control over the Canal would have disastrous consequences for the economic life of the Western Powers and for their standing and influence in the Middle East. The Cabinet should now consider what courses of action were open to us to safeguard our interests. Our first aim must be to reach a common understanding on the matter with the French, as our partners in the Canal enterprise, and with the United States Government. The French Foreign Minister, M. Pineau, was due to arrive in London on 29th July; and he proposed that he should send an urgent message to the President of the United States Government inviting him to send a representative to take part in discussions early in the following week. The Cabinet were given the following information of the importance of the Suez Canal to trade and the flow of supplies and of Egypt's financial position: –

1 Oil – Of a total of some 70 million tons of oil which passed annually from the Persian Gulf through the Suez Canal, 60 million tons were destined for Western Europe and represented two-thirds of Western European oil supplies. To move this volume of oil by the alternative route round the Cape would require twice the tonnage of tankers. If the Egyptian Government decided to interfere with the passage of oil through the Canal, it would be necessary for Western Europe to turn to the Western hemisphere for supplies; as much as 10 million tons might be involved, and it would be necessary to ask the Americans to divert to Western Europe the supplies they now received from the Persian Gulf. We ourselves had supplies sufficient to last for about six weeks. In order to conserve these it would be necessary at an early date to introduce some arrangement for the restriction of deliveries to industry and to garages.

2 Trade – Interference with traffic passing through the Suez Canal would not seriously affect the flow of imports other than oil into this country, but it would seriously hamper the export trade, particularly to India. Our exports costs would also rise as freight charges would go up.

3 Egypt's Sterling balances – Egypt had £102 million in her blocked account, of which no more was due to be released until January 1957. In addition she probably had £14 millions available on current account of which some £7 millions was held by the Bank of England and the remainder by commercial banks. The blocking of the current balances would probably not seriously incommode Egypt at the present time. Her cotton crop, of which about one-third went to Soviet countries and little was purchased by us would be coming on to the market shortly and proceeds from this would tend to put her in funds.

The Cabinet next considered the legal position and the basis on which we could sustain and justify to international opinion, a refusal to accept the decision of the Egyptian Prime Minister, Colonel Nasser, to nationalise the Canal.

The Cabinet agreed that we should be on weak ground in basing our resistance on the narrow argument that Colonel Nasser had acted illegally. The Suez Canal Company was registered as an Egyptian Company under Egyptian law; and Colonel Nasser had indicated that he intended to compensate the shareholders at ruling market prices. From a narrow legal point of view his action amounted to no more than a decision to buy out the shareholders. Our case must be presented on wider international grounds: our argument must be that the canal was an important international asset and facility and that Egypt could not be allowed to exploit it for a purely internal purpose. The Egyptians had not the technical ability to manage it effectively; and their recent behaviour gave no confidence that they would recognise their international obligations in respect of it. Moreover, they would not be able to provide the resources needed for the capital development needed in widening and deepening the Canal to enable it to carry the increased volume of traffic which it should carry in the years ahead. The Canal was the vital link between the East and the West and its importance as an international waterway, recognised in the Convention signed in 1888, had increased with the development of the oil industry and the dependence of the world on oil supplies. It was not a piece of Egyptian property but an international asset of the highest importance and it should be managed as an international trust.

The Cabinet agreed that for these reasons every effort must be made to restore effective international control over the Canal. It was evident that the Egyptians would not yield to economic pressures alone. They must be subjected to the maximum political pressure which could be exerted by the maritime and trading nations whose interests were most directly affected. And, in the last resort, this political pressure must be backed by the threat – and, if need be, the use – of force.

The Cabinet then considered the factors to be taken into account in preparing a plan of military operations against Egypt. In this part of the discussion the following points were made

1 Egypt's military forces consisted mainly of three infantry divisions and one armoured division. She had about 500 tanks and a great deal of armoured and wheeled equipment which was of doubtful efficiency. There were some 600–800 Polish and Czech technicians at present employed in the Egyptian Army, but it could not be predicted whether they would be willing to help the Egyptians in active operations. If they were, the Egyptian Army would be a dangerous force. About two-thirds of the Egyptian forces were in the Sinai area; the armoured division, however, straddled the Canal.

2 A military operation against Egypt, including consequential responsibilities for keeping the Canal in operation and controlling the area, would require the

equivalent of three divisions. The necessary forces could be made available for this purpose; but as a great quantity of vehicles and the heavy armoured equipment would have to be transported to the area by sea, the necessary preparations for mounting the operation would take several weeks. It would be necessary, moreover, to requisition ships and direct labour.

3 While the military plan was being worked out, preparations would be made to build up a ring of bomber forces at points around Egypt. Fighter squadrons would also be sent to Cyprus. It would be a week before the full resources of Transport Command could be mobilised. The size of the air forces needed would depend on the type of bombing to be carried out.

4 The naval forces available in the Mediterranean consisted of a carrier, a cruiser of the New Zealand Navy, 3 Daring Class Destroyers, 7 destroyers and an amphibious warfare squadron. Another cruiser was approaching the Canal from the Red Sea, and after discussion it was agreed that she should be diverted to Aden. Summer leave in the Home Fleet was due to begin in the following week; it would be necessary to consider whether this should be stopped.

5 In preparing any plan for military operations account must be taken of the possible effects upon our Arab allies in the Middle East and the Persian Gulf if force were used against Egypt. It was important that the operations should be so planned as to reduce to the minimum the risk that other Arab states would be drawn into supporting Egypt.

6 Consideration should be given to the possibility of cutting the oil pipeline from the Canal to Cairo which was vital to the economic life of Egypt's capital.

The Prime Minister said that against this background the Cabinet must decide what our policy must be. He fully agreed that the question was not a legal issue but must be treated as a matter of the widest international importance. It must now be our aim to place the Suez Canal under the control of the Powers interested in international shipping and trade by means of a new international Commission on which Egypt would be given suitable representation. Colonel Nasser's action had presented us with an opportunity to find a lasting settlement of this problem, and we should not hesitate to take advantage of it. An interim note of protest against the decision to nationalise the Canal should be sent forthwith to the Egyptian Government and this should be followed up, as soon as possible, by more considered representations concerted with the Americans and the French. We should also consider inviting other maritime and trading countries to support this diplomatic pressure. Commonwealth Governments might suggest that the matter should be referred to the Security Council. He did not favour this course, which would expose us to the risk of a Soviet veto. It would be necessary, however, to consider denouncing the Canal Base Agreement of 1954 in view of the fact that Egypt had given an undertaking in this Agreement not to interfere with the Canal. The fundamental question before the Cabinet, however, was whether they were prepared in the last resort to pursue their objective by the threat or even the use of force, and whether they were ready, in default of assistance from the United States and France, to take military action alone.

The Cabinet agreed that our essential interests in this area must, if necessary, be safeguarded by military action and that the necessary preparations to this end must be made. Failure to hold the Suez Canal would lead inevitably to the loss one by one of all our interests and assets in the Middle East and, even if we had to act alone, we could not stop short of using force to protect our position if all other means of protecting it proved unavailing. . . .

The Cabinet –

1 Agreed that Her Majesty's Government should seek to secure, by the use of force if necessary, the reversal of the decision of the Egyptian Government to nationalise the Suez Canal Company. . . .

3 Invited the Prime Minister to send a personal message to the President of the United States asking him to send a representative to London to discuss the situation with the representatives of the Governments of the United Kingdom and France.

4 Appointed a Committee of Ministers consisting of –

> The Prime Minister (in the Chair)
> Lord President
> Chancellor of the Exchequer
> Foreign Secretary
> Commonwealth Secretary
> Minister of Defence

to formulate further plans for putting our policy into effect.

5 Instructed the Chiefs of Staff to prepare a plan and timetable for military operations against Egypt should they prove unavoidable. . . .

8 Invited the President of the Board of Trade, in consultation with the Minister of Fuel and Power, to consider what arrangements might need to be made for the restriction of oil deliveries.

9 Invited the President of the Board of Trade to consider, in consultation with the Minister of Transport, what action might need to be taken to ensure an adequate supply of shipping for any military operations that might become necessary. . . .

Source: PRO CAB 128/30 Pt II, CM 54(56), 27 July 1956

This record of a meeting of the full Cabinet set the tone for the attitude of the British government for the next few months. It is clear from this that the Cabinet was cognisant of the necessity for action against Egypt being taken on a joint basis with the French and the United States. This action was seen as being necessary, in part, because of the supposed dependence of Britain and Western Europe on oil supplies which transited the Canal. The Cabinet recognised, however, that it would be on dubious ground in terms of the legality of any intervention and accordingly adopted the prescription of the inability of the Egyptian government to manage a vital international asset. Given the attitude of previous British governments this was at best misplaced and at worst rank hypocrisy. While the Cabinet concluded that it was determined to use force, the document clearly reveals that even at this early stage mounting an operation against Egypt could not be done quickly; this was due in part to planning for a 'worst-case scenario' which by over-estimating the military capacity of Egypt precluded a quick counter-strike and forced the military planners into a lengthy and more substantial operation. The Cabinet decided to give responsibility for managing the crisis to a sub-committee, the Egypt Committee, which was overwhelmingly hawkish in its composition. Eden's determination to settle with Nasser was expressed in an immediate telegram to the American President.

Document 3.2 Eden to Eisenhower on the Threat Posed by the Nationalisation of the Suez Canal, 27 July 1956

This morning I have reviewed the whole position with my Cabinet colleagues and the Chiefs of Staff. We are all agreed that we cannot afford to allow Nasser to seize control of the Canal in this way, in defiance of international agreements. If we take a firm stand over this now, we shall have the support of the other maritime powers. If we do not, our influence and yours throughout the Middle East will, we are all convinced, be destroyed.

The immediate threat is to the oil supplies to Western Europe, a great part of which flows through the Canal. We have reserves in the United Kingdom which would last us six weeks; and the countries of Western Europe have stocks, rather smaller as we believe, on which they could draw for a time. We are, however, at once considering means of limiting current consumption so as to conserve our supplies; and if the Canal were closed we should have to ask you to help us by reducing the amount which you draw from the pipeline terminals in the Eastern Mediterranean and possibly by sending us supplementary supplies for a time from your side of the world.

It is, however, the outlook for the longer term which is more threatening. The Canal is an international asset and facility, which is vital to the free world. The maritime Powers cannot afford to allow Egypt to expropriate it and to exploit it by using the revenues for her own internal purposes irrespective of the interests of the Canal and the Canal users. Apart from the Egyptians' complete lack of technical qualifications, their past behaviour gives no confidence that they can be trusted to manage it with any sense of international obligation. Nor are they capable of providing the capital which will soon be needed to widen and deepen it so that it may be capable of handling the increased volume of traffic which it must carry in the years to come. We should, I am convinced, take this opportunity to put its management on a firm and lasting basis as an international trust.

We should not allow ourselves to become involved in legal quibbles about the rights of the Egyptian Government to nationalise what is technically an Egyptian Company, or in financial arguments about their capacity to pay the compensation which they have offered. I feel sure that we should take issue with Nasser on the broader international grounds. . . .

As we see it we are unlikely to attain our objectives by economic pressures alone. I gather that Egypt is not due to receive any further aid from you. No large payment from her sterling balances here are due before January. We ought in the first instance to bring maximum political pressure to bear on Egypt. For this, apart from our own action, we should invoke the support of all the interested powers. My colleagues and I are convinced that we must be ready, in the last resort, to use force to bring Nasser to his senses. For our part we are prepared to do so. I have this morning instructed our Chiefs of Staff to prepare a military plan accordingly.

However, the first step must be for you and us and France to exchange views, align our policies and concert together how we can best bring maximum pressure to bear on the Egyptian Government.

Source: PRO PREM 11/1177, Eden to Eisenhower, 27 July 1956

This first message from Eden to his ex-war-time colleague Eisenhower was couched in friendly terms and is a clear attempt to persuade the American administration to back a forceful response to the nationalisation. Eden stressed the importance of the Canal but also minimised the legal aspect of the nationalisation, no doubt recognising that Britain was on shaky ground.

The experienced American diplomat Robert Murphy, another war-time colleague of Harold Macmillan, recorded rather different impressions of the British attitude towards Nasser's action.

Document 3.3 The Private Views of Eden, Lloyd and Macmillan, 31 July 1956

Today and this evening Barbour and I have had private separate and lengthy talks with Eden and Macmillan. . . . They said British Government has decided to drive Nasser out of Egypt. The decision they declared is firm. They expressed simple conviction military action is necessary and inevitable. In separate conversations each said in substance they ardently hoped US would be with them in this determination, but if we could not they would understand and our friendship would be unimpaired. If we were with them from beginning chances of World War III would be far less than if we delayed. They seem convinced USSR will not intervene but they assert that risk must be taken. Macmillan repeated over and over in language similar to that employed by Eden that Government had taken the decision and that Parliament and British people are with them. They both repeated wish that the President clearly understand decision is firm and has been arrived at calmly without emotion. They see no alternative. Macmillan in referring to our close wartime association in French North Africa emphasised several times his belief that as a former adviser and member of President's wartime staff he felt he could assure the President that Britain had no intention of submitting to Nasser's dictation, that British stake in ME is vital, that a demonstration of force provided only solution. Macmillan described some of the military planning which contemplates he said the landing of three British divisions in Egypt in an operation which would take six weeks to mount. The British estimate of importance of Egyptian resistance is low. Macmillan talked about costs. He said this operation would cost £4–500 million which they couldn't afford but would pay. All British shipping would be allocated to it except the two Queens.

During these conversations I advanced I believe all of the considerations which you and the President as well as the Under Secretary have raised. Eden, Macmillan and Lloyd showed throughout unexpected calm and no hysteria. They act as though they really have taken a decision after profound reflection. They are flexible on procedures leading up to showdown but insist over and over again that whatever conferences, arrangements, public postures and manoeuvres might be necessary, at the end they are determined to use force. They hope we will be with them and believe French are with them.

Macmillan indulged in much graphic dissertation on British past history and stressed that if they had to go down now the government and he believed British people would rather do so on this issue and become perhaps another Netherlands. To do another Munich leading to progressive deterioration of ME position and in end the inevitable disaster is he said something he Eden and his colleagues in Government are simply not prepared to do. At dinner Macmillan and Field Marshal Alexander (Harold Caccia only other person present) urged repeatedly that President as their former C in C fully appreciate finality of British decision. Macmillan several times expressed wish he could explain all this orally to President.

I apologise for length of this message but I am persuaded that flavor of these calm and very serious statements should be conveyed urgently as they request to the President.

Source: FRUS (C), 1988, Murphy to Dulles, 31 July 1956, document 33, pp. 60–62

From this American account it is clear that certain members of the Cabinet, notably the Prime Minister and the Chancellor, were committed to a military solution and invoked the spectre of pre-Second World War appeasement to justify their position. It is also noteworthy that, for whatever reason, Macmillan's estimate of the likely costs of military intervention given to Murphy were considerably higher than any figure ever given by him to the Cabinet or Parliament.

Despite the attitude of Eden, and the enthusiastic support of the French, it rapidly became apparent that there were a number of constraints upon Eden's freedom of action. In the first place, on 26 July the British Chiefs of Staff had informed Eden that a *coup de main* was an extremely high risk strategy and that a more conservative military operation would take some six to seven weeks to put in place. Therefore, the Prime Minister was forced down the diplomatic route in the absence of a swift military option. Given Eden's preference for a military solution he was now presented with two problems. First, what if a diplomatic solution were to be achieved, and, second, what was the *casus belli* for military action to be months after the nationalisation of the Canal?

Nor was the diplomatic route to be without its problems. In the first place, while the Leader of the Opposition, Hugh Gaitskell, did liken the act of nationalisation to the activities of Mussolini and Hitler in the 1930s, in a similar vein to Eden and Macmillan, he was insistent that the issue should be dealt with in accordance with international law and under the auspices of the United Nations.

Document 3.4 Hugh Gaitskell Calls for United Nations Involvement, 2 August 1956

It is all very familiar. It is exactly the same that we encountered from Mussolini and Hitler in those years before the war. . . .

I must, however, remind the House that we are members of the United Nations, that we are signatories to the United Nations Charter, and that for many years in British policy we have steadfastly avoided any international action which would be in breach of international law or, indeed, contrary to the public opinion of the world. We must not, therefore, allow ourselves to get into a position where we might be denounced in the Security Council as aggressors, or where the majority of the Assembly were against us.

If Colonel Nasser has done things which are wrong in the legal sense then, of course, the right step is to take him to the International Court. Force is justified in certain events. Indeed, if there were anything which he had done which would justify force at the moment, it is, quite frankly, the one thing on which we have never used force, namely, the stopping of the Israel ships [*sic*]. We have not done that; and it would, I think, be difficult to find – I must say this – in anything else he has done any legal justification for the use of force. What he may do in the future is another matter.

I come, therefore, to this conclusion. I believe that we were right to react sharply to this move. If nothing at all were done, it would have very serious consequences for all of us, especially for the Western Powers. It is important that what we do should be done in the fullest possible co-operation with the other nations affected. We should try to settle this matter peacefully on the lines of an international commission, as has been hinted. While force cannot be excluded, we must be sure that the circumstances justify it and that it is, if used consistent with our belief in, and our pledges to, the Charter of the United Nations and not in conflict with them.

Source: Frankland (ed.), 1959, pp.131–137

Much has been made of Gaitskell's use of the analogy of fascist dictators to suggest that he and the Labour Party reversed policy over Suez. However, it is abundantly clear that his line was consistent throughout the crisis, that force was an absolute last resort and had to carry a United Nations mandate. This speech in the House was to cause a good deal of friction between the Prime Minister and the Leader of the Opposition and was to lead to a breach in their already cool relationship. One of Eden's hopes, bipartisan support for a military operation, was thus ruled out: indeed, Eden would later be forced to recall Parliament, further opening the possibility of dissent from the government's line in the House of Commons, the press and the country.

More seriously, the first reactions from President Eisenhower and Secretary of State Dulles indicated that the United States government was also opposed to any use of force without having exhausted all diplomatic options. A telegram from the British Ambassador in Washington, Sir Roger Makins, reported a conversation with Dulles on 30 July 1956. Dulles was quoted as saying

> the United States Government would not be in sympathy with any attempt to make the Egyptian Government rescind their nationalisation decrees or, to regard them as inoperative, under the threat of force ... so long as the Egyptian action was limited to the nationalisation of the Company and did not interfere with navigation etc., there was no case which could be put to the Congress or which would gain the support of the United States public opinion, in justification of American intervention

As Makins commented 'in ... [the] ... prevailing conditions we can look for little help from Washington' **(PRO PREM 11/1018, 30 July 1956)**.

This unambiguous statement of American policy was re-emphasised by a letter from Eisenhower to Eden.

Document 3.5 Eisenhower Warns Eden Against Use of Force, 31 July 1956

From the moment that Nasser announced nationalisation of the Suez Canal Company, my thoughts have been constantly with you. Grave problems are placed before both our governments, although for each of us they naturally differ in type and character. Until this moment I was happy to feel that we approaching decisions as to applicable procedures somewhat along parallel lines, even though there were, as would be expected, important differences as to detail. But early this morning I received the messages, communicated to me through Murphy from you and Harold Macmillan, telling me on a most secret basis of your decision to employ force without delay or attempting any intermediate and less drastic steps. . . .

For my part, I cannot over-emphasise the strength of my conviction that some such method must be attempted before action such as you contemplate should be undertaken. If unfortunately the situation can finally be resolved only by drastic means there should be no grounds for belief anywhere that corrective measures were undertaken merely to protect national or individual investors or the legal rights of a sovereign nation were ruthlessly flouted. A conference, at the very least, should have a great educational effect through-out the world. Public opinion here and, I am convinced in most of the world, would be outraged should there be a failure to make such efforts. Moreover, initial military successes might be easy but the eventual price might become far too heavy.

I have given you my personal conviction, as well as that of my associates, as to the unwisdom even of contemplating the use of military force at this moment. . . . I personally feel sure that the American reaction would be severe and that great areas of the world would share that reaction. On the other hand, I believe we can marshal that opinion in support of a reasonable and conciliatory, but absolutely firm position.

Source: FRUS (C), 1988, Eisenhower to Eden, 31 July 1956, document 35, pp. 69–71

This is the first warning by the President of the United States to Eden that in the view of the American administration the use of force to resolve the dispute was unacceptable. These would be repeated consistently throughout the crisis and it has been a matter of some debate as to how Eden and others in the Egypt Committee could have calculated that any American support, either diplomatic or economic, would be forthcoming. This trenchant view was driven home by Dulles when he arrived in London for meetings with Eden and his ministers on 1 August 1956.

Document 3.6 Dulles Warns Eden of the Consequences of Use of Force, 1 August 1956

Eden said that while, of course, they would like to have the United States take part militarily in the Suez operation with them, they did not count on this. They did want our moral support and economic support in terms of petroleum products diverted from our side, and would want us to neutralise any open participation by the Soviet Union. If we could keep Russia out of open intervention, by the assurance that if Russia came in we would be in, they and the French could and would take care of the rest.

I said that I agreed that Nasser should not 'get away with it' but the question was how his course should be reversed and he could be brought to 'disgorge'. I said that United States public opinion was not ready to back a military venture by Britain and France which, at this stage, could be plausibly portrayed as motivated by imperialist and colonialist ambitions in the general area, going beyond the Canal operation itself, which was still open, I felt that for the British and French to undertake such an operation without at least the moral support of the United States would be a great disaster because it opened the way for many future evil consequences. I also pointed out that whereas the initial Egyptian resistance to a military operation might not be considerable, the long-term opposition would be very great. I recalled the position of the British at the Suez Base in 1953 when I was there, and that 88,000 U.K. troops had difficulty in defending themselves against the infiltration and assassination tactics of the Egyptians. Now the situation would be much worse. Egypt was much stronger militarily, and was getting moral and material support from the Soviet Union and Egypt's prestige and influence in the Arab World was much greater. I said they would have to count not merely on Egyptian reaction but on Egyptian reaction backed by assistance from the Soviet Union at least in the form of military weapons and supplies, and perhaps 'volunteers'. All the Arab, and parts of the Moslem world would be arrayed against the United Kingdom and France. Also they would be in trouble in the United Nations. I could not see the end of such an operation and the consequences throughout the Middle East would be very grave and would jeopardise British interests, particularly in the production and transportation of oil even more than the present action of Nasser. I felt that it was indispensable to make a very genuine effort to settle this affair peacefully and mobilize world opinion which might be effective.

Source: FRUS (C), 1988, memorandum of a conversation between Prime Minister Eden and Secretary of State Dulles, 10 Downing Street, London, 1 August 1956, 12.45 p.m., document 42, pp. 98–99

In this conversation, Dulles was not only reiterating the warnings of his President, but, aware of the views of Eden and Macmillan, as expressed to Murphy, he was at pains to emphasise that the use of force was totally unacceptable. These developments represented a grave set-back to Eden's avowed aim on the 27 July of securing American support for any British military action. Thus, only four days after Nasser's speech and Eden's response a number of what Eden felt were the key elements of his strategy were already highly questionable. He was therefore compelled, following the meetings with Dulles in London, to agree to the issuing of the tripartite statement by the governments of the UK, France and the USA. This proposed the holding of a conference in London to which over twenty nations including Egypt would be invited.

In the two weeks prior to the meeting of the London Conference, Eden and his 'War Cabinet', the Egypt Committee, took advantage of the hiatus to refine the political aims of the military strategy and to attempt to convince domestic public opinion, the American administration and Commonwealth governments of the verities of their case. On 5 August Eden returned to the issue with Eisenhower in a telegram that painted the situation created by the nationalisation in apocalyptic terms.

Document 3.7 Eden Attempts to Persuade Eisenhower, 5 August 1956

I do not think that we disagree about our primary objective. As it seems to me, this is to undo what Nasser has done and to set up an international regime for the Canal. The purpose of this regime will be to ensure the freedom and security of transit through the Canal, without discrimination, and the efficiency and economy of its operation.

But this is not all. Nasser has embarked on a course which is unpleasantly familiar. His seizure of the Canal was undoubtedly designed to impress opinion not only in Egypt but in the Arab World and in all Africa too. By this assertion of his power he seeks to further his ambitions from Morocco to the Persian Gulf. In this connection you have no doubt seen Nasser's own speech at Aboukir on August 1 in which he said 'we are very strong because we constitute a limitless strength extending from the Atlantic Ocean to the Arab Gulf'.

I know that Nasser is active wherever Muslims can be found even as far as Nigeria. The Egyptians tried to get one of the Nigerian Amirs who was on his way through Cairo to sign a message endorsing Nasser's deeds. The man tore it up, but if Nasser keeps his loot how long can such loyalty last. At the other end of the line the Sheikh of Kuwait has spoken to us stoutly of his views of Nasser. But all these men and millions of others are watching and waiting now.

I have never thought Nasser a Hitler, he has no warlike people behind him. But the parallel with Mussolini is close. Neither of us can forget the lives and treasures he cost us before he was finally dealt with.

The removal of Nasser and the installation in Egypt of a regime less hostile to the West must therefore also rank high among our objectives. We must hope, as you say in your message, that the forthcoming conference will bring such pressures upon Nasser that the efficient operation of the Canal can be assured for the future. If so, everyone will be relieved and there will be no need of force. Moreover, if Nasser is compelled to disgorge his spoils, it is improbable that he will be able to maintain his internal position. We should thus have achieved our secondary objective.

Nevertheless I am sure you will agree that we must prepare to meet the eventuality that Nasser will refuse to accept the outcome of the conference. Or, no less dangerous, that he, supported by the Russians, will seek by stratagems and wiles to divide us so that the conference produces no clear result in the sense we both seek. We and the French Government could not possibly acquiesce in such a situation. I really believe that the consequences of doing so would be catastrophic and that the whole position in the Middle East would thereby be lost beyond recall. But by all means let us first see what the conference can do – on the assumption that Nasser commits no further folly meanwhile.

You know us better than anyone, and so I need not tell you that our people here are neither excited nor eager to use force. They are, however, grimly determined that Nasser shall not get away with it this time because they are convinced that if he does their existence will be at his mercy. So am I.

Source: PRO PREM 11/1098, Eden to Eisenhower, 5 August 1956

Again invoking the parallel with Mussolini, Eden changed the emphasis of the proposed British action, from re-securing the Canal to bringing about the downfall of President Nasser and installing a more pliant and pro-western successor. In a similar vein Eden broadcast to the nation on 8 August 1956. After pointing out the importance of the Canal to British and international trade and contrasting unfavourably Nasser's act of nationalisation with those of the Labour government, Eden launched a personal attack on Colonel Nasser.

Document 3.8 Eden Broadcast to the Nation, 8 August 1956

Our quarrel is not with Egypt, still less with the Arab world; it is with Colonel Nasser . . . he has shown that he is not a man who can be trusted to keep an agreement. . . .

The pattern is familiar to many of us, my friends. We all know this is how fascist governments behave and we all remember only too well, what the cost can be in giving in to fascism. . . .

If Colonel Nasser's action was to succeed, each one of us would be at the mercy of one man for the supplies on which we live, we could never accept that. With dictators you always have to pay a higher price later on, for the appetite grows with feeding. Just now Colonel Nasser is soft pedalling; his threats are being modified. But how can we be sure that next time he has a quarrel with any country he will not interfere with that nation's shipping, and how can we be sure that next time he is short of money he will not raise the dues on all the ships that pass through the Canal? If he is given the chance of course he will.

So, my friends, the alternatives are now clear to see. If we all join together to create an international system for the Canal and spend its revenues as they should be spent to develop it rapidly, that can bring growing prosperity to East and West alike, the countries that produce the oil and the countries which buy it. There will then be wealth for all to share, including Egypt. There is no question of denying her a fair deal or a just return; but if anyone is going to snatch and grab and try to pocket what really belongs to the world, the result will be impoverishment for all, and a refusal by some countries at least to lead their life at such a hazard.

Meanwhile, we have too much at risk not to take precautions. We have done so. That is the meaning of the movements by land, sea, and air of which you have heard in the last few days. My friends, we do not seek a solution by force, but by the broadest possible international agreement. That is why we have called the conference. We shall do all we can to help its work, but this I must make plain. We cannot agree that an act of plunder which threatens the livelihood of many nations shall be allowed to succeed. And we must make sure that the life of the great trading nations of the world cannot, in the future be strangled at any moment by some interruption to the free passage of the Canal. These are our intentions.

Source: Frankland (ed.), 1959, pp. 159–160

Despite the confidence of Dulles that the United States had 'introduced a valuable stop gap into a dangerous situation' **(FRUS (C), 1988, doc. 51)**, these inflammatory statements, on the eve of a conference designed to promote a peaceful solution to the crisis, were indicative of a consistently hard line in British government circles. At an Egypt Committee meeting of 7 August 1956, which considered changes to British military plans, the Chancellor of the Exchequer, Harold Macmillan, argued that an operation which simply occupied the Canal Zone was insufficient as 'we had already learnt from bitter experience that we could not control Egypt from there. If, as he believed, our real aim was to overthrow Nasser's Government, it might be wiser to undertake an operation more directly related to that objective'. British military plans were, therefore, to be redrafted to take into account that 'our ultimate objective was to overthrow Nasser's Government' **(PRO CAB 134/1216, 7 August 1956)**.

Document 3.9 British War Aims in Egypt, 7 August 1956

EGYPT

4 Our common aim in Egypt should be to occupy the Canal Zone so as to ensure free and open traffic for all users who would during the period of occupation pay their dues into the account of the old Suez Canal Company, and to provide for suitable military government in the towns of Ismailia, Port Said and Suez and in such additional areas adjacent to the Canal as it proves necessary to occupy. We should aim at evacuating the occupied Zone within the shortest possible period of time after a satisfactory agreement has been reached with an Egyptian Government for the future control of the Canal and after arrangements have been made for a new international organisation to take over the offices and installations of the Suez Canal Company.

5 Military occupation of the Canal may involve us in military occupation of the whole of Egypt. It may also bring about or contribute to the downfall of Colonel Nasser and the establishment of a new regime in Egypt. These possibilities and their implications should be carefully considered in your discussions with the French, but it is not our present intention that they should be included in the directive which will eventually be required as a basis for action. It is most important, from the point of view of public opinion, especially in the United States and in Asia that the purpose of our action should appear to be confined to establishing the security of the inter-national waterway across the Isthmus of Suez, and not as being complicated by political designs against the Egyptian regime. It follows that the leakage of a document appearing to define our objective in wider terms could be disastrous.

Source: PRO CAB 134/1216, note by the Secretary of State for Foreign Affairs with draft instructions to Sir G. Jebb, 7 August 1956

Given that this is a memo giving instructions to the British Ambassador to France, it is significant that Eden's personal antipathy to Nasser had by now hardened into official policy; however, this was not to be widely advertised. This did raise the problem of how such an objective could be squared with both a military operation directed at occupying the Canal Zone and a diplomatic process that ostensibly envisaged substantive negotiations with Colonel Nasser's government. Such concerns were raised by the Minister of State for Foreign Affairs, the Marquess of Reading, in a memorandum to Selwyn Lloyd:

> I assume at the outset that it is our genuine desire and purpose that the conference should achieve its purpose and that, as you told me recently, we do not regard it merely as a time-consuming device until a military operation can be effectively launched.

(Kyle, 1991, pp. 185–186)

This was the nub of the issue as current military and diplomatic plans summarised by the Cabinet Secretary, Sir Norman Brook, for the Egypt Committee on 14 August envisaged the inevitable failure of the London Conference to secure a peaceful settlement and an invasion, preparations having been made in the interim, in early September. This timetable was, however, dislocated, first, by the fact that the British could not totally control the outcome of the London Conference, and, second, by the fact that a fresh pretext for invasion was required. These issues had already been raised in an earlier full Cabinet meeting on the morning of 14 August.

Document 3.10 Eden's Hopes for the London Conference, 14 August 1956

The Prime Minister said he had had a discussion that morning with Leaders of the Opposition, who had had asked for Parliament to be recalled and had indicated their opposition to the use of force to impose on Egypt any conclusion reached by the forthcoming conference. They considered that any international action should be considered at a special session of the United Nations and that the new authority should be set up under that Organisation. They had, however, recognised that if any new incidents occurred, such as interference with ships using the Canal, a new situation would arise in which force might be justified. . . .

The Prime Minister suggested that, if the conference endorsed the need for establishing an international authority for the Suez Canal, the countries mainly concerned might agree that, pending the establishment of an international authority, no further transit dues should be paid to any Egyptian authority. Colonel Nasser was at present getting between 30 and 35 per cent of the transit dues mostly from payment by American shipping companies which had always paid their dues in Cairo. Agreement to pay all dues to a blocked account with, say, the International Bank pending the establishment of the new international authority should quickly cause Colonel Nasser to lose prestige. If he were to retaliate by stopping ships from using the Canal or by taking action against the employees of the Suez Canal Company a new situation would have arisen which would warrant the use of force against Egypt.

Source: PRO CAB 128/30 Pt II, CM 59 (56), 14 August 1956

The London Conference of Maritime Nations met from 16 to 23 August. In the absence of Egypt, who had declined to attend following the bellicose rhetoric from London in the previous two weeks, the Conference did not represent negotiations between the participants in the dispute. Proposals first put forward by Egypt on 12 August 1956 were ignored; instead the Conference was forced into the position whereby whatever proposals it adopted would have to be conveyed to the Egyptian government. The tone of the conference was set by John Foster Dulles and, indeed, the resolution he advanced was the only one given serious consideration.

Document 3.11 The Eighteen Nations Proposals, 23 August 1956

1 They affirm that, as stated in the Preamble to the Convention of 1888, there should be established 'a definite system destined to guarantee at all times, and for all the powers, the free use of the Suez Maritime Canal'.

2 Such a system, which would be established for due regard to the sovereign rights of Egypt should assure;

(a) Efficient and dependable operation, maintenance of the Canal as a free, open and secure international waterway in accordance with the principles of the Convention of 1888.

(b) Insulation of the operation of the canal from the influence of the politics of any nation.

(c) A return to Egypt for the use of the Suez Canal which will be fair and equitable and increasing with enlargements of its capacity and greater use.

(d) Canal tolls as low as is consistent with the foregoing requirements and, except for c above, no profit.

3 To achieve these results on a permanent and reliable basis there should be established by a convention to be negotiated with Egypt:

(a) Institutional arrangements for co-operation between Egypt and other interested nations in the operation and maintenance and development of the Canal and for harmonising and safeguarding their respective interests in the Canal. To this end, operating, maintaining and developing the Canal and enlarging it so as to increase the volume of traffic in the interests of world trade and of Egypt, would be the responsibility of a Suez Canal Board. Egypt would grant this Board all rights and facilities appropriate to its functioning as here outlined. The status of the Board would be defined in the above-mentioned convention.

The members of the board, in addition to Egypt, would be other states chosen in a manner to be agreed upon from among the States parties to the Convention, with due regard to use, pattern of trade and geographical distribution; the composition of the board to be such that its responsibilities would be discharged solely with a view to achieving the best possible operating results without political motivation in favour of, or in prejudice against, any user of the Canal.

The Board would make periodic reports to the United Nations.

(b) An Arbitral Commission to settle any disputes as to the equitable return to Egypt or other matters arising in the operation of the Canal,

(c) Effective sanctions for any violation of the Convention by any party to it, or any other nation, including provisions for treating any use or threat of force to interfere with the use or operation of the Canal as a threat to the peace and a violation of the purposes and principles of the United Nations Charter.

(d) Provisions for appropriate association with the United Nations and for review as may be necessary.

Source: Eayrs (ed.), 1964, pp. 102–103

This rather legalistic formulation of both the problem and the solution, bears the characteristic stamp of John Foster Dulles, who was a lawyer by training. The extent to which it could prove an adequate framework within which the dispute could be settled was highly dubious given that Egypt was not attending the conference. From the British point of view, this was not a particularly satisfactory outcome for it left them no further forward. As the British Chancellor of the Exchequer, Harold Macmillan, morosely observed to Dulles

> there are only three choices: (1) Nasser voluntarily takes a proposal along the lines of US paper; or (2) We compel Egypt to take it; (3) we accept Nasser's refusal. In the last event, Britain is finished and so far as I am concerned I will have no part in it and will resign.

(FRUS (C), 1988, doc. 97)

In the face of the insistence of the United States on a peaceful settlement, notwithstanding British attempts to persuade Dulles otherwise, they had no choice but to accept the outcome of the London Conference.

Despite the attempts of the British to have Dulles act in the role of emissary to Nasser, thus further embroiling the United States in the Suez affair, the Australian Prime Minister, Sir Robert Menzies, was dispatched as head of a five-man mission to seek the reactions of the Egyptian government. Prolonged meetings took place in Cairo between 3 and 9 September 1956 but Nasser's response was held by the Menzies mission to be a rejection. Even before the Menzies mission left for Cairo, the British Cabinet had been considering what its options would be if Nasser did not adopt the resolution of the London Conference.

Document 3.12 Differences in the British Cabinet over the Use of Force, 28 August 1956

The Prime Minister said that the United States Secretary of State and the French Foreign Minister had been consulted about possible courses of action if Egypt rejected the principle of international control over the Suez Canal. The possibility of referring the issue to the Security Council was now being considered in consultation with the Governments of the United States and France. Hitherto, the United States had been against any reference to the United Nations, but the French Government recognised that such a course would have advantages from the point of view of world opinion. It would undoubtedly involve serious risks – e.g., of delay and of embarrassing amendments; but we would certainly stand better with foreign opinion and with our own if we had shown that a majority of the Security Council were prepared to endorse the statement of principles adopted by the London Conference. A Russian veto of such a resolution would demonstrate clearly the obstructive nature of Communist tactics. . . .

In discussion there was general agreement that the balance of advantage lay on the side of making some appropriate reference to the Security Council, before any military operations were undertaken, if we could be assured in advance of the full support of the United States and other friendly Powers. In that event it should be possible to defeat any embarrassing amendments to a resolution endorsing the statement of principles adopted at the London Conference. Five of the permanent members of the Security Council had already endorsed that statement and it should be possible to secure two or three additional votes. It would be preferable to take the initiative in referring the issue to the Security Council rather than risk being arraigned before it on the ground that our military measures constituted a threat to peace.

The Chancellor of the Exchequer said that our national economy now depended on supplies of oil from the Middle East. Colonel Nasser's ambitions threatened those supplies – directly, because they jeopardised the freedom and efficiency of the Suez Canal; and indirectly because the success of his plans would inevitably impair our relations with the oil-producing countries of the Middle East.

The Minister of Defence said that, for the reason which had been stated in the discussion he agreed that we could not afford to allow Colonel Nasser to succeed in his attempt to seize control over the Suez Canal and that, if all other methods proved unavailing force would have to be used to prevent it. On the other hand, the Cabinet should weigh the disadvantages of using force. If, together with the French, we took military measures against Egypt, our action would be condemned by a substantial body of public opinion in countries overseas, including several of the independent countries of the Commonwealth. Within the United Kingdom itself opinion would be divided. Our vital interests in other parts of the Middle East would also be affected; we must, in particular, expect sabotage against oil installations in other Arab countries. Moreover, once we had sent military forces into Egypt, it would not be easy to extricate them; we might find ourselves saddled with a costly commitment. While, therefore, he was ready to agree that we must continue to be prepared to use force in the last resort, he hoped that we should first exhaust all other means of curbing Colonel Nasser's ambitions and, in particular that we should let no opportunity pass of securing a settlement by agreement. . . .

The Prime Minister, summing up this part of the discussion said that it was evident that the Cabinet were united in the view that the frustration of Colonel Nasser's policy was a vital British interest which must be secured in the last resort, by the use of force. He fully recognised that, before recourse was had to force, every practicable attempt should be made to secure a satisfactory settlement by peaceful means and it must be made clear to the public, here and overseas, that no effort to this end had been spared. At the same time we could not afford to allow these efforts to impose an undue delay. Our French allies, whose public opinion was less divided than our own would be quick to place an unfavourable interpretation on anything which could be construed as hesitancy on our part. Colonel Nasser would also be looking for signs of weakening in our attitude. Finally, the difficulties of any military operation would be increased if it were long delayed. While therefore the possibilities of a peaceful settlement would be fully explored, this should not be allowed to weaken our resolution or to reduce the weight of our pressure on the Egyptian Government.

Source: PRO CAB 128/30 Pt II, CM 62 (56), 28 August 1956

The Cabinet noted the advantages of referring the dispute to the United Nations. However, it is clear from this unusually frank discussion that divisions were beginning to open up within the Cabinet over what action to take if a peaceful solution proved impossible. Paradoxically, it was the Minister of Defence, Sir Walter Monckton, who raised grave doubts about the dilemma confronting Britain, the difficulties surrounding the military option and the effect of such an operation on Britain's international standing (this was to lead to his later resignation, ostensibly on the grounds of ill-health). It should also be noted that in summing up the Cabinet discussion, Eden, conscious of the need for a united front, obscured the developing differences between his colleagues but none the less remained committed to the military option.

Despite British wishes, however, renewed emphasis was given to the diplomatic approach by a letter from Eisenhower to Eden on 3 September 1956 in which the American President reviewed the progress made at the London Conference and considered the prospects of a referral to the United Nations. He was adamant that force must remain a last resort.

Document 3.13 Eisenhower Again Cautions Against the Use of Force, 3 September 1956

As to the use of force or the threat of force at this juncture, I continue to feel as I expressed myself in the letter Foster carried to you some weeks ago. Even now military preparations and civilian evacuation exposed to public view seem to be solidifying support for Nasser which has been shaky in many important quarters. I regard it as indispensable that if we are to proceed solidly together to the solution of this problem, public opinion in our several countries must be overwhelming in its support. I must tell you frankly that American public opinion flatly rejects the thought of using force, particularly when it does not seem that every possible peaceful means of protecting interests has been exhausted without result. Moreover, I gravely doubt we could here secure Congressional authority even for the lesser support measures for which you might have to look to us.

I really do not see how a successful result could be achieved by forcible means. The use of force would, it seems to me, vastly increase the area of jeopardy. I do not see how the economy of Western Europe can long survive the burden of prolonged military operations, as well as the denial of Near East oil. Also the peoples of the Near East and of North Africa and, to some extent of all of Asia and all of Africa, would be consolidated against the West to a degree which, I fear, could not be overcome in a generation and, perhaps, not even in a century particularly having in mind the capacity of the Russians to make mischief. Before such action were undertaken, all our peoples should unitedly understand that there were no other means available to protect our vital rights and interests.

Source: PRO PREM 11/1100, Eisenhower to Eden, 3 September 1956

See document 3.5, pp. 65–66.

Dulles, increasingly perturbed by the Anglo-French insistence on military action, identified a further delaying tactic when he put forward CASU (Co-operative Association of Suez Canal Users), later known as SCUA (Suez Canal Users Association). The principal features of this scheme were outlined by Dulles to Lord Harcourt of the British Embassy in Washington.

Document 3.14 Dulles and the Genesis of SCUA, 5 September 1956

3 The fact was, however, that the Convention of 1888 gave us all the rights we required. Why should not the users club together and themselves hire the pilots, manage the technical features of the Canal and organise the pattern of navigation? He [Dulles] believed that, though it might be inconvenient, it might be quite feasible, and would lead in due course to some accommodation with Egypt. He cited in particular Article 8 of the Convention which gave broad powers to the agents of the signatories; it could not perhaps be applied literally (for instance the United Kingdom had made a reservation) but it was illustrative of the rights conferred by the Convention on the users of the Canal. The Convention gave powers to deal with obstructions, object to fortifications and station warships. If Egypt interfered with these rights, then she would put herself in the wrong.

4 It was a fatal and unnecessary weakness to assume that if Egypt did not voluntarily accept our proposals we must resort to force. On the other hand, we should be in a much stronger position with Nasser if we could show him that, supposing he rejected our proposals, we had an alternative other than war, namely that the signatories or the users would run the Canal themselves by virtue of their rights under the Convention. The Convention gave Nasser no right to make a profit out of the operation of the Canal, and he would thus see the money slipping out of his hands. He was much more likely to be deflated by the loss of these revenues than by the threat or the use of force. Our position in the United Nations would also be much stronger if we made no demands for additional rights, but relied on the Convention as giving us all we wanted in the face of Egyptian interference.

Source: PRO PREM 11/1100, Sir Roger Makins to the Foreign Office, 5 September 1956

See Document 1.1.3, pp. 3–6.

This document represents a reformulation by Dulles of the original eighteen Nation Proposals (document 3.11, pp. 72–73). It is once again heavily legalistic in tone and approach and harks back to the Convention of 1888. Dulles, concerned to head off any use of force, here provides an alternative for the British and French which could potentially return the operation of the Canal to the *status quo ante*. Both Selwyn Lloyd and Eden were unconvinced about the ultimate efficacy of this scheme but saw considerable merit in acceptance for, as Lloyd stated,

> the great tactical advantage of Mr Dulles's proposal is that if the Americans were to participate in the actual setting up of an international body after Nasser's refusal, they would have committed themselves much further towards a policy of compelling the Egyptian Government by some means or other to accept international control.

(PRO PREM 11/1100, 6 September 1956)

Moreover, Eden replying to Eisenhower on 6 September was concerned to dwell on what he saw as the continuing threat posed by Nasser in the event of the failure of the Menzies mission and SCUA.

Document 3.15 Eden again Solicits the Support of Eisenhower and the United States, 6 September 1956

In the 1930s Hitler established his position by a series of carefully planned movements. These began with the occupation of the Rhineland and were followed by successive acts of aggression against Austria, Czechoslovakia, Poland and the West. His actions were tolerated and excused by the majority of the population of Western Europe. It was argued either that Hitler had committed no act of aggression against anyone or that he was entitled to do what he liked in his own territory or that it was impossible to prove that he had any ulterior designs or that the covenant of the League of Nations did not entitle us to use force and that it would be wiser to wait until he did commit an act of aggression.

In more recent years Russia has attempted similar tactics. The blockade of Berlin was to have been the opening move in a campaign designed at least to deprive the Western powers of their whole position in Germany. On this occasion we fortunately reacted at once with the result that the Russian design was never unfolded. But I am sure you would agree that it would be wrong to infer from this circumstance that no Russian design existed. Similarly the seizure of the Suez Canal is, we are convinced, the opening gambit of a planned campaign designed by Nasser to expel all Western influence and interests from Arab countries. He believes that if he can get away with this and if he can successfully defy eighteen nations his prestige in Arabia will be so great that he will be able to mount revolutions of young officers in Saudi Arabia, Jordan, Syria and Iraq. . . . These new Governments will in effect be Egyptian satellites if not Russian ones. They will have to place their united oil resources under the control of a united Arabia led by Egypt and under Russian influence. When that moment comes Nasser can deny oil to Western Europe and we here shall all be at his mercy. . . .

The difference which separates us today appears to be a difference of assessment of Nasser's plans and intentions and of the consequences in the Middle East of military action against him.

You may feel that even if we are right it would be better to wait until Nasser has unmistakably unveiled his intentions. But this was the argument which prevailed in 1936 and which we both rejected in 1948. Admittedly there are risks in the use of force against Egypt now. It is however clear that military intervention designed to reverse Nasser's revolutions in the whole continent would be a much more costly and difficult undertaking. I am very troubled as it is, that if we do not reach a conclusion either way about the Canal very soon, one or other of these Eastern lands may be toppled at any moment by Nasser's revolutionary movements.

I agree with you that prolonged military operations as well as the denial of Middle East oil would place an immense strain on the economy of Western Europe. I can assure you that we are conscious of the burdens and perils attending military intervention but if our assessment is correct and if the only alternative is to allow Nasser's plans quietly to develop until this country and all Western Europe are held to ransom by Egypt acting at Russia's behest it would seem to us that our duty is plain. We have many times led Europe in the fight for freedom. It would be an ignoble end to our long history if we tamely accepted to perish by degrees.

Source: PRO PREM 11/1100, Eden to Eisenhower, 6 September 1956

Once again Eden responded to Eisenhower's warnings with a blend of painful historical memory and contemporary Cold War fears. The yoking of Hitler, Nasser and the Soviet Union, was clearly designed to persuade the reluctant President of the merits of Eden's position, which remained what it had been since July, that force could and should be used. This despairing picture was swiftly refuted by Eisenhower. Although the President acknowledged that 'eventually there may be no escape from the use of force' he again rejected Eden's vision and his insistence on the use of force.

Document 3.16 Eisenhower Informs Eden of the Need for a Peaceful Resolution, 8 September 1956

The use of military force against Egypt under present circumstances might have consequences even more serious than causing the Arabs to support Nasser. It might cause a serious misunderstanding between our two countries because I must say frankly that there is as yet no public opinion in this country which is prepared to support such a move and the most significant public opinion that there is seems to think that the United Nations was formed to prevent this very thing.

It is for reasons such as these that we have viewed with some misgivings your preparations for mounting a military expedition against Egypt. We believe that Nasser may try to go before the United Nations claiming that these actions imply a rejection of the peaceful machinery of settling the dispute, and therefore may ask the United Nations to brand these operations as aggression. . . .

It seems to Foster and to me that the result that you and I both want can best be assured by slower and less dramatic processes than military force. There are many areas of endeavour which are not yet fully explored because exploration takes time. . . .

I assure you that we are not blind to the fact that eventually there may be no escape from the use of force. Our resolute purpose must be to create conditions of operation in which all users can have confidence. But to resort to military action when the world believes there are other means available for resolving the dispute would set in motion forces that could lead, in the years to come, to the most distressing results.

Source: PRO PREM 11/1100, Eisenhower to Eden, 8 September 1956

These exchanges merely highlighted the increasing gulf between London and Washington's interpretations of the situation. To Eisenhower and Dulles, SCUA represented a genuine diplomatic effort which made the use of force less likely. To Eden and Lloyd SCUA potentially represented the exhaustion of diplomatic initiatives that would in turn make eventual American support, tacit or otherwise, for the use of force inevitable. In what Selwyn Lloyd called in his memoirs a 'critical' Cabinet meeting the British reviewed the situation following the rejection of the Menzies mission by Colonel Nasser.

Document 3.17 Divisions in the British Cabinet, 11 September 1956

The Prime Minister . . . said that it was evident that the Cabinet were in favour of proceeding with the plan for establishing an organisation to enable the principal users of the Canal to exercise their rights under the 1888 Convention provided that the United States Government were willing that this project should be announced in the forthcoming debate in the House of Commons and brought into operation without delay; and that the Cabinet were further agreed that in this event, the situation should be formally notified to the Chairman of the Security Council under Article 35 of the United Nations Charter. . . .

The Minister of Defence said that he hoped that the adoption of this plan for the establishment of a users' organisation would not be regarded solely as a step towards the use of force. He did not exclude the possibility that, if the Canal could be brought under effective international control, the present regime in Egypt might be overthrown by means short of war. Any premature recourse to force, especially without the support and approval of the United States was likely to precipitate disorder throughout the Middle East and to alienate a substantial body of public opinion in this country and elsewhere throughout the world. . . .

The Prime Minister, summing up this part of the discussion said that it was clear that the Cabinet were agreed that Egypt's disregard of her international obligations could not be tolerated and that effective international control over the Suez Canal must be re-established; that every reasonable effort must be made to secure this objective by peaceful means; but that, if these should all fail, we should be justified in the last resort in using force to restore the situation. It would be a difficult exercise of judgement to decide when the point had been reached when recourse must be had to forceful measures. In determining this we should weigh not only the state of public opinion in the United States, but also the views of the French, who were eager to take firm action to restore the situation and were increasingly impatient of delay.

Source: PRO CAB 128/30 Pt II, CM 64 (56), 11 September 1956

See Document 3.12, pp. 74–76, for Monckton's previous arguments on these lines.

The significance of this Cabinet discussion is the very clear gulf that was opening up between the hawks in the Cabinet led by the Prime Minister and the doves personified by the Minister of Defence. Monckton stressed the necessity for American support, and therefore the need to take SCUA seriously, while Eden continued to push the Cabinet towards the use of force, using the argument of an impatient France as a further justification for action.

Even as the invitations were being issued for a second London conference to discuss Dulles's proposals to form SCUA, the gulf between London and Washington was becoming embarrassingly public. On 13 September 1956 at a press conference given by Secretary of State Dulles, he was repeatedly pressed by journalists to outline American policy in certain scenarios, and particularly on the issue of whether SCUA was effectively an 'organised boycott' of Egyptian control of the Canal. To these questions he responded

It is not a boycott of the Canal, as far as I know, to refrain from using force to get through the Canal. If force is interposed by Egypt, then I do not call it a boycott to avoid using force to shoot your way through. We do not intend to shoot our way through. It may be we have the right to do it but we don't intend to do it as far as the United States is concerned . . . if we are met by force, which we can only overcome by shooting, we don't intend to go into that shooting. Then we intend to send our boats around the Cape. But that is certainly not a boycott of the Canal.

(Frankland, 1959, p. 215)

This further intimation of American thinking was to cause Eden difficulties in the House of Commons when the Opposition seized upon Dulles's untimely exposition to reinforce its support for a referral to the UN and to embarrass the government still further.

Document 3.18 Gaitskell Attacks Eden in the House of Commons, 13 September 1956

Mr Gaitskell: . . . Is he [the Prime Minister] prepared to say on behalf of Her Majesty's Government that they will not shoot their way through the Canal?

The Prime Minister: I said that we were in complete agreement with the United States Government about what to do. I read out from this paper, and I said – [Hon. Members: 'Answer'] – and I repeat that the first action – I said this yesterday – was to ask the Egyptian Government. We cannot do this without some co-operation with the Egyptian Government. We propose to ask for that co-operation. We have said here that if they do not give it, they are, in our view, in default under the 1888 Convention, but if they are so in default, we should take them to the Security Council – [Interruption] –

Mr Speaker: Order.

Source: HC Deb. Vol. 558 Col. 3038, 13 September 1956

See Documents 3.15 and 3.16, pp. 78–80.

This exchange is further evidence of the increasing division between the two frontbenches on how to respond to the growing crisis. It is significant that as Eden found it increasingly difficult to get American support for the use of force, in public, at least, he was concerned to stress the unanimity between London and Washington.

Document 3.19 A Satirical View of Relations Between Gaitskell and Eden, 17 September 1956

Despite the continued and entirely consistent warnings from the United States, Anglo-French military preparations continued apace. The delays caused by the diplomatic manoeuvrings of August and September had seriously affected the original timetable for military action. Increasing concern had also been registered, not least by the Service chiefs, about the possible scale of civilian casualties if the plan to invade Egypt at Alexandria was executed. The military plan was therefore recast by General Keightley, the overall Commander-in-Chief, to focus on Port Said and the Canal Zone: MUSKETEER became MUSKETEER (Revise) in mid-September 1956.

The image of Eden and Gaitskell as two halves of a pantomime lion reflects their initial agreement and subsequent divergence of views. Here, Eden is portrayed as striding resolutely forwards while Gaitskell attempts to slow his progress

Source: Punch, *17 September 1956*

A separate branch of the British strategy, which sought to establish a *casus belli* for intervention, was represented by Operations PILE-UP and CONVOY. In essence, these schemes envisaged proving that the Egyptian administration was incapable of operating the Canal by creating the maximum amount of through traffic at any given time; on 16 September fifty ships were sent to Port Said and Suez in an attempt to swamp the piloting system. In the event this was a failure as the Egyptian pilots proved capable of clearing this increased Canal traffic in a day. Because PILE-UP failed, CONVOY, a scheme to shepherd these ships through under British control, was redundant and the hoped for pretext remained elusive **(Kyle, 1991, pp. 249–250)**.

Between 19 and 21 September 1956, the Second London Conference met to discuss Dulles's proposals, and these were formalised into the Suez Canal Users Association. Once again, Egypt did not attend the conference and in many respects the situation therefore represented no advance on the first London Conference: SCUA was essentially a holding operation. Even as the conference drew to a conclusion the patience of the British with the apparent prevarications of Dulles became exhausted. Eden and Lloyd considered that SCUA, which they had cared little for in the first place, had become 'much watered down from its original conception . . . [and was] . . . widely held . . . to be more feeble in its plans for execution than was expected' **(PRO, PREM 11/1102, 23 September 1956)**. This impression was later confirmed by a statement by Dulles in a news conference on 2 October when he stated that 'There is talk about "the teeth" being pulled out of it [SCUA]. There were never "teeth" in it, if that means the use of force' **(Frankland, 1959, p. 248)**.

Therefore, in the face of mounting international and domestic political pressures and with few remaining diplomatic or military options, Eden and Lloyd decided to take their problems to the United Nations. This option had been discussed with the United States in late August but had been rejected on the grounds that this would mean Soviet involvement in any discussions on the Suez Canal.

Document 3.20 Lloyd on the Referral of the Dispute to the United Nations

During the next two days it became clear to the Prime Minister and myself that we must act. We had wanted to go to the United Nations since the beginning of the month. We had been obliged to put it off because of the SCUA plan. We had tried to play fair with Dulles by not leaking that there was a difference of opinion between us. Another reason was the nature of my talk with Dulles. He appeared to have understood our difficulties at last and, provided we did not try to rush proceedings in the Security Council, I thought that he would not disagree provided the United States were not associated with the reference. One thing that I was not going to do was to continue the discussion with him by telegram. The French agreed with us.

They thought that the exercise at the United Nations would be futile but they agreed to act in concert with us.

Source: Lloyd, 1978, pp. 148–149

This extract from the memoirs of Selwyn Lloyd, written some twenty years later but on the basis of privileged access to government papers (as an ex-Foreign Secretary), is a primary source but should be treated with some degree of circumspection as Lloyd is clearly seeking to put the best interpretation on his own and the government's actions. Lloyd is at pains here to stress the government's willingness to utilise the machinery of the United Nations, but the government had previously been reluctant to take this option and only did so out of frustration at the continual prevarication of the United States.

A joint Anglo-French reference to the Security Council to discuss the 'situation created by the unilateral action of the Egyptian Government in bringing to an end the system of international operation of the Suez Canal, which was confirmed and completed by the Suez Canal Convention of 1888' was made on 23 September 1956. A counter was put by the Egyptian government asking the Security Council to discuss 'Actions against Egypt by some powers, particularly France and the United Kingdom, which constitute a danger to international peace and security and are a serious violation of the Charter of the United Nations.' It was agreed that these should be discussed in the Security Council from 5 October 1956 **(Lloyd, 1978, pp. 149–150)**.

To concert strategy with the French, Eden and Lloyd visited Mollet and Pineau in Paris on 26–27 September 1956. There they found the French to be adamant about the necessity of bringing down Nasser by force as soon as possible. This was entirely consistent with French policy throughout the crisis; on 17 September 1956 the British Ambassador in Paris, Sir Gladwyn Jebb, recorded Pineau's opinion that

> recourse to the Security Council would (in his opinion) . . . be largely immaterial, except for window dressing purposes. What was material was that Nasser would clearly in the circumstances be thought to have got away with his seizure. We should thus be left with the distressing alternative of using force or of facing the fact that our two countries were 'completely finished'.

(PRO PREM 11/1102, 17 September 1956).

Eden gave the following report to the Cabinet on 3 October 1956.

Document 3.21 Eden Reaffirms Necessity of Removing Nasser, 3 October 1956

The Prime Minister said that he was impressed by the vigour of M. Mollet's Government and their uncompromising attitude towards the Suez situation. They were determined that Colonel Nasser's actions should not go uncorrected. They believed that, if his ambitions were not checked, the political as well as the economic future of Europe would be in jeopardy. For they feared that, in that event, existing regimes in other Arab states would collapse and the Middle East would pass under the influence, not so much of Egypt, but of the Soviet Union. If that happened, Europe itself would be at the mercy of the Russians. It was for these reasons that the French were impatient at the obstacles which were preventing the Western Powers from imposing a satisfactory settlement on the Egyptian Government. They were especially resentful of the attitude of the United States Government, many of whose statements were calculated to encourage the Russians to believe that they could, without undue danger, support Colonel Nasser in an intransigent attitude. There was indeed a risk that the Soviet Union might conclude a pact of mutual assistance with Egypt. If that happened it would become much more hazardous to attempt to impose a settlement of this dispute by force.

The Prime Minister said that it was difficult to forecast the course of the forthcoming discussions in the Security Council. There now seemed less reason to believe that the Egyptian Government would consider a solution on the lines which Mr Khrishna Menon had canvassed during his recent visit to London and there were no indications of the attitude which the Egyptians were likely to adopt in the Security Council. If they continued to be obdurate world opinion might be readier to support a recourse to forceful measures. If they offered to negotiate, the task of achieving a satisfactory settlement would be more difficult and more protracted. In either event the weeks ahead would be critical; and the Government's task had not been made easier by the public statements made by Opposition leaders in this country and by members of the United States administration.

In discussion the following points were raised:–

2 It was recognised that our objectives would not be fully attained if we accepted a settlement of the Suez Canal dispute which left Colonel Nasser's influence undiminished throughout the Middle East.

Source: PRO CAB 128/30 Pt II, CM 68 (56), 3 October 1956

The Prime Minister was at pains to stress to his colleagues the eagerness of the French to take military action against Nasser. From this account it would seem that the French shared Eden's apocalyptic vision, although, of course, this was Eden's own perception. Eden was clearly worried that Egyptian willingness to negotiate, combined with the attitude of the Labour Party and the United States administration, might make it impossible to secure a resolution of the crisis that removed Nasser from power.

What was apparently not recorded in these Cabinet minutes, according to some historians, was a report by Eden that there was a possibility of Israeli participation in any military action against Egypt **(Horne, 1989, p. 427; Lucas, 1991, p. 217)**. This resurrection of an option raised by Macmillan in early August, and swiftly dismissed on the grounds that this would unite all the Arab countries of the Middle East against Britain, brought back on to the agenda what was to prove one of the most contentious issues surrounding the whole affair. Contacts between France and Israel predated the Suez Crisis. In breach of the tripartite declaration of 1950 France had been secretly supplying arms to Israel since the spring of 1956 including advanced Dassault Mystere fighter aircraft. This de facto alliance, based on a common enemy in the Middle East, between the French and the Israelis led inexorably to informal talks at service level in early September. More detailed plans were hammered out at a conference in Paris attended by Foreign Minister Golda Meir and Chief of Staff General Moshe Dayan from the Israeli side and Christian Pineau the Foreign Minister and Deputy Chief of the Air Staff General Challe from the French side on 30 September and 1 October 1956. Challe accompanied the Israeli delegation on their return to Israel in early October to further investigate possibilities for co-operation and to examine Israeli equipment requirements. However, the stumbling block was that a *sine qua non* for the Israeli government was active British participation, which was unlikely to be forthcoming given that the matter was currently before the Security Council **(Kyle, 1991, p. 266)**.

Lloyd arrived in New York on 2 October 1956 and, with Pineau, met Dulles on the morning of 5 October to clarify their respective positions before the Security Council met that afternoon. Although Dulles agreed to support the Anglo-French position in the Security Council (which was that 'our objective is to get maximum endorsement in the Security Council for a settlement by negotiation on the basis of the principles underlying the 18 Power proposals'), the meeting revealed continuing difficulties between the British and the French on the one hand and the Americans on the other regarding the ultimate use of force.

Document 3.22 Dulles again Outlines the Consequences of the Use of Force, 5 October 1956

Mr Dulles . . . said [that] President Eisenhower's view was that if a war was started it would be very difficult to bring it to an end. He thought the result would be the loss of Western influence for at least a generation in the Middle East, Asia and Africa. . . .

He knew that there were suggestions that United States policy on the Suez issue was governed by the forthcoming elections. He could give the clearest possible assurance on his own behalf and on that of the President that this was not so. United States policy was the same as it would have been whether there were elections or not. . . .

Mr Dulles said that there might be circumstances when force would be the only alternative and it might have to be used even if no satisfactory outcome could be seen. He thought, however, that it would be a great illusion to suppose that the use of force would improve our position even if, as he did not accept, this position was now deteriorating. If force were used we could write off Pakistan, Iran and Ethiopia. The position in Africa would be worse and not better. The United Kingdom had been faced with that choice in 1953 and he knew that there were plans then to take over Alexandria and Cairo. The United Kingdom had decided against this then and he was sure that they were right and that today the arguments against such a course were even stronger, if only because Russian access to Egypt and ability to support Egypt were much greater. If force were used in violation of the United Nations Charter the United Nations itself would be destroyed with incalculable consequences not least in the United States.

Source: PRO PREM 11/1102, record of conversation between the Secretary of State, Mr Dulles and M. Pineau in Mr Dulles's apartment on 5 October 1956 at 10.15 a.m. in New York

On the eve of the first face-to-face negotiations with the Egyptians since the nationalisation, the American Secretary of State warned Britain and France of both America's position on the use of force and the catastrophic consequences of such an action.

The actual debates within the Security Council made no substantive progress. However, a series of meetings chaired by the Secretary-General of the United Nations Dag Hammarskjöld between Lloyd, Pineau and Fawzi were more productive. These were the first face-to-face meetings between the main protagonists since the nationalisation: after three days of often tense discussions a basis for further negotiations was proposed by Lloyd and agreed with some reservations by Fawzi and with some reluctance by Pineau. These 'Six Principles' were passed by the Security Council on 13 October 1956.

Document 3.23 'Six Principles for the Future of the Canal Proposed at the United Nations Security Council, 13 October 1956 by Britain and France'

Any settlement of the Suez question should meet the following requirements:
1 there should be free and open transit through the Canal without discrimination, overt or covert – this covers both political and technical aspects;
2 the sovereignty of Egypt should be respected;
3 the operation of the Canal should be insulated from the politics of any country;
4 the manner of fixing tolls and charges should be decided by agreement between Egypt and the users;
5 a fair proportion of the dues should be allotted to development;
6 in case of disputes, unresolved affairs between the Suez Canal Company and the Egyptian Government should be settled by arbitration with suitable

terms of reference and suitable provisions for the payment of sums found to be due.

Source: Lloyd, 1978, appendix IV, p. 276

Given what was to follow, it is ironic that these principles were to form the basis of the ultimate settlement of the Suez Canal dispute in 1957. The proposals, on the surface, represented a satisfactory reconciliation of the *public* British position and that of Egypt. What they did and could not do, however, was administer a public humiliation to Nasser that would lead to his downfall which was the *sine qua non* of the *private* British position.

Although these principles were greeted by Eisenhower with an enthusiastic endorsement that this meant that the crisis was over, no agreement was reached on the system that would administer the Six Principles. None the less, this represented a considerable advance on the diplomatic deadlock of the preceding months and Eden consented to Lloyd remaining in New York to explore further avenues of progress with Fawzi, the ultimate aim being that if sufficient progress had been made the foreign ministers should meet again at the end of the month. This was potentially embarrassing as Eden had delivered, on the very same day as the passage of the six Principles by the Security Council, a speech to the Tory Party conference at Llandudno which, in refusing to rule out the use of force, was, as Carlton notes, 'greeted with such great enthusiasm by the delegates that the Prime Minister must have realised that any compromise solution, such as Lloyd was working towards in New York, would be deeply unpopular in the Conservative Party' **(Carlton, 1988, p. 58)**. The Prime Minister now found himself in the dilemma that he had sought to avoid since 26 July 1956: at best, continued negotiations meant a delay in any military operation until spring 1957 and at worst the acceptance of Nasser's nationalisation.

Worse still, the situation in the Middle East had suddenly taken another dramatic and highly dangerous twist. On the night of 10–11 October 1956, Israeli forces attacked the Jordanian village and police post of Qualqilya as a reprisal for earlier *fedayeen* raids. This unusually heavy attack, involving the use of tanks, heavy weapons and jet aircraft, led to an anguished request from King Hussein of Jordan for British aid under the Anglo-Jordanian Treaty of 1948, including the provision of immediate air support **(PRO FO 371/121780, 11 October 1956)**. This raised a spectre which the British had considered as late as 10 October 1956, the possibility of an Anglo-Israeli confrontation or even war over Jordan at a time when the Suez affair was unresolved. As British military forces in the Middle East were put on alert against Israel, the Chiefs of Staff noted that either Operation CORDAGE against Israel could be pursued or Operation MUSKETEER could be implemented but not both. A predicament of horrendous complexity and with horrifying implications was now facing the anxious British Prime Minister **(Gorst and Lucas, 1988, pp. 391–436)**.

He was rescued from this quandary by the French, who chose this sensitive moment to approach Eden with a more concrete proposal involving tripartite co-operation between Britain, France and Israel. On 14 October Eden received two French emissaries for lunch at Chequers, M. Albert Gazier, Minister of Labour but acting Foreign Minister while Pineau was at the United Nations, and General Maurice Challe who was identified as a member of the French Prime Minister's personal staff but who was in reality a Deputy Chief of the Air Staff and who had been liaising with the Israeli defence force. Eden and Nutting were of the opinion that this French delegation was to discuss, in the light of Qualqilya, the possibility of an Israeli invasion of Jordan. In fact this aspect of the Middle East situation was disposed of rapidly and the talks instead centred on an alternative scenario raised by Gazier: if Israel were to attack Egypt, what would the British reaction be? On receiving from Eden an assurance that he held Egypt to be in breach of Security Council resolutions and that the Tripartite Declaration of 1950 therefore could not apply, General Challe set out a plan that was the result of his previous contacts with the Israelis. Under this plan Israel would attack Egypt across Sinai, Britain and France would then order both sides to withdraw to prevent damage to the Canal and an Anglo-French force would intervene to separate the combatants and secure the Canal. This provided Eden with a resolution of both the Jordanian situation and the long sought after pretext for military intervention in Egypt.

No formal record of this meeting was taken and key figures, such as Jebb, were excluded from the it. The historian is, therefore, reliant on the testimony of the participants. However, in his memoirs Anthony Eden makes no reference to this crucial meeting and one is left with the account of Anthony Nutting who was present. Nutting was horrified by the French proposals.

Document 3.24 Nutting on Eden and 'Collusion'

I knew then that, no matter what contrary advice he might receive over the next forty-eight hours the Prime Minister had already made up his mind . . . we were to ally ourselves with the Israelis and the French in an attack on Egypt designed to topple Nasser and to seize the Suez Canal. Our traditional friendships with the Arab world were to be discarded; the policy of keeping a balance in arms deliveries as between Israel and the Arab States was to be abandoned; indeed, our whole peace-keeping role in the Middle East was to be changed and we were to take part in a cynical act of aggression dressing ourselves for the part as firemen or policemen while making sure that our fire-hoses spouted petrol and not water and that we belaboured with our truncheons the assaulted and not the assaulter. And all to gain for ourselves guarantees for the future operation of the Suez canal which had only a day or so been substantially gained in Lloyd's negotiations with Fawzi in New York.

In all my political association with Eden, I had never found so unbridgeable a gulf between us.

Source: Nutting, 1967, p. 94

This account clearly indicates, even after ten years had elapsed, the shock felt by the man who had been seen as the 'heir apparent' to Eden. This meeting was the beginning of the process of 'collusion', a highly delicate process that entailed a narrowing of policy-making within Whitehall to a small circle of like-minded individuals; Nutting was excluded from this circle and later resigned over this issue.

Although apparently non-committal to the French party, Eden seized upon this opportunity and instantly recalled Lloyd from the continuing negotiations in New York. Thorpe, Lloyd's biographer, notes 'it was at this point that the rug was pulled from underneath Selwyn and all his efforts in New York set to naught', although Lloyd himself is strangely reticent about this episode in his memoirs limiting himself to the comment that 'the idea of our inviting Israel to attack Egypt was a poor one' **(Lloyd, 1978, pp. 164–166; Thorpe, 1989, p. 230)**. On his return to London on the morning of 16 October, convinced that he had a workable solution on the basis of the Six Principles, Lloyd was confronted with a wholly new development of which he knew nothing and which, moreover, had divided his closest colleagues. Nutting, allowed by Eden to draw up a brief in consultation with Ivone Kirkpatrick, Permanent Under-Secretary, and Archibald Ross, Assistant Under-Secretary Middle East at the Foreign Office, presented Lloyd with a reasoned case against the Challe plan which apparently convinced the Foreign Secretary that they must have 'nothing to do with this' **(Thorpe, 1989, p. 231)**. Eden, however, used all his considerable powers of persuasion and by the end of a luncheon meeting had brought Lloyd around to his point of view. It was agreed that Eden and Lloyd, not the dissident Nutting, should travel to Paris that afternoon to meet Mollet and Pineau to review the various options.

After some desultory discussion, about the position in New York, between the British and French participants, attention focused on the Challe Plan. There is only one note of this meeting, written soon after the event by Lloyd, which would indicate that only a very general discussion took place on Israeli intentions and Britain's likely response. However, Nutting claims that he was informed by Lloyd the day after the meeting that substantive discussions had taken place, which included consideration of detailed plans with the French and Israelis, which were to be discussed further at a later tripartite meeting **(Nutting, 1967, p. 99)**. Eden and Lloyd returned to London to seek ministerial approval on two key questions which the French had posed: first, in the event of an Israeli attack on Egypt would Britain aid Nasser, and, second, in the same event would Britain join with France in a military operation to secure the Canal? It is significant in terms of the history of collusion that although Eden put to his Cabinet colleagues the first question, in the official record the second issue was seemingly not addressed by the Cabinet.

Document 3.25 Eden Informs the Cabinet of the Results of Conversations with the French

The Prime Minister said that, when the proceedings in the Security Council were completed, he and the Foreign Secretary had visited Paris in order to discuss with French Ministers what further steps could now be taken towards a settlement of the Suez dispute. They had taken the earliest opportunity to hold these consultations, in view of the increasing tension in the Middle East. The political situation in Jordan was unstable, and there were signs that Israel might be preparing to make some military move. If the Israelis attacked Jordan, we should be in a position of very great difficulty. Despite the terms of the Tripartite Declaration of 1950, the French had made it plain that they would not be able in those circumstances to assist Jordan; and it was evident that the United States Government would be most reluctant to intervene. We, on the other hand, had our separate obligations under the Anglo-Jordan Treaty; but it would be contrary to our interests to act, at this time and alone, in support of Jordan against Israel. Therefore, in his conversations with the French, he had proceeded on the basis that every possible effort should be made to ensure that the Israelis should not at this stage attack Jordan. If they contemplated any military operations against the Arabs, it would be far better from our point of view that they should attack Egypt and he had reason to believe that, if they made any military move, it would be in that direction. He had therefore thought it right to make known to the Israelis, through the French, that in the event of hostilities between Egypt and Israel the United Kingdom Government would not come to the assistance of Egypt, because Egypt was in breach of a Security Council resolution and had repudiated Western aid under the Tripartite Declaration.

The Cabinet should therefore be aware that, while we continued to seek an agreed settlement of the Suez dispute in pursuance of the resolution of the Security Council, it was possible that the issue might be brought more rapidly to a head as a result of military action by Israel against Egypt.

Source: PRO CAB 128/30 Pt II, CM 71 (56), 18 October 1956

The Prime Minister had now revealed to the Cabinet the rationale behind his policy. With the possibility of Israeli co-operation against Egypt in mind, Eden was concerned to minimise the likelihood of a confrontation with Israel over Jordan. Eden, without consulting the Cabinet, had taken the significant step of encouraging the Israelis by waiving Britain's obligations under the Tripartite Declaration. While Eden's handling of these complex manoeuvres was technically deft, questions have been raised as to the wisdom of the action.

However, Lloyd indicates in his memoirs that after some discussion 'eventually it was accepted by Butler and the rest of the Cabinet that we and France should intervene to protect the Canal, if Israel moved against Egypt': this account is further substantiated by Kyle **(Lloyd, 1978, p. 177; Kyle, 1991, pp. 307–308)**. Moreover, encouraging answers had been sent to the French for transmission to the Israelis even before the full Cabinet met. Collusion was thus both gathering momentum and becoming increasingly enshrouded in secrecy: this is the first of a number of discrepancies that are only explicable by a tampering with the historical record.

News that the Israeli Prime Minister, David Ben-Gurion, had arrived in Paris with a delegation, including Moshe Dayan, for consultations with the French, at which they wished a British representative to be present, led Eden to convene a meeting on 21 October 1956 at which it was decided that Lloyd should travel to the next day Paris for further consultations. As Donald Logan, his private secretary travelling with him, later noted, 'he told me that we were to meet French and Israeli representatives to discuss military action against Egypt' **(SELO 6/602)**. Until this point it could be argued that Eden and Lloyd were merely exploring a hypothetical situation; the dispatch of Lloyd with this brief crossed the line into outright conspiracy as Eden and his Foreign Secretary must have known given that he was to travel incognito.

The first Sèvres meeting on 22 October revealed substantial differences between the two main protagonists, Lloyd and Ben-Gurion. Lloyd rebuffed Ben-Gurion's attempt to construct 'a grand design for the Middle East' and instead outlined likely repercussions of tripartite co-operation. The major sticking-point was the timing of British support for an Israeli attack on Egypt.

Document 3.26 'Suez Meetings at Sèvres, 22–25 October 1956'

If Israel were to open an attack against Egypt, British forces would as had been suggested take the opportunity with the French to seize the Canal, but the basis of the action must be to intervene to separate the forces and thus avert a threat which Israeli actions would pose to the Canal, its installations and the traffic through it. Egypt and Israel would be called upon to cease hostilities within twenty-four hours. Israel would have no difficulty in complying, but if Nasser did so his position would be weakened. In any case, British–French forces would regain the Canal. Britain no longer felt any obligation to Egypt under the Tripartite Declaration. But Britain would honour her Treaty obligations to Jordan if she were to be attacked by Israel.

Ben-Gurion did not like this reasoning. Israel was being asked to solve Britain's and France's problems by accepting the opprobrium of aggression followed by the ignominy of accepting an ultimatum. Responsibility should be shared equally. I think it may have been the French who suggested that the word ultimatum would be dropped; thereafter it was called an 'appel' or call. When Selwyn Lloyd again rejected a joint attack on Egypt, this time mentioning the damage it would do to Britain's relations with Arab countries such as Jordan and Iraq, Ben-Gurion's concern seemed to switch to practical matters. He greatly feared that the Egyptian Air Force equipped with Soviet aircraft would bomb Tel Aviv within hours of an attack and before British–French forces were in action. There would be panic in Israel and it might not be possible to sustain the action. This led to a discussion, in which Dayan and the French joined, of the timing of the 'appel' to the two forces and of action to immobilise the Egyptian bombers by the RAF who were best placed to do so. It seemed to have been assumed in earlier discussions that the RAF would accept this task but would not act until forty-eight or even seventy-two hours after the outbreak of hostilities. Lloyd was pressed to reduce the delay to thirty-six hours. There was then discussion of how quickly the Israeli attack would develop to constitute a sufficient threat to the Canal to justify the call to cease-fire, after which some time must be given before it could be assumed that it had been rejected and before the RAF could act. Dayan refused to describe the scale of the attack he had in mind, and said merely that we need not worry on that score. Ben-Gurion looked depressed. The French tried to keep the talks going.

There was a break for dinner, and when alone together for a moment Selwyn asked me what I thought of it all. I had just returned from a posting in Kuwait – how would the Arabs react? I replied that they would be astonished at what we were proposing to do, but they might come to accept it provided we got it over quickly. The established regimes in the Gulf and elsewhere would be secretly pleased if we managed to topple Nasser. I sensed from his question and from the way he had spoken at the meeting that he disliked the plan and the role which he had been called upon to play in it. I was not proud of my response but I was under no illusion that any other would have made any difference. It had become apparent to me that much of the detail had already been discussed between the French and the Israelis and between the French and British Ministers.

Throughout dinner Selwyn was thoughtful and I had to carry much of the British side of the conversation, which – if only for that reason – did not address the substance. I was invited to explain the role of the Private Secretary – the Israelis may have thought the title was a cover for something different. Dayan in his book 'The Story of My Life' quotes me as warning against any Israeli intention to occupy Sinai permanently. I have no recollection of that but it would have reflected suspicion of Israeli expansionism at the time. I certainly had no idea that anything I said could have been useful to him in persuading Ben-Gurion towards his plan in the way he describes.

After dinner the talks resumed to go over much the same ground as before. Lloyd could not agree that night to advance the attack on the Egyptian Air Force but he undertook to report to Cabinet and would hope to reply the next day. We left close on midnight to return to London.

Source: SELO 6/202, Suez meetings at Sèvres, 22–25 October 1956, narrative by Donald Logan, 24 October 1986

These recollections, set down by Lloyd's private secretary some thirty years after the event, constitute the fullest record of the Sèvres meetings from the British side. Although Logan was concerned to protect the reputation of his chief, this account substantiates accounts from the French and Israeli side. It is noteworthy that, at these meetings, in contrast to later protestations by Eden and others, there was a considerable degree of detailed planning discussions, largely at the instigation of the Israeli delegation, that goes far beyond mere 'foreknowledge'. The scenario presented in the first paragraph of the document is the core of the plan that was eventually carried out. Given Lloyd's clear discomfort with the subject under discussion it is little wonder that accounts written by the Israeli participants paint a rather unflattering portrait of the long-suffering and much put upon British Foreign Secretary **(Dayan, 1976, p. 180)**.

The next morning, after a pre-meeting of senior ministers at which Pineau was invited to London that evening for further discussion, the full Cabinet received Eden's account of the previous day's talks. Two versions of this important Cabinet discussion exist.

Document 3.27 Eden Briefs the Cabinet on the Progress of the Sèvres Talks, 23 October 1956

The Prime Minister recalled that when the Cabinet had last discussed the Suez situation on 18th October, there had been reason to believe that the issue might be brought rapidly to a head as a result of military action by Israel against Egypt. It now seemed unlikely that the Israelis would launch a full scale attack against Egypt. The United Kingdom and French Governments were thus confronted with the choice between an early military operation or a relatively prolonged negotiation. If the second course were followed, neither we nor the French could hope to maintain our military preparations in their present state of readiness – On our side some of the reservists would have to be released, some of the requisitioned merchant ships would have to be released for commercial trading and others would have to be reloaded – and our position of negotiating from strength would to some extent be impaired. . . .

The Foreign Secretary said that he would not exclude the possibility that we might be able to reach, by negotiation with the Egyptians a settlement which would give us the substance of our demand for effective international super-vision of the Canal. There were, however, three serious objections to a policy of seeking a settlement by negotiation. First, it now seemed clear that the French Government would not give their full co-operation in such a policy. Secondly, it was evident that some relaxation of our military preparations would have to be made and to that extent we should weaken our negotiating position. Thirdly, he saw no prospects of reaching such a settlement as would diminish Colonel Nasser's influence throughout the Middle East.

The Prime Minister said that grave decisions would have to be taken by the Cabinet in the course of the next few days.

Source: PRO CAB 128/30 Pt II, CM 72 (56), 23 October 1956

The 'Confidential Annex' recording the same meeting includes the following version of paragraph 1:

The Prime Minister recalled that when the Cabinet had last discussed the Suez situation on 18th October, there had been reason to believe that the issue might be brought rapidly to a head as a result of military action by Israel against Egypt. *From secret conversations which had been held in Paris with representatives of the Israeli Government it now appeared that the Israelis would not alone launch a full scale attack against Egypt.*

(PRO, CAB 128/30 Pt II *Confidential Annex*, 23 October 1956; italics in original)

This represented an indication to the full Cabinet that direct channels had been opened with the Israelis, although, as Carlton notes, perhaps the full sense and import of the Sèvres meeting was not conveyed to those ministers who had not been present at the pre-meeting **(Carlton, 1988, pp. 65–66)**.

In contrast to the frenzied behind the scenes activities, Lloyd's appearance before Parliament that afternoon was a bland 'holding operation' at which he simply reviewed the diplomatic activities of the previous month while Parliament had been in recess. Notably, he did not raise in Parliament the objections to a diplomatic settlement that he had advanced that same morning in Cabinet. That evening Pineau arrived in London to meet Lloyd and Eden; Lloyd rather coyly recalls in his memoirs that 'the main point was greater precision about the actions which we would take if Israel attacked Egypt'. However, it would seem that Pineau received assurances from the Prime Minister and Foreign Secretary about the timing of RAF air action, although Lloyd put on record in a letter to Pineau that the British were not asking the Israelis to invade Egypt, 'we had merely stated what would be our reactions if certain things happened' **(Lloyd, 1978, p. 186; SELO 6/602, p. 6; Carlton, 1988, p. 66)**.

In the light of Lloyd's commitments in Parliament the next day it was decided to send Patrick Dean (Assistant Under-Secretary at the Foreign Office in charge of the Permanent Under-Secretary's Department which handled the diplomatic aspects of military and intelligence matters) to Sèvres with Donald Logan.

Document 3.28   'Suez Meetings at Sèvres, 22–26 October 1956'

Next morning 24 October, Patrick Dean, Assistant Under-Secretary at the Foreign Office, was called early to 10 Downing Street where he was instructed by the Prime Minister to go to Paris to continue the discussion. In a briefing of about 15 minutes Eden said the French and the Israelis shared his opinion that Nasser intended to inflict great damage in the Middle East and it might be necessary for the three countries to take action if the Canal were further threatened by Nasser or as a result of hostilities between Israel and Egypt. British forces might have to intervene but only if there was a clear military threat to the Canal and Israeli forces had advanced towards the Canal. After a public warning British and French forces would then intervene between the Israelis and Egyptians to ensure the safety of the

Canal. Discussions had taken place on these lines and it must now be made absolutely clear before final decisions were taken that British forces would not move unless the Israelis had advanced beyond their frontiers against Egypt and there was a clear military threat to the Canal.

Patrick Dean at that point knew nothing of the contacts earlier in the week. He was not involved in the detailed planning mechanism. He knew that French and British ministers had met in Paris on 16 October but nothing of the substance of their discussion. The scenario Eden had sketched out was new to him. He went first to see the Permanent Under-Secretary, Sir Ivone Kirkpatrick, who while showing little enthusiasm said Dean must carry out the mission with which he had been charged, but should first see the Foreign Secretary. This he did and Lloyd told him I was to accompany him.

Source: SELO 6/202, Suez meetings at Sèvres 22–25 October 1956, narrative by Donald Logan, 24 October 1986

This further extract from Logan's account illustrates the narrowing of the 'inner circle' who knew the full details of collusion. It is clear that even the professional head of the Foreign Service, Kirkpatrick, had grave misgivings about the process, misgivings that were apparently widely shared within the Foreign Office and which were to culminate later in a round-robin letter of protest.

While these officials were on the way to Paris, a further meeting of the Cabinet was held, at which familiar arguments were recycled. Once again, the complexities of the military timetable were examined with the conclusion that after the end of October a new military plan would have to be drawn up and the belief that any conceivable diplomatic solution would leave Colonel Nasser in power was again forcefully aired. However, the meeting with Pineau the previous evening enabled the Prime Minister to indicate that a solution to this painful dilemma, that had dogged British policy since July, was at hand. Eden noted, in contrast to the Cabinet of the previous day, that 'It was now known, however, that, if such an operation were launched [MUSKETEER] Israel would make a full-scale attack against Egypt.' Eden ended the meeting by saying 'that the choice before the Cabinet was now clear. Before the final decision was taken, further discussions with the French Government would be required'. As with the Cabinet meeting of 23 October 1956, two versions of the minutes exist: the material quoted above is not con-tained in the main minutes but, again, in a confidential annex **(PRO CAB 128/30 Pt II, *Confidential Annex*, 24 October 1956)**. It is significant that Eden did not inform the full Cabinet that, even as he spoke, Dean and Logan were on the way to Paris to finalise arrangements by which the Israelis would attack first and Britain would then intervene. This was the reverse of the scenario presented by Eden in the Cabinet and one can only conclude that Eden was attempting to lead the full Cabinet along the lines of some form of co-operation with the Israelis while leaving them in the dark as to the precise form and nature of the collusion that had and was taking place.

At the Sèvres meetings of 24 October the full extent of collusion is revealed by Donald Logan.

Document 3.29 'Suez Meetings at Sèvres, 22–25 October 1956'

We left soon after 10 a.m. in my car for Hendon airfield and on the way I told him [Dean] what had taken place on the two previous days. We were met at Villacoublay by General Challe and taken to lunch in a restaurant on the way to Sèvres where we arrived at about 4 p.m. There we met the same French and Israeli teams. Dean handed over a letter from Lloyd emphasising that Britain had not asked the Israelis to take any action; it was merely a question of stating what reactions would be if certain things happened.

I cannot recall that the time that would elapse before RAF action was raised on this occasion, and it seems probable that Pineau had obtained a satisfactory answer from the Prime Minister. It did not figure in our brief. We pressed Dayan hard for assurance that the Israelis understood that unless their military action posed a threat to the Canal, British forces would not act. It did not come easily. The Israelis did not conceal that their main objective would be Sharm es-Shaikh on the Straits of Tiran to enable them to maintain passage for their ships to the port of Aqaba. We emphasised that a move in that direction would not pose a threat to the Canal. Eventually sketch maps were made and we were assured that there would be military activity in the region of the Mitla Pass. More than that we could not get, but the Mitla Pass being reasonably close to the Canal we concluded that the Israelis sufficiently understood the British position though they remained suspicious of our intentions.

There followed a somewhat desultory recapitulation of issues already discussed during the week which did not clarify the intentions of the three parties any further and raised no new issues. Then the French introduced a document in three identical copies which had just been typed in French in a neighbouring room. . . .

We were asked to sign each copy of the document. This was the first time any mention had been made of setting down what had been discussed. Patrick Dean asked me if it was in order to sign. I said the document seemed to me accurate, and also useful in recording the precision which we had been sent to obtain and could be signed as such. To refuse to sign a summary to which we could not take exception would increase suspicion of our intentions in an exploit to which the Prime Minister seemed wedded. Dean signed, making it clear that he did so *ad referendum*. The other two delegations also signed, and we each retained one copy. I think champagne was produced but there was little sparkle in the atmosphere and Patrick and I soon took our leave to return via Villacoublay. In the air, the stars shone as brightly as I have ever seen them. It seemed wholly incongruous.

Dean reported to the Prime Minister at about 10.30 that evening. When the document was handed to him, Eden seemed taken aback. Though he was satisfied with its contents, he had not expected a written record and seemed to think we should have realised this.

On the following day, 25 October, we were instructed by the Prime Minister to return to Paris to ask the French to destroy their copy of the document. At the Quai D'Orsay we presented the Prime Minister's request to Pineau who received it rather coldly and questioned the need and the advisability of such action. He pointed out that the Israelis had returned to Israel with their copy the previous evening. He would give us a full answer later. We were then taken to what ten years later I was to know as the Quai's grand reception suite of rooms and left on our own. Later we found that the doors had been locked – an unpleasant discovery, but perhaps justified to prevent our presence becoming accidentally known to diplomats at the Quai. We stayed there for several hours without any lunch and with nothing to drink. Eventually at about 4 p.m. we were taken to see Pineau again. He said the French Government would not accept the Prime Minister's proposal, partly because the Israelis had their copy with them and partly because the French saw no reason to destroy it. We returned to London and Dean reported to the Prime Minister. Next day the Private Office at the Foreign Office were told by 10 Downing Street to send over all copies of the document and the translation that they had made. This was done.

The Prime Minister's dismay at the production of the document would seem to indicate that he intended that no record of the talks with the French and the Israelis should be made. We were not aware of this though we knew that he had for some time kept his thinking on a solution of the Suez problem to a small group of like-thinking people. I believe that he chose to proceed by oral discussion only. Dayan in his book says that just before the Sèvres meeting the Israelis received via the French a written declaration signed by Eden which from his description could not have been very different from the document Dean signed later. Had Eden signed such a declaration it would seem unlikely that he would have sent us back to arrange the destruction of a document that largely merely repeated it. The explanation may be that what the Israelis received was a telegram from the French reporting the position Eden had taken at the meeting in Paris on 16 October and that either in transmission or otherwise this had come to be referred to as a declaration to which Eden had put his name.

Source: SELO 6/202, Suez meetings at Sèvres, 22–25 October 1956, narrative by Donald Logan, 24 October 1986

Again, this document clearly demonstrates the level of detailed discussion that preceded the Anglo–French–Israeli collusion. Given the concern of Eden to restrict the knowledge of this process, it is little wonder that he attempted to cover his tracks by destroying the evidence; this is perhaps the most blatant example of the historical record of Suez being distorted. Whatever the truth about the claim made by Dayan, it is indicative of the confusion created by the secrecy surrounding collusion that such a claim could be made.

The document that so horrified Eden has been reconstructed by Keith Kyle from French and Israeli sources and its authenticity has been attested to by Sir Donald Logan.

Document 3.30 The Sèvres Protocol, 24 October 1956

PROTOCOL

The results of the conversations which took place at Sèvres from 22–24 October 1956 between the representatives of the Governments of the United Kingdom, the State of Israel and of France are the following;

1 The Israeli forces launch in the evening of 29 October 1956 a large scale attack on the Egyptian forces with the aim of reaching the Canal zone the following day.

2 On being apprised of these events, the British and French Governments during the day of 30 October 1956 respectively and simultaneously make two appeals to the Egyptian Government and the Israeli Government on the following lines:

(a) *To the Egyptian Government*
    (i)   halt all acts of war.
    (ii) withdraw all its troops ten miles from the Canal.
    (iii) accept temporary occupation of key positions on the Canal by the Anglo-French forces to guarantee freedom of passage through the Canal by vessels of all nations until a final settlement.

(b) *To the Israeli Government*
    (i)   halt all acts of war.
    (ii) withdraw all its troops ten miles to the east of the Canal.

In addition, the Israeli Government will be notified that the French and British Governments have demanded of the Egyptian Government to accept temporary occupation of key positions along the Canal by Anglo-French forces.

It is agreed that if one of the Governments refused, or did not give its consent, within twelve hours the Anglo-French forces would intervene with the means necessary to ensure that their demands are accepted.

(c) The representatives of the three Governments agree that the Israeli Government will not be required to meet the conditions in the appeal addressed to it, in the event that the Egyptian Government does not accept those in the appeal addressed to it for their part.

3 In the event that the Egyptian Government should fail to agree within the stipulated time to the conditions of the appeal addressed to it, the Anglo-French forces will launch military operations against the Egyptian forces in the early hours of the morning of 31 October.
4 The Israeli Government will send forces to occupy the western shore of the Gulf of Akaba and the group of islands Tirane and Sanafir to ensure freedom of navigation in the Gulf of Akaba.
5 Israel undertakes not to attack Jordan during the period of operations against Egypt.
But in the event that during the same period Jordan should attack Israel, the British Government undertakes not to come to the aid of Jordan.
6 The arrangements of the present protocol must remain strictly secret.
7 They will enter into force after the agreement of the three Governments.

(Signed)

David Ben-Gurion
Patrick Dean
Christian Pineau.

Source: Kyle, 1991, appendix A. pp. 565–566

The document is the outcome of the Sèvres discussions and shows clearly the extent of deliberate planning, now enshrined in a formal agreement, that was carried out in late October 1956. What is clear is the fundamental disparity in the treatment of Egypt and Israel. While posing as neutral powers concerned merely to protect the Canal and prevent the spread of war, in clause 2 the British and the French were inviting the Egyptians to withdraw further into Egyptian territory while inviting the Israelis to advance further into Egyptian territory to within ten miles of the Canal. This in effect gave Israel free licence to occupy the whole of the Sinai.

In the Cabinet the following day, 25 October, Eden laid out the bones of the Sèvres strategy without ever mentioning the fact that face-to-face meetings with the Israelis had taken place.

Document 3.31 Eden Informs the Cabinet of Developments, 25 October 1956

The Prime Minister recalled that, at the time of the Cabinet's discussion on 18th October, there had been reason to believe that the issue might be brought rapidly to a head as a result of military action by Israel against Egypt. Later, on 23 October, he had informed the Cabinet that it no longer seemed likely that Israel would alone launch a full-scale attack against Egypt. It now appeared, however, that the Israelis were, after all, advancing their military preparations with a view to making an attack on Egypt. They evidently felt that the ambitions of Colonel Nasser's government threatened their continued existence as an independent State and that they could not afford to wait for others to curb his expansionist policies. The Cabinet must therefore consider the situation which was likely to arise if hostilities broke out between Israel and Egypt and must judge whether it would necessitate Anglo-French intervention in this area. The French government were strongly of the view that intervention would be justified in order to limit the hostilities and that for this purpose it would be right to launch the military operation against Egypt which had already been mounted. Indeed, it was possible that if we declined to join them they would take military action alone or in conjunction with Israel. In these circumstances the Prime Minister suggested that, if Israel launched a full-scale military operation against Egypt, the governments of the United Kingdom and France should at once call on both parties to stop hostilities and to withdraw their forces to a distance of ten miles from the Canal; and that it should at the same time be made clear that, if one or both Governments failed to undertake within twelve hours to comply with these requirements, British and French forces would intervene in order to enforce compliance. Israel might well undertake to comply with such a demand. If Egypt also complied, Colonel Nasser's prestige would be fatally undermined. If she failed to comply, there would be ample justification for Anglo-French military action against Egypt in order to safeguard the Canal. We must face the risk that we should be accused of collusion with Israel. But this charge was liable to be brought against us in any event; for it could now be assumed that, if an Anglo-French operation were undertaken against Egypt, we should be unable to prevent the Israelis from launching a parallel attack themselves; and it was preferable that we should be seen to be holding the balance between Israel and Egypt rather than appear to be accepting Israeli co-operation in an attack on Egypt alone.

Source: PRO CAB 128/30 Pt II, CM 74 (56), 25 October 1956

Eden was obviously eager to push his colleagues down the line that had already been agreed at Sèvres. He was cognisant, however, of the likelihood of charges of collusion being laid at his door. These he dismissed, with a considerable amount of casuistry, as he argued that the allegation would be made anyway.

The Prime Minister received the support of Lloyd, who emphasised the threat posed by Nasser to the props of British interest in the Middle East, Jordan, Iraq and Libya, and from other ministers who noted that such an action would be 'defensible in international law' as ensuring the 'free flow of traffic through the Canal'. In any case it was suggested that as 'a crisis in the Middle East could not now be long delayed' it was as well to act sooner rather than later. Kyle suggests that a heated exchange of views took place, with the main sceptics being Monckton, now Paymaster-General, Derick Heathcote Amory, the Minister of

Agriculture and Fisheries, and Iain Macleod, the Minister of Labour. However, against the assembled weight of the senior members of the Cabinet, none of these ministers ultimately dissented from collective responsibility **(Kyle, 1991, pp. 334–335)**. The Cabinet

> agreed in principle that, in the event of an Israeli attack on Egypt, the Government should join with the French Government in calling on the two belligerents to stop hostilities and withdraw their forces to a distance of ten miles from the Canal; and should warn both belligerents that, if either or both of them failed to undertake within twelve hours to comply with these requirements, British and French forces would intervene in order to enforce compliance.

(PRO CAB 128/30 Pt II, 25 October 1956)

With this conclusion the Cabinet had agreed, wittingly or unwittingly, to the setting in motion of the Sèvres strategy. Forces in the Middle East were stood down from CORDAGE and switched back to MUSKETEER (Revise). They were heavily reinforced with bomber aircraft in preparation for the first phase of operations against Egypt. Force commanders, such as General Stockwell, assembled in the Middle East as preparations for an invasion of Egypt were finalised. A major problem confronting the military in this confused situation was the restricted number of officers who were cognisant of the full strategy. For example, Stockwell only found out about the forthcoming Israeli invasion from his French deputy Beaufre while flying from London to Malta via Villacoublay; Stockwell then briefed the naval and air commanders informally. Further, the delicacy of the timing meant that naval movements had to be restricted in order not to alert the world that something was afoot: although the aircraft carrier covering force could sail from Malta for the eastern Mediterranean on the morning of 29 October under cover of a previously scheduled communications exercise, the invasion force could not sail from Malta until 31 October. Moreover, the maximum speed of the assault convoys was limited to 6 knots meaning that it would take six days to effect a landing **(Kyle, 1991, pp. 339–342)**.

In Israel, somewhat to the bewilderment of the British Ambassador, Sir John Nicolls, who, like most of the Foreign Office, was not privy to the Sèvres secret, mobilisation for Operation Kadesh – the Sinai campaign – gathered momentum from Friday, 26 October. These preparations alerted the Americans to the fact that something was going on in the Middle East, but doubts existed as to the direction of the potential Israeli attack. It was only on 28 October that the CIA concluded that Egypt was the likely target. Given the increase in communications traffic and the arrival of reinforcements, the Americans considered it possible that Britain and France might take advantage of this situation to settle the Canal dispute by force. Following the Israeli parachute drop at Mitla Pass which opened the Sinai campaign at 5 p.m. on 29 October, Eisenhower was moved to telegraph Eden to seek clarification of British policy.

Document 3.32 Eisenhower Regrets Possible Breach in Anglo-American Alliance, 30 October 1956

All this development, with its possible consequences including the possible involvement of you and the French in a general Arab war, seems to me to leave your government and ours in a very sad state of confusion, so far as any possibility of unified understanding and action are concerned. It is true that Egypt has not yet formally asked this government for aid but the fact is that if the United Nations finds Israel to be an aggressor, Egypt could very well ask the Soviets for help – and then the Middle East fat would really be in the fire. It is this later possibility that has lead us to insist that the West must ask for a United Nations examination and possible intervention, for we may shortly find ourselves not only at odds concerning what we should do, but confronted with a de facto situation that would make all our present troubles look puny indeed.

Source: PRO PREM 11/1105, Eisenhower to Eden, 30 October 1956

Unfortunately, this telegram arrived after a Cabinet meeting on the morning of 30 October at which the terms of the ultimatums to Israel and Egypt had been approved.

Document 3.33 The Cabinet Discusses the Possible American Attitude, 30 October 1956

Discussion then turned on the attitude which the United States were likely to take towards these developments. *The Foreign Secretary* said that he had been informed by the United States Ambassador in London that the United States Government were proposing to ask the Security Council to consider urgently a resolution condemning Israel as an aggressor. He had suggested to the Ambassador that such a resolution would be open to criticism on the grounds that Israel was acting in self-defence; and he had emphasised the assurances which we had received that Israel did not contemplate any attack on Jordan. He was not certain, however, that the United States Government would be influenced by these arguments and it was for consideration whether, if the French Government agreed, we should attempt to persuade them to support the action which we and the French were proposing to take to bring to an end the hostilities between Israel and Egypt. As there had been little fighting so far between Israeli and Egyptian forces, it seemed possible that our action might be deferred for twenty four hours; and in that event there would be time to make such an appeal to the United States Government.

Discussion showed that the Cabinet were in general agreement with this suggestion, even though it was unlikely that the United States Government would respond to such an appeal, we should do our utmost to reduce the offence to American public opinion which was liable to be caused by our notes to Egypt and Israel. Our reserves of gold and dollars were still falling at a dangerously rapid rate; and, in view of the extent to which we might have to rely on American economic assistance we could not afford to alienate the United States Government more than was absolutely necessary.

Source: PRO CAB 128/30 Pt II, CM 75 (56), 30 October 1956

Here, for the first time, there was some recognition within the Cabinet of the likely effect of carrying through military action unsupported by the United States. Given the repeated warnings from Eisenhower and Dulles it seems remarkable that the government could have deluded itself to the extent that it clearly had. Nothing was more likely to alienate the US government than proceeding with the use of force, and given that the Cabinet had noted that reserves were already falling, this should have alerted them to the possible consequences. With Anglo-American relations in a state of considerable confusion and no little disrepair, the British, together with the French, duly issued their ultimatums to Israel and Egypt in the late afternoon of 30 October 1956.

If Eden had expected an easy time in the Commons when he presented the case for the ultimatum, he was to be sadly disappointed, as he was subjected to a rigorous cross-examination by Labour members. This did not auger well for the solidity of British public opinion. Worse still, a message from Eden to Eisenhower giving the sense of his speech in Parliament was delayed with the result that the American administration learnt of the ultimatums from the press.

Document 3.34 Eden Attempts to Reassure Eisenhower, 30 October 1956

I can assure you that any action which we may have to take to follow up the declaration is not part of a harking back to the old colonial and occupational concepts. We are most anxious to avoid this impression. Nothing could have prevented this volcano from erupting somewhere, but when the dust settles, there may well be a chance for our doing a really constructive piece of work together and thereby strengthening the weakest point in the line against Communism.

Source: PRO PREM 11/1105, Eden to Eisenhower, 30 October 1956

Eden, attempting to put the best possible face on British actions, returned to a previous theme, that of anti-communism. However, even the attempt by Eden to enlist the dynamics of the Cold War did not mollify the American administration which was outraged by what it is saw as the deceit of the British government. Eisenhower, in the crucial final week of a presidential campaign in which he had been presented as a 'peacemaker', was no doubt sorely embarrassed by the fact that barely a day after he had announced consultations with the British and French to place the Israeli aggression before the Security Council, they had delivered a slap in the face by issuing the ultimatums. Eisenhower, after issuing a stinging rebuke to Eden through the press to the effect that 'peaceful processes can and should prevail', authorised Henry Cabot Lodge, US Representative to the United Nations, to place the following resolution before the Security Council.

Document 3.35 United States Resolution in the Security Council (UN Doc. S/3710) on Middle East Aggression, 30 October 1956

The Security Council,

Noting that the armed forces of Israel have penetrated deeply into Egyptian territory in violation of the armistice agreement between Egypt and Israel;

Expressing its grave concern at this violation of the armistice agreement;

1 Calls upon Israel and Egypt immediately to cease fire;
2 Calls upon Israel immediately to withdraw its armed forces behind the established armistice lines;
3 Calls upon all members
    (a) to refrain from the use of force or threat of force in the area in any manner inconsistent with the Purposes of the United Nations;
    (b) to assist the United Nations in ensuring the integrity of the armistice agreements;
    (c) to refrain from giving any military, economic or financial assistance to Israel so long as it has not complied with this resolution;
4 Requests the Secretary-General to keep the Security Council informed of compliance with this resolution and to make whatever recommendations he deems appropriate for the maintenance of international peace and security in the area by the implementation of this and prior resolutions.

Source: Frankland (ed.), 1959, p. 264

For Eden and the British Cabinet this resolution was a clear indication that American criticisms in private were to be paralleled by public action. The resolution was a clear attempt by the United States administration to prevent the escalation of the conflict by Anglo-French intervention on the behalf of Israel. This resolution was vetoed by both Britain and France as was a subsequent Soviet resolution, although by the next day the Middle East situation was referred through the 'Uniting for Peace' procedure to an emergency session of the General Assembly. (The Uniting for Peace procedure was developed at the time of the Korean War and allowed the General Assembly to act when the Security Council was deadlocked.) Clear signs of the widening Anglo-American rift were revealed by a series of telegrams from John Coulson, the British chargé d'affaires in Washington (who had been left in charge of the vital Washington embassy at this crucial moment as the incoming ambassador Sir Harold Caccia was still *en route* by ship).

Document 3.36 Dulles on the Ultimatums and Possible Consequences, 31 October 1956

Mr Dulles described the ultimatums as 'a pretty brutal affair'. The message from the Prime Minister to the President this afternoon expressed the hope that it would be accepted. He thought this hope 'highly visionary'. The Egyptians, because they were attacked would have to give up a large part of their territory under this ultimatum whereas the Israelis would only have to go back ten miles in Egypt. The Egyptians could hardly be expected to accept occupation once again. He remarked that ironically enough he had been reading a message earlier today about a talk between Mr Aldrich and yourself [Lloyd] yesterday about the possible resumption of negotiations with the Egyptians regarding the Suez Canal; and he recalled that you had expressed the view that had M. Pineau been more forthcoming at the beginning in New York it might have been possible to achieve at least the Heads of Agreement. It was part of our deliberate purpose through all these talks to urge a peaceful solution and he felt that this had been within our grasp.

Mr Dulles continued that he did not know whether the Israeli move came as any surprise to Her Majesty's Government. It certainly was not to the French. He had noted the build-up of forces in Cyprus at this juncture and the timing suggested we had some special reason for doing this. The plan could hardly have been worked out so quickly if it had not been concocted with the French Government before the Israeli action.

He thought we were facing one of the greatest tragedies not only for our trust in each other but also for the world situation. Just when the Soviet orbit was crumbling and we could point to a contrast between the Western world and the Soviet, it now looked as though the West was producing a similar situation.

He could not foresee the outcome but we might have on our hands a conflagration which would sweep through the whole Moslem world. He was most pessimistic about the outcome.

I said that I found it impossible to believe that we had had any part in urging the Israelis into their present action. All the evidence I had seen was precisely the opposite. Instructions to Her Majesty's representative in Tel Aviv, as I had pointed out at previous meetings, had all been to prevent the Israelis from taking action. The purpose of this ultimatum, as Mr Dulles had called it, was to stop the fighting. I said that the purpose of moving in forces rapidly was to prevent fighting across the Canal. I also read extracts from the Prime Minister's replies in the House emphasising the temporary nature of any occupation by Anglo-French forces. Mr Dulles was quite unmoved by any of these points.

Source: PRO PREM 11/1105, 31 October 1956

From this almost verbatim account of a most unsatisfactory conversation from the British point of view, it is clear that the American administration had seen through Eden's transparent deception without difficulty. Diplomats on the spot, such as Coulson, were placed in a thoroughly invidious position because of this, as, on the basis of inadequate knowledge, they denied collusion and were thus forced, unwittingly, to lie to their host governments. It is little wonder that Coulson was misled by the messages going to Nicholls in Tel Aviv: the real messages dealing with Anglo-Israeli collusion were going through separate MI6 channels.

Sir Pierson Dixon, British Representative at the United Nations, informed the Foreign Secretary on 30–31 October 1956 of the developing split between Britain and America.

Document 3.37 British Reaction to the American Resolution in the United Nations, 31 October 1956

It was perhaps the open split between ourselves and the Americans which has excited most attention. Mr Lodge did his best, but was clearly under firm instructions to oppose us at every point. I have already reported . . . our differences over the wording of the United States item this morning. Later during the debate I urged Mr Lodge . . . not to submit his resolution until he had considered the Prime Minister's statement and the representations made to the United States Ambassador in London. He not only tabled it forthwith, but included in it a paragraph . . . clearly directed against the Anglo-French action. In my opening speech . . . I made a public appeal to him not to press this resolution to a vote but his only response was to urge the Council to take the vote at once and to declare that the United States was gravely concerned over the Anglo-French ultimatum.

After consulting you by telephone I, together with my French colleague, registered a negative vote on the United States resolution which failed with 7 votes in favour and two abstentions (Australia and Belgium).

Source: PRO PREM 11/1105, New York to Foreign Office, 31 October 1956

This report of developments within the United Nations demonstrates the growing willingness of the United States administration to publicly disassociate themselves from the actions of their partners in the 'special relationship'. It is noteworthy that the British considered American pressure to be so strong that they were forced for the first time to use their veto in the Security Council against a resolution proposed by an ally.

In the midst of this frenzied diplomatic activity, Nasser, as expected, duly rejected the Anglo-French ultimatum. After some three months of military preparations, often hindered by false hopes of a diplomatic settlement, Britain was now committed to war against Egypt in alliance with France and Israel in all but name.

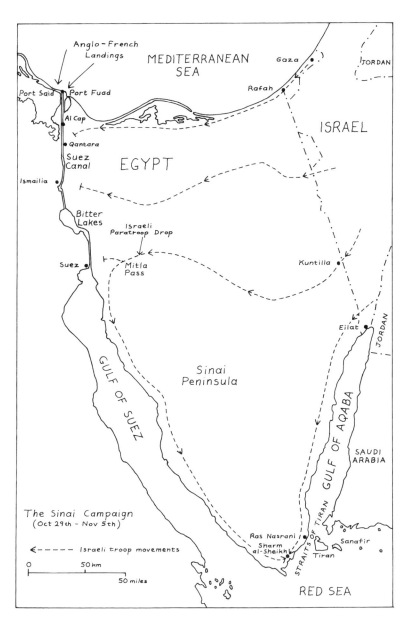

Map 2 The Sinai Campaign

Chronology July–October 1956

31 July	Dulles arrives for talks in London: Eisenhower warns Eden against use of force
2 August	British government announces recall of selected groups of reservists
3 August	Britain, France and the United States call for a conference to be held in London
8 August	Treasury delivers first economic warning to Macmillan
16–23 August	First London Conference
3 September	Eisenhower again warns Eden against the use of force
3–9 September	Menzies mission in talks with Nasser in Cairo
4 September	Dulles proposes idea of Suez Canal Users Association
7 September	Treasury issues second economic warning to Macmillan
8 September	Eisenhower again warns Eden against use of force
12 September	SCUA publicly announced
19 September	Second London Conference opens
21 September	Users Association approved by Second London Conference; Treasury issues further warnings on economy to Macmillan
23 September	Britain and France refer dispute to the United Nations
29 September	Treasury warnings on economic front
30 September–1 October	Meir and Dayan meet French for high-level talks
5 October	Lloyd meets Pineau and Dulles prior to beginning of Security Council debate
10–11 October	Israeli raid on Qualqilya in Jordan
13 October	Six Principles passed by Security Council
14 October	Gazier and Challes meet Eden at Chequers to discuss Israeli participation

15 October	Lloyd recalled from New York
16 October	Eden and Lloyd fly to Paris for talks with Mollet and Pineau
18 October	First mention of possible Israeli action against Egypt in Cabinet
22 October	Lloyd to Sèvres to meet French and Israeli representatives
24 October	Dean signs Sèvres protocol
25 October	Cabinet approves plan for 'collusion'
26 October–2 November	Treasury discussing 'crash' and emergency action
29 October	Israelis begin attack on Egypt
30 October	Britain and France send ultimatums to Egypt and Israel; Britain and France veto American and Soviet resolutions calling for cease-fire; Eisenhower reiterates warnings to Eden about use of force.

Invasion and withdrawal
November–December 1956

Military operations against Egypt were intended to begin with air attacks against Egyptian airfields on the expiry of the ultimatum at midnight of 30–31 October. However, a delay was ordered by the Prime Minister while the Valiant bombers were *en route* to their targets from Malta in order to allow American citizens to be evacuated from Cairo unharmed. In the event, the first bomber waves of Canberra aircraft from Cyprus attacked Egyptian airfields in the late afternoon of 31 October; unfortunately some aircraft missed their intended targets, military airfields near Cairo, and hit the adjacent civilian airfield, Cairo International.

Document 4.1 Headlines of National British Press, 31 October 1956

News of these attacks triggered scenes of considerable disorder in the House of Commons which was sitting in a continuing debate on government policy in the Middle East. Eden, having initiated hostilities against Egypt, was in the uncomfortable position of facing such Opposition criticism that the House had to be suspended following heated exchanges on whether in fact a state of war now existed between Britain and Egypt. These attacks from the opposition, which continued throughout the period of military action, centred on what Gaitskell perceived as an abandonment of the three fundamental bases of British foreign policy since 1945: the Anglo-American Alliance, the United Nations Charter and the Commonwealth. Moreover, the ugly charge of collusion began to be aired at Westminster. To this charge, Selwyn Lloyd replied with breathtaking insouciance, 'it is quite wrong to state that Israel was incited to this action by HMG. There was no prior agreement between us.' (see documents 3.26 (pp. 93–94), 3.28 (pp. 96–97), 3.29 (pp. 97–99) and 3.30 (pp. 100–101)). Thus began the protracted process of misleading the House of Commons and, by extension, the country: as Keith Kyle has observed, 'it still remains astonishing that the man who spoke these words was elected Speaker of the House of Commons.' (**Kyle, 1991, p. 379**)

Worse was to follow for Eden and the government. As the bombing attacks continued and the invasion convoy steamed slowly from Malta to the beaches of Port Said, Britain and her allies faced growing condemnation in the Security Council for their military action in the Middle East from a wide range of countries including the United States and the Commonwealth. On the evening

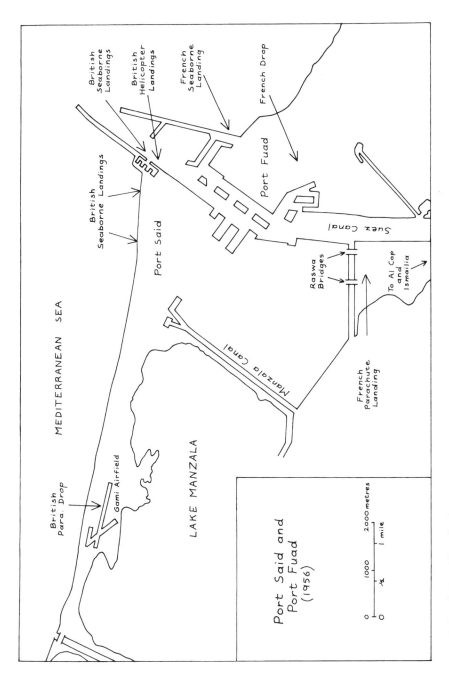

Map 3 Port Said and Port Fuad

A photomontage of British headlines, illustrating the, albeit limited, range of responses

Source: Hulton-Deutsch Collection

of 31 October the issue, on a Yugoslavian motion, was referred to an emergency special session of the General Assembly, a procedural move on which neither Britain nor France could employ their veto. Eden was to be hoist by his own petard, for on 1 November, to defuse the confrontation in the House of Commons, he indicated that Britain was willing to see United Nations involvement in a resolution of the conflict, including a peacekeeping role following a cease-fire.

Such was the anger at the Anglo-French action in the Middle East that the General Assembly met for the first time ever in emergency session and to the dismay of London passed an American resolution calling for a cease-fire on 2 November 1956. Introducing the resolution Dulles stated:

> I doubt that any delegate ever spoke from this forum with as heavy a heart as I have brought here tonight. We speak on a matter of vital importance, where the United States finds itself unable to agree with three nations with whom it has ties, deep friendship, admiration, and respect, and two of whom constitute our oldest, most trusted and reliable allies.

Document 4.2 General Assembly Resolution 997 (ES-1), Adopted 2 November 1956

1 *Urges* as a matter of priority that all parties now involved in hostilities in the area agree to an immediate cease-fire and as part thereof halt the movement of military forces and arms into the area;

2 *Urges* the parties to the armistice agreements promptly to withdraw all forces behind the armistice lines, to desist from raids across the armistice lines into neighbouring territory and to observe scrupulously the provisions of the armistice agreements;

3 *Recommends* that all Member States refrain from introducing military goods in the area of hostilities and in general refrain from any acts which would delay or prevent the implementation of this resolution;

4 *Urges* that upon the cease-fire being effective steps be taken to re-open the Suez Canal and to secure freedom of navigation;

5 *Requests* the Secretary-General to observe and promptly report on the compliance with this resolution to the Security Council and to the General Assembly for such further action as they may deem appropriate in accordance with the Charter;

6 *Decides* to remain in emergency session pending compliance with this resolution.

Source: Frankland (ed.), 1959, pp. 270–271

From the point of view of the increasingly beleaguered British government, of special concern was that the only support in the General Assembly for the tripartite military action came from Australia and New Zealand and, moreover, that the United States and the Soviet Union had combined to condemn British actions.

The pressure on Eden was increased by the receipt of a telegram from Dixon in New York, who pointed out the mounting hostility to Britain in the UN following reports of an imminent extension of the bombing offensive to telecommunications targets in civilian areas. The respected diplomat argued that

> our position here will become untenable ... if we bomb open cities with resulting loss of civilian life or engage in battle with Egyptian forces, there is not the faintest chance of

receiving any sympathy. On the contrary it would make our offer seem completely cynical and entirely undermine our position here. In these circumstances the only honest course for HMG and the French Government would be to withdraw their representatives and leave the United Nations.'

(PRO PREM 11/1105, 3 November 1956)

Despite these troubles Eden held firm. On the evening of 3 November 1956 he broadcast to the nation in an attempt to justify his policy. From the transcript it would appear that little had happened to change the mind of the Prime Minister.

Document 4.3 Sir Anthony Eden Broadcast to the Nation, 3 November 1956

What should we do? We put the matter to the Security Council. Should we have left it to them? Should we have been content to wait and see whether they would act? How long would this have taken? And where would the forest fire have spread in the meantime? Would words have been enough? What we did was to take police action at once: action to end the fighting and to separate the armies. We acted swiftly and reported to the Security Council, and I believe that before long it will become apparent to everybody that we acted rightly and wisely. . . .

The other reflection is this. It is a personal one. All my life I have been a man of peace, working for peace, striving for peace, negotiating for peace. I have been a League of Nations man and a United Nations man, and I am still the same man, with the same convictions, the same devotion to peace. I could not be other, even if I wished, but I am utterly convinced that the action we have taken is right. . . .

So finally, my friends, what are we seeking to do? First and foremost, to stop the fighting, to separate the armies, and to make sure there is no more fighting. We have stepped in because the United Nations could not do so in time. If the United Nations will take over the police action we shall welcome it. Indeed, we proposed that course to them. And police action means not only to end the fighting now but also to bring a lasting peace to an area which for ten years has lived, or tried to live, under the constant threat of war. . . .

Source: Eayrs (ed.), 1964, pp. 214–215

Eden's reference to a United Nations peacekeeping force to replace Anglo-French forces was probably made in the expectation that the UN would be unable to act in this way very quickly. The fact that the UN was able to act speedily left Eden in an exposed position as, having made the commitment publicly, he could not reasonably retract it. Eden's remarks had already been pre-empted by the initiative of Lester Pearson, the Canadian Foreign Minister, who had raised the possibility of the creation of a United Nations Emergency Force to police any cease-fire on

2 November. This had been seized upon by Dulles and a formal resolution to this effect was passed on 4 November 1956.

Taken in conjunction with a resolution proposed by India, which reaffirmed the resolution of 2 November and called on the Secretary-General to obtain compliance within 12 hours, this presented the British government with a stark dilemma as Eden's bluff had now been called. Further disquieting developments were reported to the Egypt Committee on 4 November 1956, although the Committee sanctioned a parachute drop on Port Said the following day, 24 hours ahead of schedule.

Document 4.4 Lloyd on the Mounting Pressure on Britain

We were also told that inclusion of Anglo-French troops in the UNEF [United Nations Emergency Force] was unacceptable. It was added that the Israeli representative at the United Nations had said that Israel would accept the cease-fire if Egypt agreed to do so, and the Egyptians had so agreed. After further enquiry it appeared that this was not as simple as it seemed. The Israelis had not agreed to withdraw behind the former border, the armistice lines, nor had they agreed to the introduction of a UNEF.

The Committee decided that we should press again for the inclusion of Anglo-French troops in the UNEF. We did not see how otherwise it would ever come into being. In the event, it was only our logistic support which did make it capable of functioning. The question was then raised of postponing the Anglo-French airborne landing for twenty-four hours to give time for an answer on this point, this led to a further question, whether if there were this twenty-four hour postponement it would be possible for it ever to take place.

It was at this meeting that a report came in from Dixon that there had been some discussion in New York about oil sanctions. Macmillan threw his arms in the air and said, 'Oil sanctions! That finishes it.' Two of those present remember this.

Source: Lloyd, 1978, p. 206

It should be noted, however, that neither the Egypt Committee minutes nor the full Cabinet minutes of the same evening record any mention of sanctions or economic pressures.

As Eden noted, these developments placed the onus squarely on the British for 'unless they accepted a cease-fire, they would alone be responsible for the continuance of hostilities which it had been the professed intention of their intervention to stop'. Eden canvassed several possibilities: first, that Britain could not accept the suggestion that the UNEF should not include Anglo-French troops; second, that the parachute landings could be suspended for 24 hours in order to give time for the governments of Egypt and Israel to accept a UNEF and in turn the

United Nations time to consider whether Anglo-French troops could constitute an advance guard of the UNEF; and third, that military action could be indefinitely deferred and that political and diplomatic pressure could be utilised to produce a settlement under the auspices of the United Nations. **(PRO CAB 128/30 Pt. II, CM 79(56), 4 November 1956)**.

Document 4.5 Eden Stands Firm, 4 November 1956

The Prime Minister, summing up the discussion, said that it was evident that the overwhelming balance of opinion in the Cabinet was in favour of allowing the initial phase of the military operation to go forward as planned. This being so, he proposed that the United Nations should be informed that it remained necessary in the view of the Governments of the United Kingdom and France, to interpose a force between Egypt and Israel in order to prevent the continuance of hostilities, to secure the speedy withdrawal of Israeli forces, to restore traffic through the Suez Canal and to promote a settlement of the outstanding problems of the area. For this purpose certain Anglo-French operations with strictly limited objectives would continue; but, as soon as the Israeli and Egyptian Governments accepted a plan, endorsed by the United Nations, for an international force with the above functions the United Kingdom and France would stop all military action. A new and constructive solution of the problems of the Middle East would, however, remain urgent. To this end an early meeting of the Security Council should be called, at Ministerial level, in order to work out an international settlement which would be likely to endure together with the means to enforce it.

Source: PRO CAB 128/30 Prt II, CM 79 (56), 4 November 1956

These bland minutes, however, conceal a crucial development in the nature of the support for the operation. For the first time a vote had been taken in Cabinet which revealed that some six Cabinet ministers had serious reservations about continuing with the military action and of the three Service Ministers only one, Hailsham, was for continuing the operation. **(Rhodes James, 1987, pp. 566–567)**. According to some accounts this sudden split, which included two previously fervent supporters of the military option, Kilmuir and Salisbury, led Eden to tell his senior colleagues that 'if they wouldn't go on then he would have to resign' **(Carlton, 1988, pp. 74–75)**. Eden was saved, albeit temporarily, from this indignity by the news that the Israelis had refused the cease-fire and, therefore, the British and the French were able to press on with their invasion. In the early hours of 5 November 1956 an Anglo-French paratroop force landed on the outskirts of Port Said and had little difficulty in securing their objectives. They were followed one day later by the long-awaited seaborne invasion of Port Said. Such military successes were, however, of little avail in the light of sustained and ever-mounting pressure from internal and external sources for an early cessation of hostilities.

Document 4.6 Anti-War Demonstrations in London, 5 November 1956

Source: Hulton-Deutsch Collection

On the evening of 4 November 1956 Gaitskell made his reply to Eden's broadcast. In this controversial television broadcast, which followed the demonstration in Trafalgar Square addressed by Aneurin Bevan, the Labour leader launched a savage attack on Government policy.

Document 4.7 Broadcast to the Nation by Hugh Gaitskell, 4 November 1956

Make no mistake about it: this is war – the bombing, the softening up, the attacks on radio stations, telephone exchanges, railway stations, to be followed, very soon now, by the landings and the fighting between ground forces.

We are doing all this alone except for France: opposed by the world, in defiance of the world. It is not a police action; there is no law behind it. We have taken the law into our own hands. . . .

The Prime Minister has said we were going in to separate the two sides, but you do not separate two armies by bombing airfields and landing troops a hundred miles behind one side only. No. This is a second onslaught on a country that was already the victim of an attack.

Now a new idea has been put forward: the idea that we are going in to make way for a United Nations force. But nothing was said about this in the ultimatum to Egypt. Nothing was said about this at the Security Council. If this was the Government's plan, why on earth did they not put it forward before? Why did they not propose it right at the beginning, accepting the rest of the Security Council's resolution? I will tell you why they did not do this. If the Prime Minister had agreed to this Britain would not have been able to occupy the Canal; for the idea of the United Nations police force, proposed by Canada yesterday is quite different. It would not give us control of the Canal. . . .

What are the consequences? We have violated the charter of the United Nations . . . [and created] . . . a deep division in the Commonwealth. . . .

We should, surely, without qualification, argument or conditions, accept the resolution of the General Assembly of the United Nations calling for an immediate cease-fire. . . . We should also give full support to the new resolution on which we abstained today, for a United Nations force to police the Arab–Israel borders until a proper peace settlement has been reached.

But – make no mistake – this means abandoning the idea which has been at the root of this policy: the idea of trying to solve the Suez Canal problem by force. It means going back to negotiating. . . .

I do not believe the present Prime Minister can carry out this policy. I bear him no ill will . . . but his policy this last week has been disastrous; and he is utterly, utterly discredited in the world. Only one thing now can save the reputation and honour of our country. Parliament must repudiate the Government's policy. The Prime Minister must resign. . . .

Source: Eayrs (ed.), 1964, pp. 217–218

This speech was dramatic evidence of the growing polarisation of opinion within Britain. Although this broadcast could be seen as an extension of Gaitskell's line throughout the crisis, given that British troops were about to go into action it was viewed in some quarters as unpatriotic. However, Gaitskell was to receive support from elements of the British press, notably the *Observer* but including *The Times* which had previously supported the government.

Document 4.8 *Observer* Editorial on Eden, 4 November 1956

We wish to make an apology. Five weeks ago we reported that although we knew our government would not make a military attack in defiance of its solemn international obligations, people abroad might think otherwise. The events of last week have proved us completely wrong. If we misled anyone at home or abroad, we apologise unreservedly. We had not realised that our government was capable of such folly and crookedness.

Whatever the Government now does, it cannot undo its air attacks on Egypt, made after Egypt had been invaded by Israel. It cannot undo the deliberate employment of haste so that our nearest allies had no opportunity to express disagreement. It cannot live down the dishonest nature of its ultimatums, so framed that it was certain to be rejected by Egypt.

Whether the Conservative Party can save itself from obliteration for a generation now depends on whether it produces an honest party rebellion that contributes to retrieving the national situation. But whatever the Conservative Party may do, it is essential that the world should know that the Eden Administration no longer has the nation's confidence. Unless we can find means of making that absolutely clear, we shall be individually guilty of an irresponsibility and a folly as great as that of our government.

The Eden Administration has, throughout the Summer, shown that it does not understand the sort of world we live in. It is no longer possible to bomb countries because you fear that your trading interests may be harmed . . . the sanctity of human life is the best element in the modern world.

It is for every individual in this country who is against the government's attack on Egypt to say so by writing to his M.P., lobbying him, demonstrating in every legitimate way. Nations are said to have the governments they deserve. Let us show that we deserve better.

Source: Observer, *4 November 1956*

Worse was to follow the next day. Even as the paratroop force consolidated their hold on the drop zones, leading to abortive cease-fire discussions with the Governor of Port Said and as the Anglo-French seaborne invasion prepared to land the following day, an agitated telegram arrived from Dixon in New York reporting likely developments in the United Nations General Assembly.

Document 4.9 Warnings from Dixon at the United Nations, 5 November 1956

5 These developments make it absolutely certain in my view that at the inevitable assembly meeting later today and tonight, delegations will concentrate their attention on our failure to comply with the cease-fire and in particular of the reported bombings of populated areas in apparent contradiction to our declared policy. They will be in a very ugly mood and out for our blood and I would not be surprised if the Arab–Asians and the Soviet blocs did not try to rush through some resolution urging collective measures of some kind against us. Between them they might well cook up an appeal by the Arabs to the Soviet Union to come in and help them.

6 You will recall that two days ago . . . I felt constrained to warn you that if there was any bombing of open cities with resulting loss of civilian life it would make our proposals seem completely cynical and entirely undermine our position here. Again . . . I urged that, unless we could announce that Anglo-French forces were suspending all further military activities until we knew that the United Nations were prepared to deal with the whole situation effectively, there would be no chance of our being able to move towards our objectives without alienating the whole world.

7 I must again repeat this warning with renewed emphasis.

8 For the purposes of today's proceedings it would be useful if I could have
  (a) A governmental statement on our bombing policy
  (b) Up-to date figures, if available, of Egyptian casualties so far caused in our operations, in particular of civilian personnel;
  (c) Information as to when our limited operation with its limited objectives is going to stop.

9 You will realise that monstrously unjust as it may be in the light of the precautions which General Keightley is taking . . . we are inevitably being placed in the same low category as the Russians in its bombing of Budapest. I do not see how we can carry much conviction in our protests against the Russian bombing of Budapest . . . if we ourselves are bombing Cairo.

Source: PRO PREM 11/1105, New York to Foreign Office, 5 November 1956

By now, the experienced Dixon was worried that the military action in the Middle East was leading to the almost complete isolation of Britain within the international community. For Dixon, his position was made worse by the fact that, as recounted in his memoirs, he opposed the use of force in the Suez Crisis: as a professional diplomat he was left defending a position in which he did not personally believe. In a subsequent telephone conversation with the Prime Minister, Dixon amplified this telegram, pointing out the very real probability that the General Assembly would pass a resolution imposing economic sanctions on the British and French unless they agreed to an immediate cease-fire and suspended military operations. This alarming news was to have considerable bearing on crucial decisions that were to be taken in the Cabinet the following day.

   A further concern for the government was the arrival of a letter from the Soviet leader Nikolai Bulganin which made the following allegations.

Document 4.10 Letter from Mr Bulganin to the Prime Ministers of Britain, France and Israel and the President of the United States, 5 November 1956

The Suez Canal issue was only a pretext for British and French aggression, which has other and far reaching aims. It cannot be concealed that in actual fact an aggressive predatory war is now unfolding against the Arab peoples with the object of destroying the national independence of the states of the

Near and Middle East and of re-establishing the regime of colonial slavery rejected by the peoples.

There is no justification for the fact that the armed forces of Britain and France, two Great Powers that are Permanent Members of the Security Council, have attacked a country which only recently acquired its national independence and which does not possess adequate means for self-defence.

In what situation would Britain find herself if she were attacked by stronger states, possessing all types of modern destructive weapons and such countries could, at the present time, refrain from sending naval or air forces to the shores of Britain and use other means – for instance, rocket weapons. Were rocket weapons used against Britain and France you would, most probably, call this a barbarous action. But how does the inhuman attack launched by the armed forces of Britain and France against a practically defenceless Egypt differ from this?

. . . The war in Egypt can spread to other countries and turn into a Third World War.

The Soviet Government has already addressed the United Nations and the President of the United States of America with the proposal to resort, jointly with other United Nations member-states, to the use of naval and air forces in order to end the war in Egypt and to curb aggression. We are fully determined to crush the aggressors by the use of force and to restore peace in the East.

Source: Frankland (ed.), 1959, p. 289

This veiled threat by the Soviet Union to use weapons of mass destruction against the vulnerable British Isles had little or no effect on Eden. Of more concern to the British, especially the Chiefs of Staff and the MUSKETEER commanders, was the possibility of Soviet intervention directly in the Middle East through the resupply of weapons and 'volunteers' to utilise them. This concern, despite some false alarms in Cyprus, was never to be realised. Bulganin's letter was at best bluster and at worst hypocrisy, as at the same time Soviet troops were in the process of brutally suppressing the Hungarian nationalist government of Imre Nagy using tanks and heavy weapons on the streets of Budapest.

Document 4.11 *Punch*'s View of the UN and the Suez Crisis, November 1956

Although the linking causality between Suez and Hungary may in retrospect be doubtful, the connection had been made since the end of October by Dulles, much to his fury as the champion of anti-communism. Indeed, Soviet actions at the end of October appeared to indicate a withdrawal from Hungary. This could have been interpreted in the United States as a victory for the strategy which had been pursued towards Eastern Europe. That strategy now lay in apparent ruin as the events in the Middle East overshadowed events in Eastern Europe. The

Selwyn Lloyd, Pineau and Ben-Gurion viewed as naughty schoolboys, while the United Nations, in the person of Dag Hammarskjöld, portrayed as a schoolmistress, watches over them and ignores a grinning Nasser and the Soviet attack on Hungary.

Source: Punch, *28 November 1956*

coexistence of the two events only served to increase the fury of the American administration with their European allies.

In an attempt to mollify an American President preoccupied with the final days of his re-election campaign, Eden sent a heartfelt plea for understanding. After rehearsing the familiar arguments about Nasser's supposed ambitions Eden attempted to justify the Anglo-French action in the light of the Israeli invasion of Sinai.

Document 4.12 Eden Attempts to Justify His Actions, 5 November 1956

We were of course relieved that they [the Israelis] broke in the direction of Egypt rather than of Jordan. But once they had moved, in whatever direction there was not a moment to be lost. We and the French were convinced that we had to act at once to forestall a general conflagration throughout the Middle East. And now that police action has been started it must be carried through. I am sure that this is the moment to curb Nasser's ambitions. If we let it pass, all of us will bitterly regret it. Here is our opportunity to secure an effective and final settlement of the problems of the Middle East. If we draw back now, chaos will not be avoided. Everything will go up in flames in the Middle East. You will realise, with all your experience, that we cannot have a military vacuum while a United Nations force is being constituted and is being transported to the spot. This is why we feel we must go on to hold the position until we can hand over the responsibility to the United Nations. If a barrier can be established in this way between the Arabs and the Israelis we shall then be strongly placed to call on the Israelis to withdraw. This in its turn will reduce the threat to the Canal and restore it to the general use of the world. By this means, we shall have taken the first step towards re-establishing authority in this area for our generation.

It is no mere form of words to say that we would be happy to hand over to an international organisation as soon as we possibly can. As you can imagine no-one feels more strongly about this than Harold who has to provide the money. We do not want occupation of Egypt, we could not afford it, and that is one of many other reasons why we got out of Suez two years ago.

I know how strongly you feel, as I do, the objections to the use of force, but this is not a situation which can be mended by words or resolutions. It is indeed ironical that at this very moment, when we are being pilloried as aggressors, Russia is brutally reoccupying Hungary and threatening the whole of Eastern Europe, and no voice is raised in the United Nations in favour of intervention there. It may be that our two countries can take no practical action to redress that situation. But the Middle East is an area in which we could still take practical and effective action together.

I am sending you this message in the hope that you will at least understand the grievous decisions which we have had to make. I was deeply moved by your last message before our initial action, although I was not able to reply to it as I would have liked at the time.

After a few days you will be in a position to act with renewed authority. I beg you to believe what we are doing now will in our view facilitate your action. I would earnestly ask you to put the great weight of your authority behind the proposal which we are now making to the United Nations.

I believe as firmly as ever that the future of all of us depends on the closest Anglo-American co-operation. It has of course been a grief to me to have had to make a temporary breach into it which I cannot disguise, but I know that you are a man of big enough heart and vision to take up things again on the basis of fact. If you cannot approve, I would like you at least to understand the terrible decisions we have had to make. I remember nothing like them since the days when we were comrades together in the war. History alone can judge whether we have made the right decision, but I do want to assure you that we have made it from a genuine sense of responsibility, not only to our country, but to all the world.

Source: PRO PREM 11/1177, Eden to Eisenhower, 5 November 1956

In this attempt to justify his actions, Eden misleads the American President in the first paragraph, by omission rather than by commission, by skating over the precise origins of the Israeli attack on Egypt. The Prime Minister was clearly anxious to begin rebuilding the 'special relationship' and asked for American support in the United Nations.

In Cabinet the following day it was the Foreign Secretary, not the strangely silent Prime Minister, who summarised the various pressures on the British and French to halt the action. Lloyd argued that Britain had lost the initiative in the General Assembly and had alienated American opinion. It was therefore for consideration whether the operation should continue, especially as it was pointed out that 'if we agreed to break off hostilities at once, we could maintain that we had achieved our primary objectives'. As the Cabinet minutes noted opinion had now moved towards the acceptance of a cease-fire.

Document 4.13 The Cabinet Moves Towards Accepting a Cease-fire, 6 November 1956

Discussion showed that there was general agreement in the Cabinet that, in order to regain the initiative and to re-establish relations with those members of the United Nations who were fundamentally in sympathy with our aims, we should agree, subject to the concurrence of the French Government, to stop further military operations provided that the Secretary-General of the United Nations could confirm that the Governments of Egypt and Israel had now accepted an unconditional cease-fire and that the international force to be set up would be competent to secure and to supervise the attainment of the objectives set out in the operative paragraphs of the original resolution passed by the General Assembly on 2nd November. In addition, we should state that, pending confirmation of these assumptions, the Anglo-French force would cease-fire at some point during the day, the exact time to be determined in the light of operational considerations. But we should at the same time emphasise that the clearing of the Suez Canal, which was in no sense a military operation, was now a matter of great urgency, and that we proposed that the technicians accompanying the Anglo-French force should begin this work at once.

Source: PRO CAB 128/30 Pt II, CM 80 (56), 6 November 1956

This discussion marked the acceptance by the British Cabinet, somewhat to the chagrin of the French and, indeed, British military commanders of MUSKETEER force, of the desirability of accepting a cease-fire while the aims of the operation had not in fact been met, either overtly (operations were halted when the Anglo-French forces had reached El-Kap and were therefore not in occupation of the full length of the Canal), or covertly (as Nasser remained in power). The face-saving formula for the Cabinet was Anglo-French participation in the UNEF and in the operation to clear the Canal: this participation however was to be difficult to achieve.

What was not recorded in these Cabinet minutes was perhaps the most decisive element in the equation – money. Lloyd records 'before the Cabinet met, I had spoken to Macmillan who said that in view of the financial and economic pressures we must stop' **(Lloyd, 1978, p. 209)**. Alastair Horne, Macmillan's official biographer, states

> He [Macmillan] told the Cabinet that there had been a serious run on the pound, viciously orchestrated in Washington. Britain's Gold reserves he announced, had fallen by £100 million over the past week – or by one-eighth of their remaining total. ... Telephoning Washington and then New York, Macmillan was told that only a cease-fire by midnight would secure U.S. support for an International Monetary Fund loan to prop up the pound. ... Macmillan is alleged to have warned the Cabinet that, unless there were a cease-fire, he could no longer 'be responsible for Her Majesty's Government'.
>
> **(Horne, 1989, p. 440)**

In attempting to explain the sudden conversion of Macmillan from the most hawkish supporter of the operation to the most vociferous advocate of a cease-fire, Horne has argued that 'all along, it seems that Macmillan may have been getting bad, or at least inadequate advice from those professional advisers [i.e., the Treasury and the Bank of England]' **(Horne, 1989, p. 443)**. This view is entirely at odds with the weight of evidence available in the files of the Public Record Office and is only explicable by the reliance of Horne on Macmillan's own testimony. As early as 8 August 1956 Sir Edward Bridges, Permanent Secretary of the Treasury and a former Cabinet Secretary, had warned Macmillan in no uncertain terms.

Document 4.14 The Treasury Warns Macmillan of the Need to Protect Sterling, 8 August 1956

It is already clear that our Balance of Payments and therefore our gold and dollar reserves are going to be under considerable strain over the next month or so, even if the [London] Conference reaches a successful conclusion. But if there is no clear cut conclusion to the conference and negotiations drag on for some time, our Balance of Payments position may come under even greater strain.

. . . The action to be taken is almost totally different according to the situation which we are faced with – a limited war, or a not so limited war – a war in which we go it alone, or a war in which we have the Americans with us from the onset. Frankly, I doubt whether anything much can be done under this head until we can know more clearly the assumptions which should be made . . . it may be that there are one or two essential matters that should be looked at to avoid our being caught short.

. . . This note already contains a good many uncomfortable thoughts. For good measure let me add one more. That is that even if we don't get involved in hostilities, if the crisis continues for some time with consequent disturbance of our export trade and some loss of confidence, we may well find that economic counter-measures have to be taken in the autumn. Though it is an odious thought one cannot all together rule out the possibility of an autumn budget.

Source: PRO T236/4188, Measures to Protect Sterling, *Bridges to Macmillan, 8 August 1956*

Barely two weeks after the nationalisation, the Chancellor was being informed by his chief adviser of the uncertainties surrounding the British economy in a period of crisis. The major problem was the balance of payments position, the difference between what the country imported and what it exported, including 'invisible earning' (insurance, shipping, etc.), which was a major indicator of confidence in sterling. Since the convertibility crisis of 1947, the problem of restoring sterling to a fixed exchange rate against the dollar had troubled all governments. The position of sterling was of central importance to the Bretton Woods system of fixed exchange rates, given that it acted as a reserve currency – along with the dollar, sterling effectively backed the system – and therefore international confidence in the currency was of paramount importance. The strength, or otherwise, of sterling tended to be viewed as a crude measure of the economic well-being of the country and weaknesses in the balance of payments tended to encourage speculation against the pound, thereby weakening international confidence in it. This first Treasury warning should, therefore, have been seen by the Chancellor as a serious portent of imminent economic difficulties and it is all the more surprising that the warning does not appear to have formally gone to the Cabinet.

Macmillan was therefore being left under no illusions as to the likely effect of the crisis on Britain's finances and indeed, despite his apparent confidence in Cabinet, asked Bridges to prepare a list of contingency measures including *inter alia* a 6d rise in the rate of income tax, an increase of between 6d and 1s. in petrol duty, increases in tobacco duty and, perhaps, in purchase tax and profits tax. Even these measures would not wholly meet any increased expenditure associated with the crisis. Raw material, import and exchange controls were all considered to be potentially necessary along with a recourse to fully floating exchange rates. Taken together, this package of emergency measures would have meant the ruin of the economic policy that the government had been following since 1951. The Treasury concluded that 'we are not in at all a happy position to bear any great degree of extra strain on our resources. Our reserves are still dangerously low and are certain to fall pretty sharply this month' **(PRO T236/4188, 13 August 1956)**.

In the course of discussions between the Treasury and the Bank of England it was decided that any precipitate action with respect to strengthening sterling and the reserves was to be avoided, precisely because such action would be likely to have the opposite effect and weaken confidence in the pound, provoking a run on sterling in the international markets. Bridges made the position plain to the Chancellor on 7 September 1956.

Document 4.15 The Treasury on the Necessity for United States and Commonwealth Support, 7 September 1956

. . . It seems to us that unless we can secure at least US support and a fairly unified Commonwealth then it is not possible to predict either the exact timing or the magnitude of the strains that are likely to come on our currency. At the worst, however, the strains might be so great that, whatever precautionary measures were taken we should be unable to maintain the value of the currency. . . . If we do get overt US support and support from elsewhere, including the Commonwealth, our general feeling is that our action would be regarded by world opinion as something likely to strengthen sterling. In these circumstances the broad line of our policy should be to allow things to go on as normally as possible so as to show that we have confidence both in a satisfactory and quick outcome of any military action, and in the capacity of our economy and our currency to face any strains that might come upon it. Any unusual action on our part would be likely to cast doubt on both. What this points to therefore is the vital necessity from the point of view of the currency and our economy of ensuring that we do not go it alone, and that we have the maximum US support.

Source: PRO T236/4188, Bridges to Macmillan, 7 September 1956

This second Treasury warning, with its emphasis on the necessity of American support, has a clear political message, not least because similar views were being expressed from the political and diplomatic sides while clear warnings were coming from the United States that such support would not be forthcoming in the event of the use of force. In the worst-case scenario Bridges warned of the possibility of devaluation.

The memorandum with its trenchant warnings is annotated by the Chancellor 'Yes: this is just the trouble the US are being very difficult' **(PRO T236/4188, 10 September 1956)**. Macmillan, having received copious advice over the previous six weeks which pointed to the economic difficulties which were likely to confront Britain in the event of any unilateral action, chose this moment to urge the Cabinet towards a military solution arguing that

> he regarded the establishment of this user organisation as a step towards the ultimate use of force. It would not in itself provide a solution . . . it should, however, serve to bring the issue to a head. This was of great importance to the national economy. If we could achieve a quick and satisfactory settlement of this issue, confidence in sterling should be restored but, if a settlement was long delayed the cost and uncertainty would undermine our financial position.

(PRO CAB 128/30 Pt II, 11 September 1956)

This was a remarkable reformulation of the substance of the advice tendered by Bridges.

Given the consistent warnings throughout the crisis to the Chancellor by the Treasury, these pressures should have come as no surprise to the Cabinet. However, it would appear that these warnings, for whatever reason, were not passed on formally by Macmillan to his colleagues on the Egypt Committee and in the Cabinet until 6 November. What is clear is that the pressure on sterling, orchestrated by the United States, played a fundamental role in the decision by the British to call a halt to their military operations in Egypt when the forward element of Anglo-French forces were only 23 miles down the Canal.

Although elements of the French Cabinet and military wished to continue the operation the British secured the agreement of Mollet to a cease-fire effective from midnight Greenwich Mean Time 6–7 November 1956: the Israelis had already shut down active military operations in the Sinai but a bellicose Ben-Gurion refused to countenance the insertion of a UN force, even on a peacekeeping basis, into Sinai. For the British the priority was now to salvage what they could from the wreckage of MUSKETEER by trying to retain a role in the clearance of the Canal that was closed by blockships (some of them sunk by Egypt and some by British air action) and by reconstructing relations with the United States. On the evening of 6 November, Eden spoke by telephone to Eisenhower.

Document 4.16 Conversation Between President Eisenhower and Prime Minister Eden, 6 November 1956

The President First of all, I can't tell you how pleased we are that you found it possible to accept the cease-fire, having landed.

Eden We have taken a certain risk, but I think it is justified.

The President Anthony, this is the way I feel about it. I have not ruminated over this particular situation at length. I am talking off the top of my head. You have got what you said you were going to get in that you have landed. It seems to me that from what – with regard to the cease-fire, and without going to any negotiations, I would go ahead with the cease-fire, not putting any conditions into the acceptance of the resolution and after cease-fire talking about the clearing of the Canal and so on.

Eden We are going to cease firing tonight.

The President Could you not tell Hammerskjöld that as far as the cease-fire arrangement is concerned, that that goes without condition.

Eden We cease firing tonight at midnight provided we are not attacked.

The President I see.

Eden What you may call the long cease-fire, the cessation of hostilities, that is more complicated.

The President Yes it is more complicated. Talking about the technical troops of yours.

Eden They will cooperate with us in having a cease-fire tonight.

The President If I may make a suggestion, I would offer them to Hammerskjöld – but I would not insist that he take them.

Eden It is always a bit of working out with the allies and everybody else to get this thing – with some difficulty.

The President The point I want you to have in your mind is that the cease-fire tonight has nothing to do with technical troops. You cease anyway.

Eden Unless attacked.

The President The more permanent affair – we would like to know about the other thing.

Eden I have got to go [to] my Parliament.

The President Oh, alright.

Eden In five minutes. Would you authorise me to say that you think this is helpful outside –

The President You can say that I called to say how delighted I was you found it possible to cease-fire tonight so that negotiations could start.

Eden I am just getting it down –

The President How delighted I was that you found it possible to direct a cease-fire tonight which will allow negotiations to proceed from there on.

Eden Proceed –

The President Yes. Wait a minute. Well, I will tell you what I am trying to get at. I don't want to give Egypt an opportunity to begin to quibble so that this thing can be drawn out for a week. After the cease-fire it seems like the technical thing of it would be settled very quickly, and when Hammerskjöld comes along with his people you people ought to be able to withdraw very quickly. He is getting Canadian troops – lots of troops – together.

Eden I hope you will be there. Are we all going to go out?

The President What I want to do is this. I would like to see none of the great nations in it. I am afraid the Red boy is going to demand the lion's share. I would rather make it no troops from the big five. I would say, 'Mr Hammerskjöld, we trust you. When we see you coming in with enough troops to take over, we go out.'

Eden That is not too easy unless they have good force, you know.

The President I will tell you. If they have enough – and they attack, they attack the United Nations and its whole prestige and force – then everyone is in the thing. Then you are [not] alone.

Eden May I think that one over.

The President Now that we know connections are so good, you can call me anytime you please.

Eden If I survive here tonight I will call you tomorrow. How are things going with you.

The President We have given our whole thought to Hungary and the Middle East. I don't give a damn how the election goes. I guess it will be alright.

Eden How is Foster?

The President Pretty good. He's making a pretty quick recovery.

Eden Wonderful.

The President All right. Thank you and go ahead with your meeting.

Eden Thanks so much.

Source: FRUS (C), 1988, transcript of a telephone conversation between President Eisenhower in Washington and Prime Minister Eden in London, 6 November 1956, 12.55 p.m., document 525, pp. 1025–1027.

The somewhat confused and confusing appearance of this document is explicable, in part, because it is a verbatim transcript of a transatlantic telephone conversation. While on the surface a friendly conversation, it is evident that Eden is in a somewhat supplicant position and that the face-saving compromise hoped for by the British Cabinet, the participation in the UNEF and the clearance of the Canal, did not meet with American approval. This confused conversation highlighted the difficulties that were likely to face the British in their task: as the Cabinet meeting in the morning of 6 November had noted, the overriding objectives were now a restoration of the 'special relationship' with the United States and a prominent role in the clearing of the Canal. But as Eisenhower's conversation with Eden makes clear the first objective was unlikely to be realised unless the second was entirely dropped by the British: in further telephone conversations the next day, a proposed visit by Eden to Washington was refused until British troops left Egypt. As Lucas notes, the British Prime Minister was now excluded from contact with the centre of American policy-making which increasingly, with the hospitalisation of Dulles, shifted towards the anti-British Hoover and the pragmatic American Treasury **(Lucas, 1991, pp. 299-300; Carlton, 1988, p. 82)**.

The situation confronting a British Cabinet in some disarray was made more complex by the speed with which the Secretary-General of the United Nations managed to push through the resolution authorising the constitution of the UNEF. The outcome of debates on 7 November 1956 in the Security Council was to exclude Britain and France from participation in the UNEF but to allow the Anglo-French forces to remain in Port Said until the UNEF arrived in Egypt. For the next week the British attempted to retain some shreds of dignity by insisting on the retention of a British element within the UNEF, but, in the face of the refusal of both the United Nations and the United States to countenance this, by 12 November 1956 the Egypt Committee had agreed that Selwyn Lloyd should go to New York to try and secure the best terms that he could. Again it is clear that it was financial pressures that were driving British policy.

On 7 November 1956 a meeting of Treasury officials chaired by Macmillan noted that in the previous week Britain had lost $85 million from the sterling reserves and, moreover, with the blocking of the Canal and the destruction of oil pipelines in the Middle East Britain was faced with a shortfall of oil which would cost some $800 million a year to replace from western hemisphere sources controlled by the United States. In the face of this dire prognosis, the only source of aid was from the International Monetary Fund and the Export–Import Bank, both of them effectively controlled by the United States. Therefore the essential requirement was to approach the United States as soon as possible. However, the new British Ambassador Sir Harold Caccia informed the Foreign Office on 8 November that 'there is at present no possibility of aid, which in any event would not be available until after further Congressional action and I think we must take it that there is at present no possibility of an Exim Bank loan' **(PRO T236/4189, November 1956)**.

The former British Ambassador in Washington Sir Roger Makins, who had now taken up his new position as Permanent Secretary at the Treasury, informed the Chancellor on 9 November 1956 that in the view of the Governor of the Bank of England 'Sterling [was] a major casualty of recent events and that radical treatment [would] be required to save it.' He was also of the view that the most important ameliorative measure was 'an improvement in our relations with the Americans' **(PRO T236/4189, 9 November 1956)**.

In a meeting between Bank of England and Treasury officials to consider what actions were necessary to relieve the strain on sterling the following conclusions were drawn.

Document 4.17 Treasury and Bank of England Concerns over Sterling, 12 November 1956

1 We cannot continue to lose reserves at the present rate, and continue at the same time to hold sterling at its present value. Failure to hold sterling at its present value would involve risks even wider than those of devaluation: the cohesion of the Commonwealth would be severely tested and there might be dangerous consequences to the structure of NATO arising from our inability to meet its commitments.

2 The most important and adequate measure which might be taken involves an approach to the United States and would require a friendly and compliant attitude on their part. We may not be able to rely on this for some time to come. It should be noted, however, that the time factor is of vital importance, such as to warrant our seeking action in other spheres of policy to hasten a return to more friendly relations with the United States. . . .

4 *If we can hold the present position until relations with the United States become more friendly*, it will then be possible to make a very broad approach to them for assistance, on the grounds that it is a major interest of the United States and the whole world that the sterling system should be formally maintained. The following arrangements could be discussed, given United States co-operation: –

(a) The largest possible drawing on the IMF by the United Kingdom (up to $1000 million) and drawings by other members of the Commonwealth if they could be induced to take this step in the common interest.

(b) The pledging of our holdings of United States securities as collateral for a loan from United States financial institutions.

(c) Some arrangement on the waiver.

(d) An Ex/Im Bank loan for oil purchases. . . .

7 *If United States co-operation is not available or not available in time*, we may be obliged to take 'crash' action, which would involve whatever could be managed on: –

(a) The IMF drawing or standby

(b) The sale of our present holdings of United States securities.

(c) The waiver.

Resort to these possibilities might at least offer some prospect of tiding us over immediate difficulties until such time as we are able to approach the Americans.

Source: PRO T236/4189, note of a meeting held in Sir Leslie Rowan's room, 3 p.m., 12 November 1956

The waiver applies to provisions made in the Anglo-American dollar loan agreement of 1946 whereby interest repayments could be waived in any given year in order to alleviate poor British economic circumstances. The technical terms covering this, however, were so complicated that the waiver was considered unworkable.

This very stark picture highlighted the urgency of American support by stressing the disastrous consequences that would follow if such support was not forthcoming. American support was vital for political reasons, but also because it would facilitate the raising of a loan from the Export–Import Bank. Again, this document was never formally circulated to the Cabinet.

It was therefore clear to those concerned with Britain's financial stability that salvation lay only with the United States and that whatever price had to be paid for American aid must be paid. As Rowan informed Makins on 13 November 1956:

> Clearly the most desirable course would be to make broad arrangements with the help of the Americans. We may, however, not be able to wait so long. We cannot, however, at this stage make any recommendation on the matter beyond the following:
>
> (a) We should take every practicable step in other spheres of policy, e.g. withdrawal of troops from Egypt, to ensure the opening at the earliest possible date of general conversations with the United States and preferably at the highest level.
>
> **(PRO T236/4189, 13 November 1956)**

The Treasury were therefore in no doubt as to what courses of action had to be followed, but Selwyn Lloyd, in his first meeting with American officials since mid-October, took a stance that astonished the American Representative at the United Nations, the normally urbane Henry Cabot Lodge. As Lodge reported to the Department of State, the British seemingly remained obdurate on the issues of withdrawal and Canal clearance.

Document 4.18 Continuing Anglo-American Friction, 14 November 1956

Lloyd said several times that US had 'led the hunt' against the UK and France thus far and question was whether we would do so again if they stayed in Egypt. . . . He said 'you may feel we acted rashly, immorally and behind your backs, but UK had to do what it did. There was no alternative'. Otherwise, he contended, a gradual process of shutting UK out of Middle East would have taken place over the next year or two with first their losing Jordan, next Libya, then Iraq and finally Kuwait. They simply could not take this and would rather risk loss of all at once. Dixon said this was historical moment to act and historians like Toynbee would say so in future. Both Lloyd and Dixon contended their action was necessary to save West and unless they were supported now, all gains would be lost. . . . Lloyd and Dixon both contended their action, if supported, would stop Soviet intervention in Middle East. . . . Lloyd and Dixon minimised their Charter obligations saying it was monstrous to let small nations get away with aggression against them whilst accusing Great Powers of aggression when they acted in self defence. Lloyd said US had been guilty of aggression in

Guatemala under Charter, but that we had been quite right in acting as we had there. Dixon said, in an aside, UK could not be held to so-called Charter principles they did not believe in. He felt question of force should have been argued out a month ago. Towards end of conversation, we discussed question of clearing Canal and Lloyd said a large UK fleet was converging on Canal for that purpose and would reach there in a fortnight. . . . Lloyd made it clear that he was so determined to have a strong force in Egypt – either Anglo-French or a really strong international force – that he was quite willing to risk Soviet intervention. His attitude struck me as reckless and full of contradictions. It has made me more pessimistic about the British than anything that has happened in my service here.

Recommended action:

1 He may be going to Washington this weekend to see the Secretary. I recommend that either Dulles or Hoover tell him we are strongly behind the cease-fire and withdrawal and want the Anglo-French forces withdrawn on phased basis with the entry of the international force just as fast as possible.

2 If he does not go to Washington, I recommend that I be authorised to tell him this flatly here. He is in a dangerous state of mind which could touch off a war, and which, I understand, reflects Eden's view.

3 We should be prepared to face distinct possibility that British and French will not agree to get out because of their doubts that the UN force will be strong enough to suit them.

4 A further declaration of support by the President for the speedy unobstructed entry of the international force and the speedy withdrawal of the Anglo-French force would be a powerful help. If the President decided to make such a statement he might consider making it here – which would fortify the effect.

Source: FRUS (C), 1988, telegram from the mission at the United Nations to the Department of State, 14 November 1956, document 575, pp. 1123-1125

The belligerent tone of this robust defence of Britain's actions by Lloyd no doubt reflected, in part, Lloyd's frustrations. It left Lodge, however, largely unmoved and fearful of the consequences of such an unyielding attitude on the part of the British Cabinet. Hence, his advice to the Secretary of State and the President to maintain a firm line on the desirability of British withdrawal.

Document 4.19 Aerial View of Blockships in the Canal, 26 November 1956

Source: Hulton-Deutsch Collection

In confirmation of this American hard line the British were informed on 15 November 1956 at an Organisation of European Economic Co-operation meeting that no oil supplies would be forthcoming until Britain had accepted American conditions for withdrawal from Egypt. On 17 November, however, the British Cabinet, discussing Lloyd's activities at the United Nations, still felt that it could continue to hold the line. A change was, however, not long in arriving and once again Macmillan was the key figure, not least because Eden had told his colleagues of his intention to recuperate in Jamaica and Lloyd was absent in the United States. On the afternoon of 18 November 1956 Macmillan called on the American Ambassador, Aldrich at his official residence.

Document 4.20 Macmillan and Salisbury Hint at Change of British policy, 19 November 1956

Macmillan said that it was evident that British Government may be faced within the next few days with the terrible dilemma of either (a) withdrawing from Egypt having accomplished nothing but to have brought about the entry into Egypt of a completely inadequate token force of troops representing the UN, whose only function is to police the border between Israel and Egypt, without having secured the free operation of the Canal or even being in a position to clear it, or (b) renewing hostilities in Egypt and taking over the entire Canal in order to remove the obstructions which have been placed there by Nasser and to insure its free operation and to avoid the complete economic collapse of Europe within the next few months. The danger of course in the minds of the British Cabinet of adopting the first alternative is that loss of prestige and humiliation would be so great that the govt must fall, while the second alternative would obviously involve the risk of bringing in the Russians and resulting in a third world war.

Macmillan said that faced with this desperate choice some members of the Cabinet would undoubtedly be willing to take the risk of the second alternative and go down fighting, but he said that he and Salisbury believed that if through a message from the President to Eden or in some other manner the British Government could be assured that the United States Government intends to pursue a policy of obtaining through action of the United Nations the immediate clearance of obstructions from the Canal and its operation by an international agency in accordance with the principles developed at the first London conference on Suez a majority of the Cabinet would chose the first of these alternatives and would not only withdraw the British forces but would also bring pressure on the French to withdraw their forces from Egypt at once. It would not be contemplated that the assurances to which I have just referred would be in the form of any agreement nor could they be made public.

I believe that the situation which is causing Macmillan and Salisbury to think along the lines I have just indicated is the realisation of the desperate financial position in which they will find themselves at the end of the year unless by that time they are working in the closest possible co-operation with the US in both the economic and political fields. Macmillan indicated yesterday that the month of November may show a loss of 200 or 300 millions of dollar balances and he is of course faced at the end of the year with the payment of something like $180 million of the annual payment on the British debt to the US and Canada. If in order to meet these payments he has not been able to draw on the Monetary Fund and borrow on his securities from the Federal Reserve Bank . . . he fears that there may be a real panic regarding sterling. Perhaps the above is only another way of saying that the British Cabinet is beginning to realise what a terrible mistake has been made and appreciate the fact that the only thing which can save them is the immediate and intimate co-operation with the US through the agency of the United Nations. Whether or not the government would fall under these conditions is anyone's guess, but I believe that leaders such as Macmillan and Salisbury feel that if they can make their colleagues understand that the ultimate support of the US has not been lost the government still could count on the votes of a sufficient number of Conservative backbenchers to insure a majority for the government in favour of withdrawal from Egypt in state to [spite of] the fact that no satisfactory arrangement had yet been entered into with Nasser regarding the Canal. To put it in its simplest form I would say that the British Cabinet is prepared to withdraw from Egypt now and leave to the UN the settlement of the problems involved in the relations between Israel and the Arab world and the problems relating to the operation of the Canal provided that the tremendous moral influence and power of the President will be continuously brought to bear on the UN to insure through the UN the ultimate solution of these terrible problems in accordance with justice and international law. . . .

It is perhaps interesting to note also in connection with the above, that as Secretary knows, both Macmillan and Salisbury have been among the most bellicose members of the Cabinet during entire Suez crisis.

Source: FRUS (C), 1988, telegram from the Embassy in the United Kingdom to the Department of State, 19 November 1956, document 588, pp. 1150–1152.

This remarkable account of a candid conversation between two of the most hawkish members of the British Cabinet and the American Ambassador signifies the beginning of an acceptance of withdrawal by the British government. The Chancellor appears to have realised, somewhat belatedly, the consequences of the British action and the dependence of the British on American goodwill. Moreover, this conversation also marks the beginnings of the struggle for the leadership of the Conservative Party and the government as Macmillan sought to build links with the American administration.

The full impact of the financial position was becoming more and more apparent to the British Cabinet as November wore on. On 19 November a high-level meeting of the Treasury and the Bank of England informed Macmillan that

> . . . it would probably be impossible to hold the currency and a 'catastrophe course' would have to be followed. This would involve leaving the pound to float freely with such support as might be decided from time to time. It would probably lead to the break-up of the sterling area (possibly even dissolution of the Commonwealth), the collapse of E[uropean] P[ayments] U[nion], a reduction in the volume of trade and currency instability at home leading to severe inflation. The Chancellor agreed. The right course was to maintain the currency by all means within our power and he would submit this intention to the Cabinet on the following day.
>
> **(PRO T236/4189, 19 November 1956)**

In the Cabinet Harold Macmillan for the first time appraised his colleagues fully of the dire situation confronting the country.

Document 4.21 Macmillan Reveals the Economic Position to the Cabinet, 20 November 1956

The Chancellor of the Exchequer said that the Cabinet might shortly face the grave choice of deciding whether to mobilise all our financial resources in order to maintain the sterling/dollar rate at its present level, or to let the rate find its own level with the possible consequence that sterling might cease to be an international currency. The latter course, which would lead almost inevitably to the dissolution of the sterling area, would be a severe blow to the prestige of the UK and a major victory for the Soviet Union. Moreover, there could be no certainty that even a floating rate would not need to be supported on a scale which might entail almost as great a demand on our reserves as the maintenance of a fixed rate.

The Chancellor of the Exchequer said that during the first week in December he would have to announce the loss of gold and dollars during November. This figure might be as high as $300 million and the shock both to public opinion in this country and to international confidence in sterling would be serious. Nevertheless there was a reasonable chance that if we maintained the existing sterling/dollar rate and mobilised our financial resources as rapidly and effectively as circumstances allow, we could maintain the sterling area in being and preserve sterling as a major international currency. We could not look for any assistance from the US in this course until the situation in the Middle East had been sufficiently clarified to enable us to re-establish our normal political relations with the US Government. But, although our formal approach to the US would be premature at the present time, we should endeavour to establish informal contact with them through the Treasury Delegation in Washington in order gradually to enlist their support for the loans which we should have to raise both by exercising our drawing right in the IMF and by pledging our own dollar securities in the American market. If we were assured of the goodwill of the US in this respect it might be possible for us to declare simultaneously with the announcement of the loss of gold and dollars during November, our determination to maintain the existing sterling/dollar rate and to restore the economy by means of appropriate internal and external policies.

In a brief discussion it was emphasised that there was increasing evidence that unofficial opinion in the US was showing a greater understanding of our policy in the Middle East. We should do all we could to ensure that our actions and motives were presented to public opinion in the US as fully and convincingly as possible.

Source: PRO CAB 128/30 Pt II, CM 85 (56), 20 November 1956

This exposition by the Chancellor of the economic cost of the Suez Crisis and Operation MUSKETEER must have come as something of a shock to the Cabinet although the Chancellor himself had been well aware of the likely outcome for some time. It is indicative of Macmillan's style that the American Ambassador knew about the condition of the British economy before Macmillan's Cabinet colleagues. Again, it was stressed that the only salvation lay in the hands of the United States. No doubt shocked by this bombshell, the Cabinet seemed unable to grasp the full implications of the position. It took a further, even more harsh, memorandum by the Treasury to stir the Cabinet into the necessary action. On 22 November 1956 Rowan informed Makins and Macmillan that

> if we are to have any real chance of succeeding in our crash action, or better still of avoiding the necessity for it the first essential is the re-establishment of relations with the United States. It is quite clear that there is a conflict between economic and political considerations, and that the longer political considerations are allowed to prevail the greater danger there is to the whole fabric of our currency.
>
> **(PRO T236/4190, 22 November 1956)**

A Cabinet meeting the same day began the process of acceding to American demands by authorising a 'token' withdrawal of British forces, while a full withdrawal would be contingent upon clearance of the Canal and negotiations on the future status and operation of the Canal.

This was not enough to convince the sceptics within the State Department and Treasury in Washington of the sincerity of the British: Hoover and Humphrey continually informed Caccia and Lloyd that a resumption of relations along with the provision of financial aid was contingent upon 'full compliance with UN resolutions' and that 'introduction of UN force and phased withdrawal UK–French force should take place without delay and that once this is well under way we can enter into consultation with the British on basic issues' **(FRUS (C), 1988, doc. 605)**. Although an increasingly cordial relationship between Macmillan and the administration was being built up through the channel of Aldrich, a frosty atmosphere continued to mar Anglo-American contacts in New York and Washington. As Selwyn Lloyd reported to R.A. Butler, acting Prime Minister in Eden's absence,

> ... the hard core of policy-makers some of whom have been strongly pro-British in the past are now against us. This will continue until we have made what they would regard as the *amende honourable* by rapid withdrawal. Their feeling is that we have to purge our contempt of the President in some way ... if we are going to have difficulty with the Party over announcing withdrawal I think we may have to tell certain selected individuals that the Americans have no intention of lifting a finger to help preserve us from financial disaster until they are certain that we are removing ourselves from Port Said quickly.
>
> **(PRO PREM 11/1106, 27 November 1956)**

For a week, with Cabinet meetings virtually every day, the British attempted to work towards some face-saving compromise that would allow them to withdraw from the ill-fated enterprise with as much dignity as possible. However, the build up of financial and diplomatic pressures was by now irresistible, particularly because early in December the full extent of Britain's parlous economic position would be made embarrassingly public with the customary monthly release of the statement on reserves. As the Cabinet noted on 27 November,

> it was urgently necessary that we should re-establish satisfactory political relations with the United States. We should have to announce early in the following week, the extent of the drain on our reserves of gold and dollars during November and it was desirable that we should have secured by then the support of the United States Government for the action which we should need to take to support sterling.
>
> **(PRO CAB 128/30 Pt II, 27 November 1956)**

The direct contacts between the ad hoc British team of Butler and Macmillan was successful in buying time to make the necessary painful decisions because Eisenhower, a convalescent Dulles, Hoover and Humphrey were now prepared to allow the British a short period of grace: the unacceptable alternative for the American administration was to accept potential long-term damage to the western diplomatic alliance and the international economic system.

The fateful decisions were taken somewhat ambiguously in two Cabinet meetings on 28 and 29 of November. Lloyd, having returned from New York in the morning, briefed the Cabinet in the afternoon of 28 November about the position in the United Nations.

Document 4.22 The Cabinet Accepts Defeat, 28 November 1956

The Foreign Secretary said that in his judgement the economic considerations were now even more important than the political. We could probably sustain our position in the United Nations for three or four weeks; but, so far from gaining anything by deferring a withdrawal of the Anglo-French force which we could, if we wished, complete within the next fortnight, we should thereby risk losing the good will of public opinion, which in all countries wished the clearance of the Canal to proceed as rapidly as possible. On the other hand if we withdrew the Anglo-French force as rapidly as was practicable, we should regain the sympathy of the United States Government. We should be better placed to ask for their support in any economic measures which we might need to take; and we should have removed as far as lay within our power all impediments to the further clearance of the Canal. But we could not properly maintain (and should not seek to do so) that our withdrawal of the Anglo-French force was dependent on a firm guarantee that clearance of the Canal would proceed forthwith. It was unlikely that the Secretary-General of the United Nations would be either able or willing to give such a guarantee and it would be preferable that we should base our action on our previous undertaking that the Anglo-French force would be withdrawn as soon as its place was taken by an effective United Nations force, which was competent to carry out the functions assigned to it by the General Assembly. This point would shortly be reached and it would therefore be possible for the Cabinet, if they agreed, to authorise the withdrawal of the Anglo-French force while emphasising that this action was based on our confident expectation that rapid progress would now be made by the United Nations towards the clearance of the Canal, an agreement about its satisfactory administration thereafter and a comprehensive settlement of the long-term problems of the Middle East.

The Chancellor of the Exchequer said that it would be necessary to announce early in the following week the losses of gold and dollars which we had sustained during November. This statement would reveal a very serious drain on the reserves and would be a considerable shock both to public opinion in this country and to international confidence in sterling. It was therefore important that we should be able to announce at the same time that we were taking action to reinforce the reserves both by recourse to the International Monetary Fund and in other ways. For this purpose the good will of the United States Government was necessary; and it was evident that this good will could not be obtained without an immediate and unconditional undertaking to withdraw the Anglo-French force from Port Said. He therefore favoured a prompt announcement of our intention to withdraw this force, justifying this action on the ground that we had now achieved the purpose for which we had originally launched the Anglo-French military operation against Egypt and that we were content to leave the United Nations, backed by the United States, the responsibility, which the General Assembly could now be deemed to have accepted for settling the problems of the Middle East. . . .

The Lord Privy Seal said that it appeared to be the preponderant view of the Cabinet that we should announce, in the next few days, that we were now prepared to withdraw the Anglo-French force from Port Said as rapidly as possible, in the faith that the United Nations had now accepted responsibility for securing the objectives for which we had originally begun military operations against Egypt. It would, however, be necessary to secure the agreement of the French Government to this proposal and to take such steps as time allowed to secure United States and Commonwealth support for action on these lines.

Source: PRO CAB 128/30 Pt II, CM 90 (56), 28 November 1956

Here, at last, the condition of the economy took precedence over face-saving operations on the ground in Egypt: Harold Macmillan led the *volte face* by the British Cabinet by agreeing to withdraw the British forces from the Canal area in the hope of securing American aid.

At the Cabinet meeting the next day, Macmillan, having received a number of trenchant Treasury papers spelling out the magnitude of the disaster confronting the government, informed his colleagues of the position at the end of November.

Document 4.23 The Continuing Necessity for American Aid, 29 November 1956

The Chancellor of the Exchequer said that during November there had been a serious drain on our reserves of gold and dollars . . . in November, the final net loss which would be announced was likely to be about $270 million. In the third week of the month alone we had lost over $100 million . . . the announcement of the November figures, which must be made no later than 4th December, would shake confidence in sterling still further, and would be a severe shock to the stability of the sterling area. These effects could only be mitigated if it were possible, when the announcement was made, to indicate plainly the government's intention to take firm measures to remedy the situation. The Chancellor of the Exchequer said that these measures fell under three heads. Firstly, he wished to be able to say that we were at once proceeding to exercise our drawing rights in the IMF and to seek dollar loans against the collateral security of government held stocks. Secondly, it must be apparent that we were taking effective steps to repair the breach in our political relations with the United States Government. . . . Thirdly, some measures for strengthening our domestic economy should be announced at the same time. It was not enough that we should seek to overcome our difficulties merely by borrowing dollars: it must also be apparent that we were ready to accept some measure of sacrifice at home. . . .

The Cabinet recognised the gravity of the situation disclosed by this statement and agreed that urgent action must be taken to remedy it. They supported the measures which the Chancellor proposed to take to this end. In particular, they endorsed his view that the Government should not appear to be seeking to meet the situation solely by borrowing dollars and that supplementary action should be taken at the same time to strengthen the national economy.

Source: PRO CAB 128/30 Pt II, CM 91 (56), 29 November 1956

Two days later Macmillan informed the Cabinet that the position was even worse, that the reserves had fallen below the benchmark figure of $2,000 million and that the month of December would commence with a net loss of $300 million. In the light of this 'no fundamental improvement in the situation could be expected unless we succeeded in re-establishing normal political relations with the United States' **(PRO CAB 128/30 Pt II, 1 December 1956)**. On the morning of 3 December 1956 the Cabinet drafted an announcement of withdrawal which was delivered by the unfortunate Selwyn Lloyd in the House of Commons that afternoon. Although, as Kyle notes, Lloyd attempted to claim MUSKETEER was a success which now enabled the Anglo-French forces to withdraw, their 'peace-keeping' task complete, it was a clear statement of defeat **(Kyle, 1991, p. 514)**. Anglo-French forces were to be withdrawn unconditionally from Port Said as soon as possible on a schedule to be agreed with the new commander of the UNEF, General Burns.

Having secured this act of contrition the American administration moved swiftly to provide the support so desperately needed by the British. Indeed high-level negotiations in both London and Washington had taken place since the last week of November to ensure that there should be no hiatus between the British statement of withdrawal and the beginning of American assistance: the previously hostile Humphrey informed Caccia on 2 December 1956 that 'if and when the green light was given [Britain] could look forward to "massive support"' **(PRO FO 371/120816, 3 December 1956)**. American coffers were now opened to the financially embarrassed British: Britain could draw $561 million from the IMF, with the possibility of further credit of $738 million in the future, to replenish the depleted dollar reserves. A loan of $500 million was raised with the Exim Bank to purchase dollar products, notably oil. The scheduled repayment of the Anglo-American loan was waived. In addition to this financial largesse, the hitherto absent verbal support was now forthcoming from Washington from figures such as Vice-President Nixon as well as Eisenhower and Dulles **(Johnman, 1989, pp. 176–177; Kyle, 1991, p. 514; Lucas, 1991 p. 318)**.

With the last troops of the Anglo-French forces leaving Egypt on 22 December 1956, and with the Anglo-French salvage fleet allowed only a minimal role in the clearance of the Canal, MUSKETEER came to an ignominious conclusion. The Anglo-French operation had achieved precisely the opposite of what Eden and his colleagues had intended in late July 1956. The attempt to ensure free transit through the Canal resulted in a six-month blockage and the aim of international-ising the Canal ended in failure. Oil supplies from the Middle East were so disrupted that petrol rationing had to be instituted in Britain. Nasser, the main target of the operation, remained firmly in power in Cairo with enhanced prestige throughout the Arab world. More seriously, the limitations of Britain's power were starkly revealed by the actions of the United States in November 1956. After Suez, the 'illusion' of Britain as an independent world power could no longer be sustained, although Conservative and Labour governments were to try to do precisely that with decreasing success for the next twelve years.

Chronology November–December 1956

31 October   Anglo-French air attacks against Egyptian targets; UN Security Council calls emergency meeting of General Assembly; Selwyn Lloyd denies collusion in House of Commons

1 November   Gaitskell attacks government; Commons suspended in disorder; Israelis defeat Egyptian forces in Sinai; Commonwealth countries denounce British actions in General Assembly; American cease-fire resolution passed by General Assembly

2 November   General Assembly calls for cease-fire

3 November   Israel apparently accepts cease-fire on condition that Egypt does the same

4 November   Suez Canal blocked; Israel rejects cease-fire; Cabinet split on launching of invasion

5 November   British and French paratroop invasion launched; Bulganin note threatens rocket attacks; Israel accepts cease-fire

6 November	Anglo-French seaborne landings begin; sterling in crisis – reserves critical; Macmillan counsels acceptance of cease-fire; Eden announces cease-fire for midnight
7 November	General Assembly authorises UN Expeditionary Force for Egypt; Treasury officials inform Macmillan that $85 million has been lost from sterling reserves in the previous week
8 November	Vote of confidence in the House of Commons
15 November	Egypt Committee informed that no US aid forthcoming until withdrawal of Anglo-French from the Canal Zone commenced
20 November	Macmillan apprises colleagues of 'dire' economic position
22 November	Cabinet agrees to token withdrawal of forces pending further negotiations on future clearance and operation of Canal; Treasury warns that political considerations are overriding economic considerations
23 November	Eden flies to Jamaica for 'rest'
30 November	Cabinet accepts unconditional withdrawal from Egypt
1 December	Macmillan informs Cabinet that no US economic assistance would be forthcoming unless complete withdrawal announced
3 December	Cabinet authorise public announcement of withdrawal of troops
14 December	Eden returns to London
20 December	Eden lies to House of Commons on 'foreknowledge'
22 December	Evacuation of British troops from Egypt completed
9 January 1957	Eden resigns as Prime Minister – replaced by Macmillan.

The Suez Crisis of 1956 has been commonly seen as a pivotal moment in post-war British history, the moment at which Britain's pretensions to world power status were stripped away. The impact of Suez is, however, perhaps more ambiguous than would appear at first glance. This chapter will examine the two main areas of concern: British domestic politics and Britain's external policies.

5.1 The Domestic Impact of the Suez Crisis 1957–1959

The most spectacular casualty of Suez was, of course, the Prime Minister, Anthony Eden. Eden had returned from his rest-cure in Jamaica on 14 December 1956 and was initially quite recalcitrant in his attitude towards Suez, appearing confident that he could and should remain in office. On 18 December, addressing the influential 1922 Committee of the Conservative Party, the Prime Minister implied that lack of American support was the main reason for the failure at Suez: 'we have been patient with the United States over a long-time . . . we might have expected something in return' **(Thomas, 1986, p. 224)**.

The Prime Minister's bullishness was however to be rapidly undermined by developments in two quarters. First, as was only to be expected, the Labour Party attempted in the House of Commons, with some degree of success, to exploit the issue of collusion to apply pressure to the tottering government. On 20 December Eden was forced into a straightforward lie saying that 'There were no plans got together to attack Egypt . . . there was not foreknowledge that Israel would attack Egypt – there was not' **(Hansard, 20 December 1956)**. This was to be Eden's last appearance as Prime Minister before the House. Second, Eden rapidly realised that there was a move to displace him as Prime Minister from within his own Cabinet. During Eden's absence in Jamaica, Macmillan had used the channels opened through Aldrich to Eisenhower to discuss not only the financial position but also the question of Cabinet changes. As Winthrop Aldrich observed following a conversation with Macmillan on 18 November, the very day Eden announced his intention to recuperate in Jamaica 'I cannot help wondering whether . . . some sort of movement is on foot in the Cabinet to replace Eden' **(FRUS (C), 1988 doc. 588)**. He repeated this in a wire to Washington the following day in much more dramatic terms.

Document 5.1.1 Macmillan Forecasts Eden's Downfall, 19 November 1956

Macmillan came to residence tonight at his request. . . . Eden has had physical breakdown and will have to go on vacation immediately, first for one week and then for another, and this will lead to his retirement. Government will be run by triumvirate of Butler, Macmillan and Salisbury. While Macmillan did not say so specifically, I gather that eventual set up will be Butler Prime Minister, Macmillan Foreign Secretary, Lloyd Chancellor of the Exchequer, with Salisbury remaining Lord President of Council. Possibly Macmillan might be Prime Minister. First action after Eden's departure for reasons of health will be on withdrawal of British troops from Egypt. Macmillan said, 'if you can give us a fig leaf to cover our nakedness I believe we can get a majority of the Cabinet to vote for such withdrawal without requiring conditions in connection with location of United Nations forces and methods of re-opening and operating Canal although younger members of the Cabinet will be strongly opposed'.

Source: FRUS (C), 1988, telegram from the Embassy in the United Kingdom to the Department of State, 19 November 1956, document 593, p. 1163

A few days later, Aldrich would also wire the astonishing information that Macmillan had indicated to him that 'British Cabinet changes which he [Macmillan] has previously forecast will take place within the next few days' **(FRUS (C), 1988, doc. 602)**. Eisenhower was prepared to deal with either Macmillan or Butler or both, although he had a strong preference for Macmillan, his former colleague from the Second World War campaign in North Africa.

In the event the removal of Eden was to take longer than the 'conspirators' envisaged. By the end of the year Eden's health had deteriorated further and he himself had begun to realise that perhaps it was time to leave office, given that he could no longer count on the support of backbenchers in the House or his senior colleagues in the Cabinet. On 8 January 1957 Eden saw the Queen at Sandringham and proffered his resignation formally the next day. It is ironic that a politician noted for his sure touch in foreign affairs was brought down by the field in which he had made his reputation and which was supposedly his forte. Forced to relinquish the premiership, to which he had succeeded after five years as Churchill's deputy, his reputation never fully recovered despite his elevation to the House of Lords as Lord Avon.

The question remained, who would be the leader of the party and the Cabinet. The two main contenders were Butler and Macmillan. In November it had seemed as if Butler was the natural successor, but opinion on the backbenches increasingly shifted towards the apparently more resolute Macmillan. However, leaders of the Conservative Party in the 1950s were not elected by the ballot box: instead the patrician figure of Lord Salisbury was invited by the Queen to take soundings among the Cabinet and senior party figures with the result that

Macmillan was invited to take over as Prime Minister. It is also ironic that the man who had been one of the most hawkish supporters of military action, in the full knowledge of the dire consequences that this would have for the British economy for which he was responsible as Chancellor of the Exchequer, was the major beneficiary of the political upheaval caused by Suez. His succession to the premiership no doubt owed much to his sudden *volte face* in early November; he was characterised by the acerbic Brendan Bracken as 'leader of the bolters' **(Kyle, 1991, p. 508)**, which allowed him to pose as a resolute figure able and willing to take harsh decisions: the fact that the necessity for these harsh decisions was due in no small part to his own posturing was left conveniently obscure.

The new Cabinet differed little from the Eden Cabinet; only two junior ministers had resigned over Suez, Nutting and Edward Boyle, and consequently only a minor reshuffle was necessary to accommodate the elevation of Macmillan to Prime Minister. Macmillan's first priority had to be to stabilise the government and party in the wake of Suez. The party that Macmillan was leading was still essentially that of Churchill, wedded to the Empire and certain of Britain's world role; any substantial change in such fundamental policies required that Macmillan be master in his own house by fashioning a government more in his own image and having that government receive the mandate of a general election victory.

Document 5.1.2 Macmillan as the 'New Manager', January 1957

Curiously, the Suez débâcle had little effect on the electoral fortunes of the Conservative Party. Despite the continuing attempts of the Labour Party to make political capital out of the affair, aided by the fact that the same personnel were in the Cabinet, the Conservative Party proved remarkably resilient. Foreign affairs is rarely a matter that excites domestic political passion and exercises influence on voting intentions in Britain, and as Epstein's study of British politics 1956–1959 reveals the Suez issue was no exception to this. The issue was confined broadly to the normal lines of party politics: that is to say the normal supporters of the Conservative Party would continue to support the Conservative Party and the normal supporters of the Labour Party would continue to support Labour. Suez, while arousing considerable partisan feelings, was not an issue that was likely to generate large shifts in voting patterns; indeed, Epstein's studies of opinion polls and by-elections in the period 1956–1959, in addition to the general election of 1959, show little or no perceptible impact. It was therefore no surprise that the Conservative Party went on to win the 1959 election, which was fought almost solely on domestic issues. **(Epstein, 1964, pp. 199–210)**. Periodically Suez and notably 'collusion' was raised in the House of Commons but to little effect as Suez was a non-issue in party political terms.

Source: Punch, *16 January 1957*

5.2 'Winds of Change': The Suez Crisis and Britain's World Role 1957–1968

The decade after the Suez crisis was perhaps the most dramatic in terms of Britain's role in the world since the Second World War. It saw the rapid decolonisation of Britain's empire in Africa, the first application to join the EEC and the final withdrawal from bases East of Suez. Yet, historians are divided over the influence that the catastrophe of the Suez débâcle had on the course of British external policy: Brian Lapping has argued that Suez was at the root of these radical changes in British policy, while Anthony Low has posited that the only impact of Suez was perhaps to accelerate changes that were already in train, in real terms he argues Suez had little or no effect **(Lapping, 1987; Low, 1987 pp. 31–33)**. While it is difficult for the historian to prove a negative without erecting a sterile counterfactual model, it would seem that Suez had the effect of revealing reality and forcing the new Macmillan administration to take painful steps that had been foreshadowed.

Immediately prior to his resignation Anthony Eden set out his thoughts on the lessons of Suez for future British policy. Sent to senior Cabinet ministers, this informal letter represented a radical statement by the still Prime Minister and an acknowledged expert in foreign affairs.

Document 5.2.1 Eden on the Lessons of Suez, 28 December 1956

We have to try and assess the lessons of Suez. The first is that if we are to play an independent part in the world, even on a more modest scale than we have done heretofore, we must ensure our financial and economic independence. Since we have no raw materials but coal, this means that we must excel in technical knowledge. This in its turn affects our military plans.

Too many of our scientists are working for the fighting Services. I think that I have seen a figure of two-thirds. Anything of this order cannot be accepted at the present time. On the other hand, some progress with the military aspects of the development of the hydrogen bomb can no doubt be useful for civil purposes also. It seems therefore that we have need to keep the balance between civil and military development, leaning rather more towards the former in our nuclear programme.

In the strategic sphere we have to do some re-thinking about our areas of influence and the military bases on which they must rest. Some of the latter seem of doubtful value in the light of our Suez experience.

What return for instance do we get for our armoured division in Tripoli and Libya? If the purpose is to prevent this part of North Africa falling under Egyptian dominion could that not be ensured more cheaply? We shall still need the air facilities at El Adem as well as Cyprus if we are to be sure of reaching the Persian Gulf, which is today our most important overseas commitment. But do we need armour in Tripoli itself? And would not a smaller garrison be sufficient if one is needed at all? If we apply the same considerations to the Indian Ocean can we not now dispense with the Ceylon Naval base altogether, using the Maldives instead for the air? Can we not increase the integration of the Services so far as concerns our requirements at Singapore? Do we need so many troops in Malaya? It is at least certain that we must at once put an end to the Korean commitment. I would hope that we could move that battalion to Hong Kong.

One of the lessons of Suez is that we need a smaller force that is more mobile and more modern in its equipment. This probably means that we have in proportion to our total army too much armour and too much infantry and too small a paratroop force. We cannot contemplate keeping an army in Germany which is numerically much more than half its present numbers and the cost will have to come down proportionately. Mobility and quality in training rather than numbers would be our need.

[Passage deleted and retained under Section 3(4).]

At home the events of these months must create some deflation, though probably in geographically limited areas, eg the motor car industry in the West Midlands. This again may not be entirely unhealthy and if and when the oil begins to flow again the economy may be the healthier as a result. The most anxious fact on the home front is I think the alarming increase in the cost of the welfare state. Some of this, eg education, is a necessary part of our effort to maintain a leading position in new industrial developments. Other aspects of this spending are less directly related to our struggle for existence. I have long been anxious, as I know have the Lord Privy Seal and the Chancellor, to do something to encourage our younger and gifted leaders in science and industry to stay with us. The present burden of taxation leaves them with little incentive except patriotism. We shall not have adjusted our problems until the younger generation here can feel that they live in a community which is leading in industrial development and can reasonably expect a fair reward for their brains and application.

The conclusion of all this is surely that we must review our world position and our domestic capacity more searchingly in the light of the Suez experience which has not so much changed our fortunes as revealed realities. While the consequences of this examination may be to determine us to work more closely with Europe, carrying with us, we hope our closest friends in the Commonwealth in such development, here too we must be under no illusion. Europe will not welcome us simply because at the moment it may appear to suit us to look to them. The timing and the conviction of our approach may be decisive in their influence on those with whom we plan to work.

Source: PRO PREM 11/1138, Sir Anthony Eden, 'Thoughts on the general position after Suez', 28 December 1956

The deletion above illustrates a new trend in release policy under the Thirty Year rule. Although this document should technically have been released in 1987, it was considered too sensitive to release at that time. Under the Open Government policy this document was released in 1993 with a passage deleted: instead of retaining the whole document, the trend is now towards 'censoring' the relevent passages.

The shocks of early November 1956 had clearly driven Eden to acknowledge the necessity for a wide-ranging review, embracing domestic as well as external policy. This was a continuation of a trend that was marked even before Suez in that since 1945 periodically British governments, struggling to balance the expenditure on a world role with the creation and maintenance of the welfare state, had periodically indulged in similar exercises. In the summer of 1956 the Policy Review Committee had just such terms of reference but was temporarily derailed by the Suez Crisis itself. Further committees, including the Future Policy Committee, were established in the wake of Suez but had a very low priority and indeed did not produce their final reports until 1961.

In January 1957 Lloyd picked up on Eden's note and proposed in Cabinet a fresh approach to Europe involving British participation in political and economic initiatives. His colleagues were sharply divided about both the merits and the timing of this proposal and left this initiative to hang. In the meantime the new Cabinet was forced to respond to the gravity of the country's immediate situation. The economic and financial crisis created by Suez had exacerbated the already shaky foundations of Britain's budgetary position, and in January 1957 Macmillan and his new Chancellor, Peter Thorneycroft, were forced into a realisation that drastic measures would be necessary if a balanced budget was to be achieved for the next financial year starting in April 1957. The Prime Minister gave the following summary to the Cabinet in April 1957.

Document 5.2.2 Macmillan on the Need for Economies, 21 January 1957

Defence and Social Services, however desirable they might be in themselves, would be of no avail if the attempt to sustain them at unrealistic levels resulted in the collapse of the economy. If the necessary retrenchment in expenditure could be achieved, the nation could reasonably look forward to better times when the immediate crisis had been overcome and the massive programmes of investment began to bear fruit. The problem of achieving essential economies in the short term must be solved in such a way so as not to prejudice the formulation of sound policies for the long-term, especially in the case of defence.

Source: PRO CAB 128/31, CC (57)2, 21 January 1957

The two areas of saving identified were the social services, notably education and the National Health Service, and defence. In the intense debates that followed it was concluded that the welfare budget could not be cut, that any shortfall in this area had to be made up by an increase in insurance contributions, and that it was in the area of defence policy that savings could and should be made. This was the background to the influential Sandys White Paper on Defence of April 1957.

Document 5.2.3 The Sandys White Paper, April 1957

3 . . . The time has now come to revise not merely the size, but the whole character of the defence plan. The Communist threat remains, but its nature has changed; and it is now evident that, on both military and economic grounds, it is necessary to make a fresh appreciation of the problem and to adopt a new approach towards it. . . .

DEMANDS ON ECONOMIC RESOURCES

6 Britain's influence in the world depends first and foremost on the health of her internal economy and the success of her export trade. Without these, military power cannot in the long run be supported. It is therefore in the true interests of defence that the claims of military expenditure should be considered in conjunction with the need to maintain the country's financial and economic strength.

7 Over the last five years, defence has on average absorbed ten per cent of Britain's gross national product. Some seven per cent of the working population are either in the Services or supporting them. One-eighth of the output of the metal-using industries, upon which the export trade so largely depends is devoted to defence. An undue proportion of qualified scientists and engineers are engaged on military work. In addition, the retention of such large forces abroad gives rise to heavy charges which place a severe strain upon the balance of payments. . . .

NUCLEAR DETERRENT

12 It must be frankly recognised that there is at present no means of providing adequate protection for the people of this country against the consequences of an attack with nuclear weapons. Though, in the event of war, the fighter aircraft of the Royal Air Force would unquestionably be able to take a heavy toll of enemy bombers, a proportion would inevitably get through. Even if it were only a dozen, they could with megaton bombs inflict widespread devastation. . . .

15 The free world is to-day mainly dependent for its protection upon the nuclear capacity of the United States. While Britain cannot by comparison make more than a modest contribution, there is a wide measure of agreement that she must possess an appreciable element of nuclear deterrent power of her own. British atomic bombs are already in steady production,

and the Royal Air Force holds a substantial number of them. A British megaton weapon has now been developed. This will shortly be tested and thereafter a stock will be manufactured.

16 The means of delivering these weapons is provided at present by medium bombers of the V-class, whose performance and speed and altitude is comparable to that of any bomber aircraft now in service in any other country. It is the intention that these should be supplemented by ballistic rockets. Agreement in principle has recently been reached with the United States Government for the supply of some medium-range missiles of this type. . . .

MANPOWER REQUIREMENTS

40 Provided that the services are reshaped and redistributed on the lines indicated above and that commitments are curtailed in the manner proposed, the Government are satisfied that Britain could discharge her overseas responsibilities and make an effective contribution to the defence of the free world with armed forces much smaller than at present. . . .

43 National Service inevitably involves an uneconomic use of manpower, especially in the training organisation. There are at present no less than 150,000 men training or being trained in the establishments of the three Services. This high figure is due, in large measure, to the continuous turnover inseparable from National Service, the abolition of which would make possible substantial savings in manpower. . . .

46 In the light of the need to maintain a balanced distribution of the national resources the Government have made a comprehensive review of the demands of defence upon the economy and of the country's military responsibilities. They have concluded that it would be right to aim at stabilising the armed forces on an all-regular footing at a strength of about 375,000 by the end of 1962. This does not take account of Colonial troops and other forces enlisted overseas, which at present amount to about 60,000.

SWITCH OF RESOURCES

67 The new defence policy set out in this paper involves the biggest change in military policy ever made in normal times. In carrying it through a certain amount of disturbance is unavoidable.

68 The large reduction in the size of the armed forces will inevitably create some surplus of officers and NCOs. The proportion will differ for each Service and for the various ranks and branches. Those whose careers are to be prematurely terminated will be given fair compensation and will be helped in every way possible to find suitable employment in civilian life.

69 The volume of defence work of many kinds will be curtailed and some establishments will have to be closed. The manpower and industrial resources released must be absorbed into productive use as quickly as

possible; and the Government Departments concerned will do all they can to ensure that the switch is effected smoothly.

EXPENDITURE

70 The Defence Estimates for the year 1956/7 amounted to about £1,600 million, before deducting receipts from Germany and the United States. Had the programme as planned a year ago been allowed to continue unchanged, the figure for 1957/8 would have risen to about £1,700 million.

71 However, as a result of strenuous efforts to effect economy it has been found possible to keep the defence estimates for the coming year down to a total of £1,483 million. From this must be deducted receipts from Germany and the United States which are expected to be about £50 million and £13 million respectively. Thus the net estimate of total defence expenditure for 1957/8 will amount to about £1,420 million.

Source: Defence: Outline of Future Policy, *Parliamentary Papers, Cmd 124, April 1957*

This seemingly radical approach which stressed Britain's nuclear deterrent forces, the V bomber force, at the expense of conventional forces deployed overseas, including the ending of national service by 1960, was the culmination of a long-standing trend in British defence policy: defence spending was supposed to fall from 10 per cent of GNP in 1957 to 7 per cent in 1960. Again, Suez was the catalyst but not the primary cause of these changes. Moreover, the Sandys White Paper was simply an attempt to maintain Britain's position in the world in a more cost-effective way rather than a thoroughgoing reassessment of that position: the assumption of Britain's world role remained essentially unchanged.

The key to Britain's position in the world was the special relationship with the United States. The Bermuda Conference in March 1957 by which Britain was to receive some sixty Thor intermediate-range ballistic missiles from the United States (albeit controlled under a dual-key arrangement) publicly symbolised the restoration of the Anglo-American special relationship after the strains of the previous year, but in a very different context defined by the Eisenhower Doctrine of January 1957. The rationale behind the Eisenhower Doctrine was set out by Dulles on 2 January 1957 when he appeared before the Senate Committee on Foreign Relations.

Document 5.2.4 Dulles on British Weakness, 2 January 1957

Secretary Dulles. The fact is that it is more and more developing to be the fact that the British and the French are not going to be able to carry even the share of the so-called free world defense which they had been trying to carry up to the present time.

Their own difficulties are weakening them. The French position is very considerably weakened by the hostilities in North Africa. The British position has been greatly weakened by the effort which they made in the recent attack on Egypt.

Now, partly that created, partly it disclosed, the vulnerability of the British economic and financial position. But it brought the British to a realisation of the fact that they have got to cut their costs more.

They have been cutting these, and this present task of their Secretary of Defense Sandys reflects what they regard as the imperative necessity of getting a sounder economy by cutting out a good many of their military burdens, and particularly their overseas commitments.

Senator Russell. Well, I was not dealing with that in this series of questions. But as they do reduce theirs, the total strength of the free world is decreased, unless we fill whatever position they abandon, militarily and economically, is it not?

Secretary Dulles. Broadly speaking, that is so, yes. . . .

Source: ESSFRC, 1979, p. 91

The result of this logic was outlined in the President's statement to Congress on 5 January 1957. After reviewing the strategic importance of the Middle East Eisenhower outlined his Middle East policy.

Document 5.2.5 The Eisenhower Doctrine, 5 January 1957

Thus, we have the simple and indisputable facts;

1 The Middle East, which has always been coveted by Russia, would today be prized more than ever by International Communism.
2 The Soviet rulers continue to show that they do not scruple to use any means to gain their ends.
3 The free nations of the Mid-East need, and for the most part want, added strength to assure their continued independence. . . .

Seldom in history has a nation's dedication to principle been tested as severely as ours during recent weeks.

There is general recognition in the Middle East, as elsewhere, that the United States does not seek either political or economic domination over any other people. Our desire is a world environment of freedom, not servitude . . . if the Middle East is to continue its geographic role of uniting rather than separating East and West; if its vast economic resources are to serve the well-being of the peoples there, as well as that of others; and if its cultures and religions and their shrines are to be preserved for the uplifting of the spirits of the peoples, then the United States must make more evident its willingness to support the independence of the freedom-loving nations of the area. . . .

. . . weaknesses in the present situation and the increased danger from International Communism, convince me that basic United States policy should now find expression in joint action by the Congress and the Executive. Furthermore, our joint resolve should be so couched as to make it apparent that if need be our words will be backed by action. . . .

The action which I propose would have the following features.

It would, first of all, authorise the United States to cooperate with and assist any nation or group of nations in the general area of the Middle East in the development of economic strength dedicated to the maintenance of national independence.

It would, in the second place, authorise the Executive to undertake in the same region programs of military assistance and co-operation with any nation or group of nations which desires such aid.

It would, in the third place, authorise such assistance and co-operation to include the employment of the armed forces of the United States to secure and protect the territorial integrity and political independence of such nations, requesting such aid, against overt armed aggression from any nation controlled by International Communism. . . .

The present proposal would, in the fourth place, authorise the President to employ, for economic and defensive military purposes, sums available under the Mutual Security Act of 1954, as amended, without regard to existing limitations. . . .

I shall . . . seek in subsequent legislation the authorization of $200,000,000 to be available during each of the fiscal years 1958 and 1959 for discretionary use in the area, in addition to the other mutual security programmes for the area hereafter provided for by the Congress. . . .

. . . If power-hungry Communists should, either falsely or correctly, estimate, that the Middle East is inadequately defended, they might be tempted to use open measures of armed attack. If so, that would start a chain of circumstances which would almost surely involve the United States in military action. I am convinced that the best insurance against this dangerous contingency is to make clear now our readiness to cooperate fully and freely with our friends in the Middle East in ways consonant with the purposes and principles of the United Nations. I intend promptly to send a special mission to the Middle East to explain the co-operation we are prepared to give.

Source: PPPUS, pp. 6–16

This extension of American power to an area that had hitherto been an agreed British preserve was a not entirely unwelcome development for the British but it did represent a set-back to the idea of an independent British role in their traditional area of influence, the Middle East and Africa. Again, however, it should be asked how far the British had in any case been able to operate independently of the United States since the Second World War?

In terms of the Empire the process of decolonisation had more or less halted after Palestine in 1948 with the solitary exception of the unique case of the Sudan in 1956. In 1956, the British were preparing to withdraw from certain colonies, notably the Gold Coast and Malaya, but little further action was contemplated. Yet in the wake of Suez there was apparently a precipitate rush by Britain to rid itself of its remaining fragments of Empire: it is tempting to conclude that this process was a direct consequence of the disaster at Suez following a 'cost–benefit' analysis conducted in London. However, a close examination of the chronology of British decolonisation would indicate that Suez was not the primary cause. In 1957 the Gold Coast became independent, but this, of course, had been long in train. The major bulk of British decolonisation took place in the early 1960s with the major shift in British policy seemingly taking place following the 1959 election, which cleared the Conservative backbenches of some of their more atavistic elements, and the appointment of the progressive Iain Macleod as Colonial Secretary. These changes allowed Macmillan to make the most public expression of this shift in policy in his famous 'winds of change' speech given in Cape Town during his tour of South Africa.

Document 5.2.6 Speech by the Prime Minister, Harold Macmillan, to the South African Parliament, 3 February 1960

In the twentieth century, and especially since the end of the war, the processes which gave birth to the nation-states of Europe have been repeated all over the world. We have seen the awakening of national consciousness in peoples who have for centuries lived in dependence on some other power.

Fifteen years ago this movement spread through Asia. The most striking of all the impressions I have formed since I left London a month ago is of the strength of this African national consciousness. In different places it may take different forms but it is happening everywhere. The wind of change is blowing through the Continent.

Whether we like it or not, this growth of national consciousness is a political fact. We must all accept it as a fact. Our national policies must take account of it. . . .

. . . As I see it, the great issue in this second half of the twentieth century is whether the uncommitted peoples of Asia and Africa will swing to the east or to the west. Will they be drawn into the Communist camp? Or will the great experiments in self-government that are now being made in Asia and Africa, especially within the Commonwealth, prove so successful, and by their example so compelling, that the balance will come down in favour of freedom and order and justice?

Source: The Times, *4 February 1960*

This clearly portended an acceleration of British decolonisation in Africa. However, a number of caveats have to be entered around the simplistic assumptions that defeat at Suez caused British decolonisation. First, the policy of decolonisation had been set in train before Suez; what altered was the timing. Second, the very rapid ending of the French and Belgian Empires in Africa was in danger of leaving Britain as the sole major power that still possessed colonies. Third, this explanation is a Eurocentric perspective that ignores the potent force of African nationalism, the rise of which predated Suez, although the victory of Nasser at Suez was undoubtedly an inspiration to the African nationalists. Fourth, in the new era introduced by the Sandys White Paper Britain was unable and unwilling to fight increasingly costly colonial counter-insurgency wars given the precedents of Palestine, Malaya and Kenya. Again, the impact of Suez is not clear-cut but the fact remains that by 1964 Britain had substantially disentangled itself from its Empire.

Despite Eden's invocation of a turn towards Europe the initial Macmillan government showed little interest in the creation of the European Economic Community; indeed it fostered a rival to the EEC in the ill-fated European Free Trade Area. Commonwealth interests and the role of the Sterling Area remained of paramount importance to the British government. By 1959, however, two things were abundantly clear. First, in economic terms, the EEC was a resounding success and Britain's economic growth rate lagged significantly behind that of its main Western European competitors. Moreover, there had been a significant shift in Britain's trade patterns away from the Commonwealth and towards Europe. Second, in diplomatic terms, the government began to worry that the political success of the EEC threatened Britain's relationship with the United States in that America could base its alliance strategy around the EEC rather than Britain. The logic and benefits of isolation were therefore dubious. Indeed, there appeared to be compelling reasons for moving towards closer and more formal links with the EEC and the Macmillan government duly applied for membership in the summer of 1961. This application, however, ran up against the formidable figure of France's President, Charles de Gaulle, who organised the vetoing of British membership of the EEC in January 1963.

It is tempting to see the hand of Suez behind this change in British orientation. Significantly, however, it was not until five years after Suez that this first application was made. It is also arguable that the application was made not in a spirit of genuine co-operation but merely as a tactical device to balance Britain's diplomatic system between the United States, Europe and the emerging Commonwealth. Finally, it is clear that there were powerful economic reasons for this shift in British policy that had nothing to do with the Suez Crisis.

It might have been expected that the new Labour government of Harold Wilson, elected in 1964, would have had a distinctive perspective on Britain's role in the world having been out of office for the previous thirteen years. Nothing could be further from the truth however. Indeed, the new Prime Minister sounded little different from Ernest Bevin or Anthony Eden when he claimed in the early days of his administration that Britain had a world role to play 'one which no-one in this House, or indeed the country, will wish us to give up or call in question' **(Ovendale, 1994, p. 133)**.

Despite Wilson's rhetoric the economic climate of the 1960s was much worse than that of the mid-1950s. Full convertibility of sterling in 1958 had meant that holders of sterling were now able to sell it and buy other currencies without restriction: this rendered sterling highly vulnerable to currency movements and to speculation. Furthermore, the balance of payments position had steadily worsened since the mid-1950s. Net government spending abroad rose by over 200 per cent to £499 million between 1957 and 1967 largely because of Britain's overseas military commitments. Therefore the economy was prone to consistent balance of payments problems which in turn raised questions as to the value of the currency which now operated in a narrow band (+ or − 2 per cent) of £1 to $2.80. Accordingly, therefore, with very limited reserves the maintenance of international confidence was of paramount importance to the stability of sterling.

By 1964 British exports were some 20 per cent less competitive than they had been in 1955 and the overall deficit on the current account in 1964 was approaching £400 million per annum whereas the deficits for 1955 and 1960 were only £150 million and £250 million respectively. Many commentators took this as evidence that the economy was facing severe structural constraints which could only be solved by a devaluation of the pound. Once again, however, as at Suez nearly a decade earlier, economics and politics would interact in a somewhat unusual fashion. The economic logic for devaluation may have been compelling but the political objections to this act, at least as far as Wilson and his closest Cabinet colleagues were concerned, were even more compelling. It was Labour which was associated in the public mind with the two previous devaluations of 1931 and 1949. Even more pressing for the political mind was the fact that the government only had a majority of four in the House of Commons and it was likely that it would have to seek a renewed mandate within two years. Therefore precipitate action in economic policy, such as devaluation and the likely accompanying package of deflationary measures, was undesirable. As Wilson himself had said as early as 1958, 'the strength of sterling must be our first and primary consideration . . . the strength of sterling and all that depends on it must take priority over all other considerations' **(Ponting, 1989, p. 65)**. Devaluation therefore was ruled out and maintaining confidence in sterling became the centrepiece of Labour's economic policy. So important was this that, according to Clive Ponting, a series of 'understandings' between the British government and the United States administration of Lyndon Johnson had been arrived at whereby American support for sterling, the stability of which they saw as essential for the continuation of the Bretton Woods economic system, was traded for a continued British presence East of Suez, particularly in South-East Asia in support of the American effort in Vietnam **(Ponting, 1989,**

pp. 40–60). This of course involved heavy overseas expenditure by the British, which in turn led to financial strain, which in turn affected confidence in sterling.

The 1957 Defence White Paper had not led to the expected savings in defence expenditure. Indeed the very basis of this review had been to maintain commitments but at a lower cost. Defence expenditure had actually risen 8 per cent in real terms between 1957 and 1963. This rise was largely a consequence of expenditure on equipment to maintain the British nuclear deterrent and the forces for Britain's commitment to NATO. A review by the Labour government in its first year in office concluded that Britain should maintain its commitments in Europe and East of Suez but would attempt to find equipment savings that would keep the defence budget within a ceiling of £2,000 million per annum for the next five years. Consequently the next year saw Harold Wilson and Denis Healey continuing to argue that Britain would not relinquish any of its commitments while simultaneously cutting orders for the equipment that was necessary for it to sustain a world role. The fifth Polaris submarine and the new aircraft carrier for the Navy, CVA-01, were cancelled and the TSR2, P1154 and the HS681 aircraft programmes were terminated. An attempt to escape from the contradictions in this policy, of maintaining commitments while cutting equipment, was made by ordering F-111 long-range strike aircraft from the United states to replace both the TSR2 programme and fulfil the role of CVA-01 East of Suez.

This dichotomy was clearly identified by Richard Crossman in his account of a small after-dinner meeting at Chequers in October 1966 which discussed the level of defence expenditure.

Document 5.2.7 The Labour Government and Defence Commitments, 22 October 1966

Denis Healey started by saying that he had now re-considered the defence budget and thought it was possible to get it down next year to something below £1,850 million. This would mean cutting between £250 million and £400 million by halving our expenditure East of Suez, cutting our costs in Germany by a third and winding up our Middle East commitment altogether. He said in rather a superior voice that intellectually it might seem to be easier to do this by cutting the East of Suez commitment altogether but our allies would never allow that. . . . What came out of a very long discussion is that the defence policy Healey proposes would mean leaving token forces in the Far East quite unable to fulfil any of the precise obligations we've undertaken in SEATO and there may well be token forces in the Middle East unable to fulfil the obligations we've undertaken under CENTO. I made this point and said, 'But surely it's far better first to make a major change in foreign policy and follow Ernest Bevin's example? You remember when he totally withdrew from Greece and Turkey and forced the Truman Doctrine on the Americans. Now isn't that the kind of thing we should now do? We should make a proper basic foreign policy change and not merely whittle away our defences while maintaining our commitments.' Again Denis said that intellectually that might be true but practically it was impossible.

Harold tried to stop me and I realised straightaway that I was alone among the seven. I'm really completely out of sympathy with the whole atmosphere of this government's attitude to foreign policy and defence – they want to maintain our commitments while cutting away the forces with which we sustain them. What George Wigg and I have argued for years and years is precisely that the one thing a Labour Government must not do is to assume huge responsibilities and then deny our troops the weapons necessary to sustain them. Just think of it. The first Defence Review isn't yet twelve months old. Already, in July, it's been cut by £100 million. Now Denis is saying he can cut it in six months' time by another £300 million while we still retain all our commitments in the Far East, in the Middle East and in Germany. Both before the meeting and at the end I was reminded in the presence of the others that I was a new member of the club and must mind my tongue especially because I couldn't yet fully understand what was involved. I'm afraid I do understand only too well. But I never suspected that when I got inside O.P.D. [Overseas Policy and Defence Committee of the Cabinet] and discovered what was actually being done by these colleagues it would be so crude, so unskillful – a futile attempt to remain Great Britain, one of the three world powers, while slicing away our defences.

Source: Howard (ed.), 1979, pp. 263–264

However, buffeted by one economic crisis after another, piecemeal reconsiderations of British overseas commitments and the associated expenditure had to take place. In totality this was to add up to nothing less than a radical departure in British defence and overseas policy. In 1966, the Labour government reluctantly decided that the expensive British commitment to the defence and internal security of Aden would end in 1968, and in 1967 the Borneo commitment was wound up. More significantly, however, in the summer of 1967 a Supplementary Statement on Defence produced by the Secretary of State for Defence, Denis Healey, indicated an imminent end to the British role East of Suez. Commitments in Singapore and Malaya were to be scaled down and brought to an end by the mid-1970s, the paper concluded in an optimistic fashion.

Document 5.2.8 Labours Continuing Optimism on Defence, July 1967

1 We have been working continuously for almost three years on a major review of defence, revising Britain's overseas policy, formulating the role of military power to support it, and planning the forces required to carry out this role. This Statement marks the end of that process. The decisions in it

have been reached after extensive consultations with our allies, to whose views we have given full weight. They spring from the best assessment we can make of Britain's interests and responsibilities as they will develop in a changing world.

2 Substantial savings will be made in the demands of defence on the nation's manpower and financial resources. More of our forces will be based in Britain. We plan no major change in the size of our contribution to NATO. The savings will be chiefly obtained from a significant reduction in our military presence outside Europe and from some changes in its deployment.

Source: Supplementary Statement on Defence Policy 1967, Parliamentary Papers, Cmnd 3357, July 1967

This optimism was misplaced as further defence reviews were soon to be forced. An air of impending economic crisis in the autumn of 1967 following poor trade figures (a deficit of £159 million in September and October) and an accelerating run on the pound led to a hurried decision to devalue sterling from an exchange rate of $2.80 to $2.40. This marked the end of one of the central ambitions of economic policy followed by all governments since the war, that of holding the value of sterling within the Bretton Woods system of fixed exchange rates.

The failure of the economic foundations of British prestige was to lead inexorably to the final collapse of the increasingly illusory 'world role'. The automatic benefits of devaluation, more competitive British exports, were inevitably slow to be realised. Indeed, devaluation had to be reinforced by a programme of swingeing deflationary measures in 1968. These measures were to lead to anguished debates in the Cabinet in January 1968 regarding where the axe should fall, on expenditure at home or abroad. The new Chancellor of the Exchequer, Roy Jenkins, argued strongly for radical cuts to be made in defence expenditure based on a fundamental reassessment of overseas commitments. He was supported by the Prime Minister, who had long been the advocate of the strong pound and the 'world role' as symbols of British power and prestige, but who in the wake of devaluation had changed his mind, and by a group of 'left-wing' ministers who were loath to see an abandonment of social and welfare provisions simply to maintain an illusion of power. Against this block, Denis Healey and the Foreign Secretary, George Brown, were unable to prevail **(Howard (ed.), 1979, pp. 440–442)**.

In January 1968 the Cabinet therefore took a series of decisions that were to mark the end of Britain's world role: the ending of the East of Suez commitment, the withdrawal from the Persian Gulf and the cancellation of the F-111 strike aircraft and the running down of naval forces and manpower in the army marked an acceptance of a more regional role, focused on Europe.

Document 5.2.9 The East of Suez Decision, 16 January 1968

11 . . . There is no military strength whether for Britain or for our alliances except on the basis of economic strength; and it is on this basis that we best ensure the security of this country. We therefore intend to make to the alliances of which we are members a contribution related to our economic capability while recognising that our security lies fundamentally in Europe and must be based on the North Atlantic Alliance. . . .

12 We have accordingly decided to accelerate the withdrawal of our forces from their stations in the Far East . . . and to withdraw them by the end of 1971. We have also decided to withdraw our forces from the Persian Gulf by the same date. The broad effect is that, apart from our remaining dependencies and certain other necessary exceptions we shall by that date not be maintaining military bases outside Europe and the Mediterranean.

Source: Speech to the House of Commons by Harold Wilson, 16 January 1968, Hansard, vol. 756, cols 1580–1581

This abandonment of the East of Suez role marked the final end of Britain's attempt to retain a distinctive world role. As the American Secretary of Defense, Clark Clifford, stated, 'the British do not have the resources, the backup or the hardware to deal with any big world problem . . . they are no longer a powerful ally of ours because they cannot afford the cost of an adequate defence effort'. As Dean Rusk pointed out, this was the 'end of an era' **(Ponting, 1989, pp. 58–59)**.

6 | The debate

Historiographical debate on the Suez Crisis has been intense and wide-ranging, beginning with the very earliest account, *Secrets of Suez* by the Brombergers, published in 1957, and has been subsequently driven by the availability of source material in the form of memoirs and official documents. Among the themes and issues raised by historians and commentators are overarching questions, such as the place of Suez in the 'decline' of Britain as a Great Power, and issues that are integral to the crisis, such as whether the issue could have been settled by negotiation rather than by the resort to force, collusion between Britain, France and Israel and the role of the Prime Minister and the Cabinet in both these areas.

One of the most controversial of all issues is the suggestion that Suez was pivotal in the rapid 'descent from power' of Britain after the Second World War. One must be careful however and not conflate cause and effect and ascribe to Suez the notion that the crisis in some way caused British decline rather than reflected it. Suez was a marker point in that it reflected very clearly the truth that the British economy could not sustain a great power role without the support of the United States. However, all British governments after 1945 were only too well aware of the changing realities of British power in the post-war world: there is a straight line from the Keynes memorandum of 1945 through to the Eden 'valedictory note' of December 1956 in terms of an awareness of the fragility of the British economy and its implications for a continued world role that was to culminate in the painful East of Suez decision in 1968. In some senses, the interest of Suez lies in the stubborn refusal of ministers and others to accept the logic of their own position, and who were therefore forced to adopt increasingly desperate and atavistic expedients in an attempt to achieve victory in a battle against the forces – nationalism, communism and American interference – that were undermining Britain's cherished status as a world power.

One key example of this atavism is the seeming dichotomy between an awareness and acceptance of Britain's post-war economic position and a lack of willingness to accept that this would act as a major constraint on Britain's world role. As Selwyn Lloyd himself noted in his memoir of Suez published in 1978:

> At a later stage it was alleged that one result of Suez was to make us realise that we could not act independently. The fact was that we knew that all the time. We were very well aware of our economic weakness and of the strain on our resources of expenditure overseas affecting our balance of payments. We had, however, to conceal that knowledge.
>
> **(Lloyd, 1978, pp. 36–37)**

Given such an interpretation it was all the more unusual that the Suez operation went ahead with almost no consideration given to the likely economic conse-quences of an action that did not have the formal support of the United States. The Suez Crisis took place against the economic background of substantial cuts in British public expenditure which were aimed at rectifying a weak balance of payments position. The crucial question therefore arises of why there was little or no consideration of the economic impact of Suez until it was too late. The issue was not discussed by the Cabinet or the Egypt Committee and the Prime Minister and Foreign Secretary appear to have been blissfully unaware of the possible impact on Britain's precarious financial position until that impact duly arrived. Alastair Horne has asserted that the blame lies not with Macmillan but with his Treasury officials, but even the most cursory reading of Treasury files at the Public Records Office reveal this to be a gross distortion of the evidence. Indeed, from the nationalisation of the Canal Sir Edward Bridges and his colleagues at the Treasury and the Bank of England were warning their minister of the likely economic damage if Britain proceeded without full American support.

This then raises the vexed question of the role of the United States. It is asserted in many memoirs and biographies, including those by Eden and Lloyd, that the United States administration of Eisenhower and Dulles consistently misled the British Cabinet about the degree of support that would be forthcoming from Washington in the event of force being used. Again, however, a reading of the archival material in both Washington and London, such as that undertaken by W. Scott Lucas (Lucas, 1991), makes it clear that while the British could complain about American delaying tactics, insisting on what the British increasingly viewed as futile negotiations, there can be little doubt as to the fact that American policy was consistently against the use of force *except* in the absolute last resort. Whether 'the last resort' had been reached when Selwyn Lloyd was recalled from New York by Eden in mid-October 1956 is a moot point. Certainly from the United States point of view there was still the possibility of further negotiations taking place: in the light of this it is ironic that the final settlement of the dispute, in April 1957, was based broadly on the Six Principles that Lloyd had so assiduously negotiated in New York in early October 1956. The British Cabinet appear to have wilfully assumed that whatever the circumstances of the intervention in Egypt, the United States would fall into line behind their faithful ally.

The recall of Lloyd was the occasion of the first British steps towards collusion with the Israelis. Although there had been desultory discussion in the Egypt Committee in August 1956 of the possibility of co-operation with the Israelis, the startling proposal of Gazier and Challe gave the idea fresh life and lead to the abandonment of any further negotiations with the Egyptians. Moreover, it is arguable that collusion made possible the resort to force that had been the aim of the Eden government from the beginning of the crisis by providing the pretext that hitherto had been lacking. The question of collusion has been the dominant feature of much of the literature on Suez, possibly to the extent of preventing the evolution of a full picture of Suez. Many of the participants have asserted that there was nothing dishonourable in the dealings that took place in October 1956, rather this was simply a process of 'co-operation' between three countries with mutual interests. As Lloyd has claimed in his memoir:

> It cannot be collusion merely to have confidential talks with other governments. This was going on all the time with the United States, France and the other countries which sent representatives to the two London conferences. Talks with the Government of Israel no more constitute collusion than our talks with these other Governments.

This distinction by the Foreign Secretary is a fine one: Lloyd, who was after all by profession a barrister, himself admits that the *Oxford Dictionary* definition of collusion as a 'fraudulent secret understanding' is the correct one, but asserts that the actions of the British government were not fraudulent and were justified by their motives **(Lloyd, 1978, pp. 247–248)**. This justification raises a number of issues. First, if collusion was just part and parcel of the normal diplomatic game similar to that of the London Conferences, why were great lengths gone to to keep the process secret? Second, if there was no 'collusion' why was it repeatedly denied within the House of Commons by government spokesmen, including Lloyd and Eden, and why was it subsequently played down in their memoirs? Third, Lloyd's argument ultimately comes down to a variant of 'the end justifies the means' and must therefore be judged accordingly in both moral and practical terms. In an age which expected high standards of probity from its politicans the fact that the Prime Minister and Foreign Secretary could 'lie' to the House of Commons and by extension the public came as a great shock. Morally, collusion was both fraudulent and dishonourable. If, as Lloyd asserts, collusion must be judged on its practical value then the results speak for themselves. An operation designed to internationalise the Canal, reduce the power of Nasser, stabilise the Middle East and reassert British power and prestige had precisely the opposite effects.

Collusion inevitably focuses attention on the actions and motives of the individuals at the centre of the policy-making apparatus within Whitehall. Again, much debate has centred on the question of who knew what and when. This debate is somewhat arid: as Professor Hennessy has alleged, 'one did not need to be a member of British intelligence to put two and two together and make four. The full Cabinet knew' **(Hennessy, 1994)**. While the onus for collusion clearly lies with senior ministers, junior ministers and most civil servants, outside of a very narrow circle of senior officials, were not actually kept fully informed but may have been able to deduce what was happening. As Lucas has established there is substantial documentary evidence across the spectrum of Whitehall to support this view.

In light of this, renewed emphasis is placed on the role of the hawks, notably Eden and Macmillan. As we have established it was the Prime Minister and his Chancellor of the Exchequer who were the most fervent advocates of intervention in Egypt. Given the outcome of the crisis, much has been written about Eden's judgement. Even his 'official' biographer has noted the increasingly irrational attitude of Eden to Nasser and the Canal. How far this was caused by his ill-health remains a matter for conjecture, although his close colleagues such as Nutting and Shuckburgh consider that his already brittle temperament was undermined by a combination of illness and overwork. While this may go some way to explaining Eden's obsession with recovering the Canal and overthrowing Nasser, there is little doubt that the policy adopted by Eden represented a genuine belief in the threat posed by Nasser to British interests. There can be no doubt, however, that Eden never favoured a negotiated settlement and was determined on the use of force to which end he was prepared to collude with France and Israel in order to bring Nasser down.

The role of Macmillan has been much less clear: it was not until the opening of the files relating to Suez at the Public Record Office in 1987 that a full picture could be drawn of the part played by the Chancellor. There is much truth in Harold Wilson's cutting assessment of Macmillan: 'first in, first out'. Throughout the crisis Macmillan was the most avid supporter of the military option despite his awareness of the fragility of Britain's financial position. It is therefore astonishing that at no stage was any serious consideration given to either the cost or the possible financial consequences of the operation: for this Macmillan must be held responsible. It is equally astonishing that it was Macmillan who was to emerge blameless from the wreckage and assume the office of Prime Minister having played a leading part in the undermining of Eden's position: as both Lucas (1991) and Kyle (1991) have pointed out, in contradistinction to Horne (1989), Macmillan was actively seeking to displace Eden as early as 16 November 1956.

Historical debate on the pivotal nature of Suez in respect of Britain's post-war 'decline' will doubtless continue. What can be said with some degree of certainty is that Britain's post-war position was relatively weaker after Suez than before precisely because Suez revealed to all 'as in a lightning flash' Britain's existing weaknesses with which it had been wrestling since the end of the Second World War. Contemporaries were divided as to the impact of Suez: some, for example Anthony Low, viewing it as an irrelevance and others such as Brian Lapping seeing it as a fundamental sea-change. Just as assessments of the course of British policy and the role of individuals during the Suez Crisis have been clarified by the availability of the official record, the ultimate consequences for Britain of Suez can only be judged once all the official records for the 1960s are available for the historian to read and reflect upon. Whatever its impact in terms of policy, for the first time since the war the myth of British power and prestige had been seriously challenged and found wanting: the gulf between reality and great power status was starkly revealed.

Dramatis personae

Titles and Positions are those held during the Suez Crisis unless otherwise stated.

Aldrich, Winthrop *United States Ambassador in London 1953–1957*

Amery, Julian *Conservative MP; founder member of the Suez Group*

Attlee, Clement *British Prime Minister 1945–1951*

Ben-Gurion, David *Prime Minister of Israel 1955–1963*

Bevin, Ernest *British Foreign Secretary 1945–1951*

Black, Eugene *President of the World Bank*

Boyle, Air Chief Marshal Sir Dermot *Chief of the Air Staff*

Boyle, Edward *Economic Secretary to the Treasury*

Bridges, Sir Edward *British Cabinet Secretary 1938–1945; Permanent Secretary to the Treasury 1945–1956*

Brook, Sir Norman *Cabinet Secretary 1945–1960*

Bulganin, Nikolai *Soviet Prime Minister*

Burns, General E.L.M. *Commander UNEF*

Butler, R.A. *Chancellor of the Exchequer 1951–1955; Lord Privy Seal 1955–1962; Leader of the House of Commons 1955–1961*

Byroade, Henry *United States Ambassador in Egypt*

Caccia, Sir Harold *Deputy Under-Secretary of State, Foreign Office; British Ambassador in Washington 1956–1963*

Challe, General Maurice *Deputy Chief of Staff of the French Air Force*

Churchill, Sir Winston *Prime Minister 1940–1945 and 1951–1955*

Clarke, William *Press secretary to Sir Anthony Eden*

Crossman, Richard *Labour Cabinet Minister of Housing and Local Government 1964–1970*

Dayan, General Moshe *Israeli Chief of Staff*

Dean, Sir Patrick *Deputy Under-Secretary at the Foreign Office 1956–1960; head of the Permanent Under Secretary's Committee*

Dickson, Marshal of the RAF Sir William *Chairman of the Chiefs of Staff*

Dixon, Sir Pierson *Permanent British Representative to the United Nations 1954–1960*

Dulles, John Foster *United States Secretary of State 1953–1959*

Eden, Sir Anthony *British Foreign Secretary 1935–1938, 1940–1945, 1951–1955; British Prime Minister 1955–1957*

Eisenhower, Dwight D. *United States President 1952–1960*

Farouk, King *King of Egypt 1936–1952*

Fawzi, Mahmoud *Egyptian Foreign Minister 1952–1964*

Gaitskell, Hugh *Chancellor of the Exchequer 1950–1951; leader of the Labour Party, 1955–1963*

Gazier, Albert *French Minister of Labour*

Glubb, General Sir John *British Chief of Staff of the Jordanian Arab Legion 1939–1956*

Hailsham, Viscount *First Lord of the Admiralty*

Hammarskjöld, Dag *Secretary–General of the United Nations 1953–1961*

Hankey, Lord *British Cabinet Secretary 1916–1938*

Harcourt, Viscount *British Minister at the Washington Embassy*

Head, Antony *Secretary of State for War 1951–October 1956; Minister of Defence October 1956–January 1957*

Healy, Denis *Labour MP 1945–1992; Minister of Defence 1964–1970*

Heath, Edward *Government Chief Whip*

Home, Lord (later Sir Alec Douglas–Home) *Commonwealth Secretary 1955–1960; Prime Minister 1963–1964*

Hoover, Herbert *United States Under-Secretary of State*

Humphrey, George *United States Treasury Secretary*

Hussein, Ahmed *Egyptian Ambassador in Washington*

Hussein, King *King of Jordan 1952–present*

Jebb, Sir Gladwyn *British Ambassador in Paris 1954–1960*

Jenkins, Roy *Chancellor of the Exchequer 1967–1970*

Keightley, General Sir Charles *Commander-in-Chief, Middle East Land Force 1953–1957; Allied Commander-in-Chief of the MUSKETEER forces*

Keynes, Lord *British economist and adviser to the Treasury 1940–1946*

Khrushchev, Nikita *Soviet General Secretary 1955–1964*

Kilmuir, Viscount *Lord Chancellor 1954–1962*

Kirkpatrick, Sir Ivone *Permanent Secretary at the Foreign Office 1953–1957*

Lampson, Sir Miles (later Lord Killearn) *British Ambassador in Egypt and later member of the Suez Group*

Lennox–Boyd, Alan *Colonial Secretary 1954–1959*

Lesseps, Ferdinand de *Engineer of the Suez Canal*

Lloyd, Selwyn *British Foreign Secretary 1955–1960*

Lodge, Henry Cabot *Permanent United States Representative to the United Nations 1953–1960*

Logan, Donald *Assistant private secretary to Selwyn Lloyd*

Macleod, Iain *Minister of Labour 1955–1959; Colonial Secretary 1959–1964*

Macmillan, Harold *Minister in Residence Mediterranean 1942–1945; Minister of Housing 1951–1954; Minister of Defence 1954–1955; Foreign Secretary 1955; Chancellor of the Exchequer 1955–1957; Prime Minister 1957–1963*

Makins, Sir Roger *British Ambassador in Washington 1953–October 1956; Permanent Secretary at the Treasury October 1956–1960*

Meir, Golda *Israeli Foreign Minister*

Menon, Krishna *Indian Minister without Portfolio*

Menzies, Sir Robert *Australian Prime Minister and emissary to Nasser in September 1956*

Mollet, Guy *French Prime Minister 1956–1957*

Monckton, Sir Walter *Minister of Defence 1955–October 1956; Paymaster–General October 1956–January 1957*

Mossadeq, Mohammed *Iranian Prime Minister at the time of the Abadan Crisis*

Mountbatten of Burma, Admiral Earl *First Sea Lord 1955–1959; Chairman of the Chiefs of Staff Committee, 1959–1964*

Murphy, Robert *Deputy Under-Secretary United States State Department*

Nasser, Colonel Gamal Abdel *Prime Minister of Egypt 1954–1956; President of Egypt 1956–1970*

Neguib, General Mohammed *Prime Minister of Egypt 1952–1954; President of Egypt 1953–1954*

Nicholls, John *British Ambassador in Israel*

Nuri es–Sa'id *Iraqi Prime Minister*

Nutting, Anthony *Minister of State at the Foreign Office 1954–November 1956*

Pearson, Lester *Canadian Foreign Minister 1948–1957*

Pineau, Christian *French Foreign Minister 1956–1957*

Salisbury, Marquess of *Lord President of the Council and leader of the House of Lords 1951–1957*

Sandys, Duncan *Minister of Housing and Local Government 1954–1957; Minister of Defence 1957–1959*

Sargent, Sir Orme *Permanent Secretary Foreign Office 1946–1949*

Shepilov, Dimtri *Soviet Foreign Minister*

Shuckburgh, Evelyn *Principal private secretary to Anthony Eden 1951–1954; Assistant Under-Secretary at the Foreign Office 1954–1956*

Stockwell, General Sir Hugh *Allied Commander of MUSKETEER Ground Forces*

Templer, General Sir Gerald *Chief of the Imperial General Staff 1955–1958*

Thorneycroft, Peter *President of the Board of Trade 1955–1957; Chancellor of the Exchequer 1957–1959*

Trevelyan, Sir Humphrey *British Ambassador in Cairo 1955–1956*

Waterhouse, Captain Charles *Tory MP and leader of the Suez Group*

Wilson, Harold *British Prime Minister 1964–1970*

Annotated bibliography

A pattern can be seen in the development of the historiography of Suez. Perhaps more than any other recent historical question, the historiography of Suez has been affected by the major difficulty afflicting contemporary history: in some measure it has been driven by the periodic release of source materials and the resulting media attention. A simple analysis of the publication dates of many of the works cited below reveals a clustering around the tenth, twentieth and thirtieth anniversaries of the Suez Crisis. The student might therefore find it instructive to compare and contrast, say, the work of the Brombergers published in 1957, with that of Hugh Thomas published in 1966 and those of Kyle and Lucas both published in 1991. The first of these is an essentially journalistic account written rapidly for publication and clearly based on interviews with mainly French participants. Thomas's work still lacked full access to government records but had the advantage of being based upon interviews with a range of senior figures in the British policy-making circle, including Selwyn Lloyd. The works by Kyle and Lucas are based heavily on archival sources, both British and American, which became available to the historian in 1987.

The framework for the historiography of Suez was established by the early appearance of memoirs of key British political figures. These are, however, of variable quality. *Full Circle*, the memoirs of Anthony Eden (1960), while apparently full, gloss over certain episodes, for example, the key meeting at Chequers in October between himself and the French emissaries Gazier and Challe is not mentioned at all. The memoirs of Lord Kilmuir (1964) attempt to paint British actions, particularly over the charge of collusion, in the best possible light. A valuable counterblast was administered by the memoirs of Anthony Nutting (1967) which for the first time made public the mechanics of collusion. The recollections of Macmillan (1971) are exceedingly sketchy on the subject of Treasury advice regarding the economy. Perhaps the most balanced memoir of those written by participants is that of the Foreign Secretary Selwyn Lloyd (1978), although on the legality or otherwise of the operation Lloyd, in common with Kilmuir, is, for a lawyer, curiously ambivalent on the finer points of international law.

There is a limited literature of memoirs by civil servants of which by far the best is that by Evelyn Shuckburgh (1986) which, as the title *Descent to Suez* suggests, is mainly concerned with the pre-Suez period, but contains fascinating insights into the character and actions of Anthony Eden from Shuckburgh's position as firstly Principal Private Secretary to Eden 1951–1954 and then Under-Secretary at the Foreign Office dealing with Middle Eastern Affairs 1954–1956. The memoirs of Pierson Dixon (1968) contain valuable material on the negotiations in the United Nations as well as indicating the strong reservations that this professional diplomat had about both the legality and the morality of Operation MUSKETEER. This latter theme is also treated in the memoirs of Paul Gore-Booth (1974) which contain an interesting passage on the supposed civil servants' 'revolt'. The recollections of William Clark (1986), Eden's press secretary, are again a good source for the actions and attitudes of the Prime Minister.

Given both the controversial nature of the Suez Crisis and the fact that a number of the key participants enjoyed lengthy careers in government spanning the middle decades of the twentieth century it is scarcely surprising that there is a rich and growing body of biographies covering this area. Randolph Churchill's (1959) often brutal assessment of Eden was inspired by the author's strong dislike of Eden whom he considered to be a political lightweight. A more balanced, although still critical, appraisal is provided by David Carlton's life of Eden (1981). Carlton was the first to use important American sources, particularly the Eisenhower papers, to shed light on the Suez affair (this is particularly the case with the struggle for the succession). The 'authorised' biography of Eden by Robert Rhodes James (1987) is an altogether more sympathetic reading which is perhaps over-reliant, where Suez is concerned, on the Avon papers. There are earlier works on the life of Macmillan, but the official biography by Alastair Horne (1989) whilst lengthy and apparently comprehensive, is seriously flawed. Again it is almost solely reliant on Macmillan's own account of his role in the Suez Crisis and ignores the wealth of primary source material which is available at the Public Record Office. The best single volume treatment of Macmillan is John Turner's 1994 study in the *Profiles in Power* series. The somewhat grey figure of the Foreign Secretary, Selwyn Lloyd, has been well-served by his biographer D.R. Thorpe who has produced a well-balanced study of his subject (1989). Anthony Howard's biography of R.A. Butler (1987) is disappointing on Suez, while John Campbell's volume on Edward Heath (1994) sheds little light on the delicate role performed in 1956 by Heath as Chief Whip. As might be expected less has been written on the 'officials'' lives: the exception is Philip Zeigler's life of Mountbatten (1985) which sheds some light on the often complex character and motivations of the First Sea Lord.

Since the opening of the British archives for the Suez period in 1987 there has been a large number of monographs and essays written on the subject. The best short introduction is David Carlton's *Britain and the Suez Crisis* (1988) which is a model of compression. Longer and more detailed is Keith Kyle's *Suez* (1991) which is comprehensive in its sweep. Lucas's *Divided We Stand* (1991) is a similarly full account focusing more sharply on the Anglo-American 'special relationship'. There are two important volumes of essays edited by Louis and Owen (1989) and Troën and Shemesh (1990) which both contain valuable thematic studies of key aspects of the crisis: the latter also has valuable first-hand material from Julian Amery and the Ben-Gurion diaries. The military aspect of the crisis is well covered in Fullick and Powell's volume (1979), the interaction between strategy and diplcmacy is the subject of Gorst and Lucas's article in the *Journal of Strategic Studies* (1988). The international economic aspects of the Suez Crisis is the subject of Diane Kunz's (1991) monograph, and the relationship between the Treasury and Macmillan is covered in the essay by Johnman (1989). The best analysis of the political impact of Suez remains Epstein's *British Politics and the Suez Crisis* (1964).

Further reading

Bar Zohar, M., *Ben Gurion: A Political Biography* (London 1978)

Beaufre, A., *The Suez Expedition, 1956* (London 1969)

Bethell, N., *The Palestine Triangle* (London 1979)

Birkenhead, Earl of, *Monckton* (London 1969)

Bowie, R., *Suez 1956: International Crisis and the Rule of Law* (Oxford 1974)

Boyle, P. (ed.) *The Churchill–Eisenhower Correspondence* (London 1990)

Braddon, R., *Suez, Splitting of a Nation* (London 1973)

Briggs, A., *A History of British Broadcasting*, vol. 5 (London 1995)

Bromberger, M. and Bromberger, S., *Secrets of Suez* (London 1957)

Butler, Lord, *The Art of the Possible* (London 1971)

Cairncross, A., *Years of Recovery* (London 1985)

Campbell, J., *Edward Heath* (London 1994)

Carlton, D., *Anthony Eden* (London 1981)

——, *Britain and the Suez Crisis* (Oxford 1988)

Casey, R.G., *Australian Foreign Minister. The Diaries of R.G. Casey 1951–60* (London 1972)

Churchill, R.S., *The Rise and Fall of Sir Anthony Eden* (Dublin 1959)

Clark, W., *From Three Worlds: Memoirs* (London 1986)

Cloake, J., *Templer: Tiger of Malaya. The Life of Field Marshal Sir Gerald Templer* (London 1985)

Colville, Sir J., *The Fringes of Power: Downing Street Diaries 1939–1955* (London 1985)

Constantine, S., *Buy and Build: The Advertising Posters of the Empire Marketing Board* (London 1986)

Darby, P., *British Defence Policy East of Suez 1947–1968* (Oxford 1973)

Darwin, J., *The End of the British Empire* (Oxford 1991)

Dayan M., *Diary of the Sinai Campaign* (London 1966)

——, *Story of My Life: An Autobiography* (New York 1976)

Dixon, P., *Double Diploma. The Life of Sir Pierson Dixon, Don and Diplomat* (London 1968)

Eayrs, J., *The Commonwealth and Suez* (Oxford 1964)

Eden, Sir Anthony, *Full Circle* (London 1960)

Eisenhower, D.D., *The White House Years*, vols 1 and 2 (New York 1963 and 1965)

Epstein, L.V., *British Politics and the Suez Crisis* (London 1964)

ESSFRC, *Executive Session of the Senate Foreign Relations Committee Vol IX, 1957* (Washington 1979)

Farnie, D., *East and West of Suez. The Suez Canal in History 1854–1956* (Oxford 1969)

Ferrell, F., *The Eisenhower Diaries* (New York 1981)

Finer, H., *Dulles over Suez* (London 1964)

Frankland, N., (ed.), *Documents on International Relations 1956* (Oxford 1959)

FRUS (A), *Foreign Relations of the United States, 1955–1957*, vol. XIV (Washington 1988)

—— (B), *Foreign Relations of the United States, 1955–1957*, vol. XV (Washington 1988)

—— (C), *Foreign Relations of the United States, 1955–1957*, vol. XVI (Washington 1988)

Fullick, R. and Powell, G., *Suez: The Double War* (London 1979)

Gilbert, M. '*Never Despair*'. *Winston S. Churchill, 1945–1965* (London 1988)

Glubb, General Sir John Bagot, *A Soldier with the Arabs* (London 1957)

Gore-Booth, P., *With Great Truth and Respect* (London 1974)

Gorst, A., 'Facing Facts? The Labour Government and Defence Policy, 1945–50', in N. Tiratsoo (ed.) *The Attlee Years* (London 1991)

Gorst, A. and Lucas, W.S., 'Suez 1956: Strategy and the Diplomatic Process', *Journal of Strategic Studies*, vol. 11, no. 4, 1988, pp 391–436

——, 'The Other Collusion', *Intelligence and National Security*, vol. 4, no. 3, 1989, pp. 576–595

Hailsham, Lord, *A Sparrow's Flight* (London 1990)

Harris, K. *Attlee* (London 1982)

Heikal, M., *Cutting the Lion's Tail* (London 1986)

Hennessy, P., *What Ever Happened to Us* (BBC Television, 11 December 1994)

Hoopes, T., *The Devil and John Foster Dulles* (London 1974)

Horne, A., *Macmillan* (London 1989)

Howard, A., (ed.), *The Crossman Diaries (Condensed Version)* (London 1979)

——, *RAB: The Life of R.A. Butler* (London 1987)

——, *Crossman* (London 1990)

Johnman, L., 'Defending the Pound: The Economics of the Suez Crisis 1956', in A. Gorst, L. Johnman and W.S. Lucas (eds), *Postwar Britain 1945–1964* (London 1989)

Johnson, P., *The Suez War* (Dublin 1957)

Kent, J., 'The Suez Canal Base Agreement', *Journal of Imperial and Commonwealth History*, vol. XXI, no. 3, 1993, pp. 45–63

Kilmuir, Earl of, *Political Adventure* (London 1964)

Kunz, D., *The Economic Diplomacy of the Suez Crisis* (New York 1991)

Kyle, K., *Suez* (London 1991)

Lamb, R., *The Failure of the Eden Government* (London 1987)

Lapping, B., 'Did Suez Hasten the End of Empire?', *Contemporary Record*, vol. 1, no. 2, pp. 31–33

Lloyd, S., *Suez, 1956. A Personal Account* (London 1978)

Louis, W.R., *The British Empire in the Middle East, 1945–1951* (Oxford 1984)

Louis, W. and Owen, R. (eds), *Suez 1956, The Crisis and its Consequences* (Oxford 1989)

Love, K., *Suez: The Twice Fought War* (London 1970)

Low, A., 'Did Suez Hasten the End of Empire?' *Contemporary Record*, vol. 1, no. 2, p. 31 (1987).

Lucas, W.S., 'The Path to Suez: Britain and the Struggle for the Middle East 1953–1956', in A. Deighton (ed), *Britain and the First Cold War* (London 1990)

——, *Divided We Stand* (London 1991)

Macmillan, H., *Tides of Fortune, 1945–55* (London 1969)

——, *Riding the Storm, 1956–1959* (London 1971)

Menzies, Sir R., *Afternoon Light* (London 1967)

Moncrieff, A. (ed.), *Suez Ten Years After* (London 1967)

Monroe, E., *Britain's Moment in the Middle East* (London 1963, 2nd edn 1981)

Murphy, R., *Diplomat Among Warriors* (London 1964)

Neff, D., *Warriors of Suez. Eisenhower takes America into the Middle East* (New York 1981)

Nutting, A., *No End of a Lesson. The Story of Suez* (London 1967)

Ovendale, R., *British Defence Policy since 1945* (Manchester 1994)

Pearson, L., *Memoirs, Vol. II, 1948–1957. The International Years* (London 1974)

Pineau, C., *1956 Suez* (Paris 1976)

Ponting, C., *Breach of Promise: Labour in Power 1964–1970* (London 1989)

PPPUS, *The Public Papers of Presidents of the United States: Dwight D. Eisenhower*, (1957)

Pressnell, L., *External Economic Policy Since the War. Volume 1: The Post-War Financial Settlement* (London 1985)

Robertson, T., *The Inside Story of the Suez Conspiracy* (London 1965)

Rhodes James, R., *Anthony Eden* (London 1987)

Shuckburgh, E., *Descent to Suez* (London 1986)

Thomas, H., *The Suez Affair* (Suez 1966)

Thorpe, D.R., *Selwyn Lloyd* (London 1989)

Troën, S.I. and Shemesh, M. (eds), *The Suez–Sinai Crisis 1956. Retrospective and Reappraisal* (London 1990)

Turner, J., *Macmillan* (London 1994)

Williams, P., *Hugh Gaitskell* (London 1979)

—— (ed.), *The Diary of Hugh Gaitskell 1945–1956* (London 1983)

Zeigler, P., *Mountbatten* (London 1985)

Index